My Farce From My Elbow

My Farce From My Elbow

An Autobiography

BRIAN RIX

Secker & Warburg
London

First published in England 1975 by
Martin Secker & Warburg Limited
14 Carlisle Street, London W1V 6NN

Copyright © Brian Rix 1975

SBN: 436 41500 3

Printed in Great Britain by
Cox & Wyman Limited,
London, Fakenham and Reading

LIST OF ILLUSTRATIONS

BETWEEN PAGES 88 AND 89

Brian's mother aged 29
Brian's father in 1930
The Rix children in 1924
Brian aged 11 in *The Rose and the Ring* [*Woodcock, Bridlington*]
Brian in *The Sorcerer*, 1935
His son Jonty aged 11
First "pro" photograph, 1942 [*Basil Shackleton, London*]
The wedding cake, 1949 [*Allan Barr, Bridlington*]
Air crew reception centre, 1944
An audience at the Whitehall Theatre
Reluctant Heroes as seen by Ronald Searle
On the set of *Love in a Mist* [*BBC, London*]
Brian Rix and Elspet Gray in *Round the Bend*
After a Royal Garden Party, 1951 [*Universal Pictorial Press & Agency, London*]
Brian and Elspet with Harold Wilson
Jonty's christening in 1961 [*Central Press Photos Ltd, London*]
"This is Your Life", 1961 [*BBC, London*]

BETWEEN PAGES 152 AND 153

Simple Spymen at the Whitehall Theatre
Brian Rix at the Garrick Theatre, 1967 [*Michael Ward*]
The two Brians in *Men of Affairs*

With Donna Reading in *A Bit Between the Teeth* [*Gilbert Photography, London*]

Brian in pensive mood [*L. Hanley, Today, London*]

Taking delivery of a new Jaguar [*David Ross Studios, East Molesey*]

Brian and Warren Mitchell in *Men of Affairs*

Brian and Elspet on holiday [*Peter G. Reed, Preston*]

Returning from Spain, 1965 [*Press Association Photos Ltd, London*]

At rehearsal for *Uproar in the House* [*Clive Limpkin, Daily Express, London*]

Brian with his daughter Louisa, 1970

The Rix family in 1972 [*Peter Dumbleton, Whittlesford*]

At the cricket nets [*Ian Tyas, Keystone Press Agency Ltd, London*]

Lord's Taverners after a game

Middlesex v Vic Lewis All Stars, 1973

Joanna Lumley learning to bat [*Eric Weller, Photoeil, Walthamstow*]

I dedicate this book, written in my own indecipherable longhand, to the members of my audience – those who love me and those who loathe me – and to my wife Elspet, the members of my family plus my friends – who've been a bit ambivalent in their time, too. To all, my gratitude for their support.

Act I

A few years ago an unkind critic, who shall be nameless (anyway, I forget his name), wrote:

"Mr Rix doesn't know his farce from his elbow."

About the same time the venerable *Sunday Times* critic, Harold Hobson (I remember *his* name), wrote:

"Mr Rix is the greatest master of farce in my theatre-going lifetime."

On the other hand a Jamaican reporter (I *never* knew his name) wrote:

"Mr Rix is London's best known fart actor."

Somewhere between the fundament and the flatus must lie the truth. On the following pages I will explore the facts, the lies, the myths and the press agents' handouts in an effort to prove to my own satisfaction just where I stand. If you care to come along with me, I should be delighted and I will try and make the going as smooth as possible. If you decide against the journey, please close the book very gently and replace it on the bookshop shelf as unostentatiously as you can for I would hate your disgruntled look to discourage any other would-be buyers.

How is it that I, the Yorkshire son of a Yorkshire shipowner, have become the actor-manager who has presented and appeared in farce ever since 1950? It is a unique record: for the majority of that time I have been in the West End of London and, to make it even more unusual, I have only played in three theatres – the Whitehall and the Garrick and the Cambridge – with a total of eleven plays. It must have been predestined.

When I was a baby my nannie had a crush on the local railway signalman. He controlled the destiny of trains going through a level crossing within walking distance of my house and quite often I would be pushed there at an opportune moment, to coincide with the closing of the gates, so that vague intimacies could be shouted up from pavement level to signalbox altitude. If I was a romantic actor no doubt this embryonic romance would have culminated in wedding bells with the bride and groom leaving the church beneath an arch of crossed sleepers. If I was a tragic actor it could be that my pram rolled in front of the oncoming express and the gallant railwayman lost his life in one despairing leap to push me clear of the thundering juggernaut.

The truth is, alas, altogether mundane. Whilst the two star-crossed long-distance lovers were deep in conversation, I fell out of my pram. Nannie was so horrified at the possibility that her dear little charge was both hurt and grubby that she rounded on the startled signalman and blamed him totally for distracting her attention from her screaming bundle of, literally, bouncing baby. And this, of course, is the very stuff of farce. No one actually ever gets it – whatever "it" might be – and authority is always undermined, whether it be nannie, civil servant, vicar, policeman or Member of Parliament. The ardent lover always ends up hiding in the cupboard; the enraged husband always ends up losing his trousers. It is a simple formula but, my God, it's a difficult one to put into practice.

But back to childish things. As a small boy I was garrulous, friendly, given to vivid flights of imagination and totally incapable of concentrating on anything I didn't like. I sometimes look at my younger son, Jonathan, and wonder where the hell he gets those annoying traits from ...

I was born at Cottingham near Hull in the East Riding of Yorkshire, on the 27th January 1924, just in time for breakfast. Cottingham is, or was, the largest village in England. We have to make grandiloquent claims like that when we come from the end of the line. By that I don't mean that I was the last child (I was: the fourth) but that the London and North Eastern Railway ended abruptly in Hull and we always felt that the rest of England rather lost interest in us by the time the train reached Doncaster or York or Leeds. This feeling was reinforced during the war. Everyone else was mentioned in the news: "Last night enemy aircraft raided London or Manchester or Liverpool." Hull had hell knocked out of it (ninety-seven per cent of *all* buildings suffered damage) but we were referred to as "Humberside" or "North Eastern England". Can you wonder I've always worried about my billing ever since?

My memories of Cottingham are brief:

a) I was happy.
b) My nannie loved me.
c) So did my parents – but I didn't realise it at the time.
d) I fell out of my pram.
e) I played with saucepan lids – clashing them like cymbals – for hours on end.
f) The house seemed huge. Actually it was semi-detached.
g) My younger sister, Sheila, squashed my finger in the car door.
h) My elder sister, Nora, squashed my finger under a see-saw.
i) I swallowed gnat-bite lotion.
j) I went to my first film, *Felix the Cat*, and caught whooping cough.
k) I was allowed to have dinner with my elder brother, Malcolm, when he returned home from school with his neck all bandaged. He'd had an operation.
l) I was given a toy gramophone on my fourth birthday, which was celebrated in my nursery at the top of the house. There was a big fireguard in front of the fire.

m) I learnt to ride a bicycle – falling off on the lawn hundreds of times.

n) We left Cottingham and moved to Hornsea. I was five. Unbeknown to me, this was the first step towards my future career.

Hornsea is a small seaside resort nineteen miles from Hull and is mainly peopled by Hull businessmen. The houses are solid and dependable – as are the people. But in 1929 religious prejudice abounded in that village of four thousand souls! Not Christian against Jew or Catholic against Protestant. No – it was merely Protestant against Protestant. *We* were the best (of course) being C of E. The narrow-minded lot (the breadth of *our* minds wouldn't have covered a sixpence) were the Methodists and those we *never* met were the Primitive Methodists or the Congregationalists. Every Sunday we were summoned to our various places of worship by multifarious bells clanging from splendidly built belfries. All except the Catholics. The twelve of *them* met in a wooden hut.

BUT, this lot separated by God were brought together by Mammon – or, more accurately, by Mama. She was mad about the theatre and with her sweet soprano voice was a natural for the leads in the local Gilbert and Sullivan productions. In addition to this, though, she organised and presented the annual Passion Play for the church – but, in the true spirit of Christianity, cast and audience *were* recruited from other denominations – as well as a Concert Party which toured the local halls. This rejoiced in the nomenclature, "Mrs Fanny Rix and her Bright Young Things". Yes, my mother *was* christened Fanny – no sniggers please – or kindly leave the book. She was also referred to once, in a Parish Magazine, as "Mrs Fanny Rix and her Bright Flowing Things". This conjures up a very interesting picture of my mother's physical attributes, but this particular vicar was obviously a bit strange for he took great exception to a harmless old Cochran sketch which was set in a Customs shed. In this ladies smuggled packages in their corsets and one of these bulging supports was revealed to the audience. Such a display was "not suitable enter-

4

tainment for a Church Hall nor did it reflect great credit on the actress who revealed her underwear". The vicar is long dead. The actress was my sister, Sheila, who under her married name of Sheila Mercier, revealed many undignified feminine garments and foibles during her years with me at the Whitehall and the Garrick. She now makes endless cups of tea as Annie Sugden in *Emmerdale Farm*.

But to go back to Fanny. Amateur Theatricals – Passion Plays, Concert Parties and Theatre Plays – presented in such jolly places as the Parish Hall, the Floral Hall, Granville Court and the Star Cinema. Visits to the Rep. at the Little in Hull. Visits to the marvellous open-air theatre in Scarborough. Can you wonder all four Rix children loved the theatre? My brother, Malcolm, and my sisters, Nora and Sheila: all older than I and all splendid, I thought, in everything they did. Being the youngest has its compensations. We are much freer than our elders to indulge in hero worship, and my brother was the best amateur I knew at acting or tennis or driving or swimming or cricket. And my father? He made the scenery and the props. He was also mad on cricket. So what hope had I? Cricket and the theatre have been the ruling passions of my life ever since those days – apart from sex, of course. However at the age of five sex was a few years away – but the theatre and cricket were always at hand. So was sex, come to think of it but we won't go into that!

So we moved to a rented house in Hornsea – hard by the seafront – to see if we liked living there. The house now is a nunnery but in those days it housed six Rixes, Florrie the maid and Allie the nannie, plus a super generator which charged the batteries to supply our home with electricity. It was a magnificent machine which had to be tended and nurtured every hour of its working life but it always seemed to fail when my father wished to impress visitors with the fact that our house, unlike others, had electricity. He would rush into the garage, start the machine with many a muffled curse, and the bulbs would flicker once again into uncertain life. A perfect set-up for the electric version of *Gas Light*. I never really knew my father well. I now realise he was a gentle, frustrated man who was given, because he was frustrated, to sudden impassioned rages. Hurling himself at the generator showed his character, as did, once, his loving creation of half a dozen Roman swords for a Passion Play. He made them out of papier mâché and they took days and days of patient endeavour. Unhappily one of us laughed at the knobs at the end of the swords – they were huge balls totally out of proportion to the blades and the scabbards. My father exploded into a monstrous rage.

"If you can make the bloody things better – make them yourselves," was his highly original comment. Unhappily he hurled the lot of them into the fire at the same time. He'd made a load of Roman armour, too, but we grabbed all this before he could wreak his revenge. In the end *he* was sorry, *we* were sorry, and my mother had to hire half a dozen Roman swords with huge balls at their ends.

Hillcrest – this was the name of our rented house – also sported a tennis court and there I learned to play cricket, began to doubt Father Christmas and lost Allie, my nannie. My nursery school was Miss Learoyd's, which was near the church. On the first day I asked Allie not to leave me. On the second day I asked her to leave me at the gate. On the third day I asked her not to kiss me good-bye. Allie was heartbroken. The writing was on the wall and, of course, eventually she had to leave. I loved Allie. She was a warm, soft creature and I used to visit her regularly until she died. Happily, her brother had left her some money so she lived in comfort throughout her retirement.

When I was seven we moved to our "own" house – Kirkdale. I also moved from Miss Learoyd's to my prep school – St Bede's. I shall crib the whole of my schooldays (as was my wont) from the magazines. They are instructive and commemorative. My sisters were there before me in the "Girls' Department":

St Ethelburga's Summer Term 1930:
"During the Easter Holidays, ten entered for the Hull Festival competitions in Elocution. Betty Jubb and Sheila Rix came third."
"Nora Rix and Sheila Rix won the three-legged race."

You will note that our family was already reaching for the heights.

St Bede's:
"D. F. Platts (The Leys) is in his house Junior XI for Cricket and 12th man for his house First XI."
"Tony Platts was placed third in his class for Violin during the Hull Musical Festival."

Dear Tony. A gentle boy, known and teased as Beaky because of his heroic nose – he was killed in Normandy in 1945 when a Tank Officer. He was picking Spring flowers . . .

His elder brother, Douglas, never made The Leys' First XI but he *could* have made the D'Oyly Carte. He had (and has) a superb light baritone – but went into his father's business – corn. He should have joined me.

I am godfather to Antony – Douglas' adopted son. A gentle boy too – like his long dead uncle – but not yet a splendid Pooh-Bah like his long dead grandfather. We thought him ideal as Lord High Everything Else, for wasn't he a Methodist?

Easter Term 1931:
"AVE, ATQUE VALE. The following new boys joined the school this term: G. Dick, B. Noall, D. Fox, D. French, A. Lancaster, B. Rix."

My memories of all these boys are few except for Douglas Fox and David French. Douglas had a withered arm and was my greatest friend. One day, fairly recently, he left his wife and family – never to be seen again. His empty car was found – nothing more. David French had a stutter and his father was then our family doctor. He ceased to be, a year later, in circumstances which I shall, all in good time, reveal.

The headmaster was Dr G. H. Bickmore – "Bickie" to all and sundry – assisted by his splendid wife, Gwen. A medical doctor by training, he was a marvellous teacher and infused great enthusiasm into everything that interested him. Cricket, Rugger, Scouts, Shooting, Theatre, and, occasionally, academic subjects. As a doctor, however, he had his limitations, for after many years of running a prep school, he was let loose on the Army during the war in a medical capacity and literally had to re-learn his Charing Cross Hospital training at the expense of the PBI. It is doubtful if the German Panzers, in full cry, created more terror in the British Army. But hindsight is no way to form a judgment. I loved old Bickie and did my best for him at all times. Of course, I was best at the things *I* liked – acting and cricket – but, *honestly*, I did do my best at Maths and Latin.

My first appearance in a school play was at Christmas 1932. Suitably impressed by my family's theatrical interests you are no doubt expecting me to spring into the lead. The reverse was the case. I began, literally, at the bottom. I was "Kaa's Tail", the third vertebra from the end. The following two Christmases saw a meteoric rise. In 1933 I was a Nymph in *Theseus* and in 1934 I spoke my first earth-shattering lines at the court of Hereward the Wake.

"Yes, my liege," croaked I as the 1st Maiden.

I say croaked quite deliberately. Such was my excitement at being given a chance to perform I lost my voice at every school play. The extraordinary thing is that this became synonymous with Christmas and has continued into my professional days. I always seem to develop a cold around December 25th and have to spend at least a month being cared for by one of those admirable Ear, Nose and Throat theatre specialists, John Musgrove or Norman Punt. How's that for a psychosomatic disorder? I also suffer dreadfully with my bowels and bladder before a first night and frankly I might just as well sit on the loo and settle for a package deal rather than attempt to delineate betwixt front and rear. Once, when I was a *very* small boy, I had to present a bouquet to Mrs Fox who was playing the piano at a Rugger Club Concert. I was very excited and duly went to the loo for a pee but realised that all was not well behind. I attempted to drop my trousers before dropping anything else but failed miserably – for I was then, promptly, sick. I did not present the bouquet but I did present a hell of a problem to my parents. How *do* you clean up such a royal flush?

This subject reminds me of another moving occasion when I was travelling on a bus from Hull to Hornsea – a distance of

8

nineteen miles. One mile out of Hull I wanted to pee. Two miles out I was bursting and the jogging up and down wasn't helping too much either. At three miles I stood up and asked the Clippie to stop. I found this a terrible request to make for I was young, impressionable and fancied her. But worse was to follow, for in broad daylight and in full view of two dozen passengers I scrambled out of the bus and red-faced with mortification and hot with horror I released the dammed-up waters against the offside rear wheel, which I believed to be the legal one when it came to relieving oneself against a vehicle in public. The courage *that* took.

You may well be scratching your heads in wonderment at my reference to the offside rear wheel being a legal urinal in public. This belief springs from my youth. We had a notorious carter in Hornsea called Finch but known locally as "Stench", because of the aroma that surrounded him and his horse and cart. Often I'd see him using the offside rear wheel and when I queried this I was told it was the one legal place where one could flash it in public or words to that effect. It may be an Old Wives' Tale, but certainly Stench got away with it. Maybe the Old Wives enjoyed the spectacle.

Another famous figure in Hornsea at that time was a tiny gardener affectionately known as "Dwarfie". He and Stench had a life-long feud.

"When art tha goin' to grow, Dwarfie?" yelled Stench one day.

"When tha washes tha bloody neck," replied Dwarfie.

Such wit, such repartee. Hornsea would buzz delightedly with their cross-talk for we considered them equal to Laurel and Hardy. My dad employed Dwarfie as a part-time gardener, and during the war we kept chickens. One night we caught a rat in a cage-trap in the chicken-run. My father looked at this and tried to drown it in a bucket of water. However, his courage failed but he then remembered that Dwarfie, who would be with us in the morning was, as well as being a part-time gardener, a part-time rat-catcher as well. My father looked at the rat. The rat looked at him. My father thought it looked hungry and, being a soft-hearted chap, gave it a few handfuls of chicken food to keep it going till its execution in the morning. At the appointed time, along came Dwarfie and had the problem of dealing with the over-fed rat presented to him.

"Leave t' bugger to me," he whistled through his droopy moustache, and found a suitable pick-axe handle. "Now open up t' cage door," he instructed my father, "and I'll belt t' bloody bugger on t' head." My father obeyed, the rat ran out, Dwarfie smote the air and fell arse over apex, missing the rat completely which escaped sleek and fit, after a very good night's board and lodging.

"You daft bugger," moaned Dwarfie to my dad. "Tha' should have waited till I told thee I weer ready. Now that mucky bugger with his horse and cart'll tell whole bloody world about this."

Stench did, of course. The story passed into the local mythology of the time. Happy innocent days . . .

Christmas 1935 was a great occasion for me. My first lead in the school play. I played Scout Napoleon Sharkey in *Nap's Adventure* which was really a crib from *Ambrose Applejohn's Adventure*. However, I was hardly conscious of plagiarism at that time, merely that I was able to overact to my heart's content. "Avast, ye Lubbers" and other shouted orders were all part of the 2nd Act when I dreamt I was a pirate. Unfortunately, the shouting was a little dimmed by my usual loss of voice, but I got through somehow and was adjudged "excellent" in the school review. Then followed two more years of Christmas bliss:

"In *The Rose and the Ring* Giglio was played by Rix [there's fame for you – none of your Christian-name rubbish] who thoroughly enjoyed his part and did it well."

The same magazine contained another gem of information:

"The Swazi-Wallah Band, which was got up by Mr Gray and performed in the interval, was composed of the following – Mr Gray at the Piano, M. Strachan, B. Rix, A. Brown, W. Barr and W. Austin. Brown and Austin performed on the

Bottle-Phone. The remainder played on their Kazoos and a remarkably good performance they gave."

What with enjoying my part and giving a remarkably good performance on my Kazoo – I must have been exhausted.

Sadly, 1937 was my last performance in a school play at St Bede's. "In *He Found Adventure* the biggest part was taken by Brian Rix as Ian Stuart and a good job he made of it." It was also my swan song at the school for the rest can be seen in the same magazine:

"Congratulations are due to the Rugger XV for its unbeaten season – no small achievement considering our numbers and those of our opponents. Congratulations are also due to Brian Rix who ended his successful cricket season last year by taking 8 wickets for 17 runs and scoring 54 not out when playing in a match organised in August by the Yorkshire CCC for E. Riding schoolboys – in which match he was the youngest boy playing." (My father nearly burst with pride that day – especially when the Bishop of Hull bestowed his apostolic blessing by saying I was the best boy cricketer he'd ever seen.)

Finally, in March: *Ave Atque Vale* –

"B. N. R. Rix, Head Boy, XI (Colours), XV (Colours), VIII (Colours) – to Bootham School, York."

I loathed Bootham. I was desperately homesick and bullied unmercifully. This may seem strange – for it was a very civilised school and held to all the best in the Quaker teachings – but the boys (or, rather, a few of them) could be monsters. One horror really crucified me and I was delighted when I heard he had been killed in the war. That's how bad it was for me. Why? Well I was different. Because of cricket, my first term was in the summer and it's a bad start to be put into the 1st and 2nd XI nets when you're a new boy, especially one aged thirteen. But my main difference was physical. My right bollock was missing – and this provided endless enjoyment for all those little darlings whether I was taking a cold bath (obligatory, first thing in the morning) or changing for games or showering after them:

> Mono – he's only got one ball
> And that one is very, very small.
> His brother, has the other
> And his father's none at all.

sung to the tune of "Colonel Bogey".

The whole thing was a balls-up anyway. When I was eight I had had to push the heavy roller at school along with several other boys. My mistake was to push too hard and next day a strange swelling appeared in my right groin. After months of staring at this – as though it would go away – my parents and our aforementioned family doctor decided the time had come for the operation. I was admitted to the local Cottage Hospital. The night before my admission I suspected the worst. Not because anyone had had the common sense to tell me, but because I was given a dose of Syrup of Figs. Normally our bowels were opened forcibly on Friday nights but this was a Sunday night – and the unaccustomed movement alerted my suspicions. You see, the same procedure had been followed the previous year when I had my adenoids and tonsils removed and children have long memories when it comes to the unpleasant. I entered the hospital with great trepidation.

My worst fears were all too soon realised. My family doctor assured me I wouldn't have to have ether – in those days administered on to a mask by a drop bottle. I went into the operating theatre quaking at the knees to be greeted by total silence from the general surgeon about to perform the op and to be greeted also by the face mask, the drop bottle and ETHER. I fought like a child possessed. It took four nurses to hold me down and twice I fell off the operating table. I often think that surly surgeon winkled out my poor little bollock through sheer spite. Anyway, winkle it out he did. It can be done too easily in a hernia operation if you're not careful, and my surgeon wasn't. My father could have sued for a large sum of money on my behalf, but because he didn't wish to cause me distress he elected never to

12

mention it to me and simply changed our family doctor. Poor dad, he sentenced his youngest to eight years of purgatory at school.

My second hernia was a much more pleasurable experience. I was 22 and in the RAF. I was also in a very pretty WAAF at the time and working away well and happily when suddenly I felt a sharp pain. Withdrawing politely, I examined the afflicted area. There on the left side this time, was the tell-tale bump. Sick Quarters in the morning. Immediate admission to Halton RAF hospital, two weeks in bed, four weeks' sick leave, a neat scar and an untouched left bollock that has served me manfully to this day.

But back to Bootham. It was there that I discovered my love of the theatre exceeded my love of Medicine, and the latter was the reason I had gone to Bootham in the first place. A great family friend was Dr Norman Rymer. He had been badly gassed in World War I but in spite of dreadful respiratory troubles he ran a huge practice in Hull and always wanted me for a partner – for I had expressed great interest in Medicine from an early age. He'd been to Bootham and he and my father thought the same path should be followed by me. Alas, I was good at all the actors' subjects – English, English Literature and History – but disastrous at Maths, Chemistry and Physics.

Bootham was years ahead in many things. It took advantage of the Friends Appointments Board – that is Vocational Guidance – long before other schools followed this line. My report of the 2nd May 1940 had a number of pertinent things to say:

"In the intelligence test we gave him he made a distinctly good score; it was well above the average for boys of his age and type of education. On this basis we would regard his level of general intellectual ability as a very satisfactory one . . .

"His essay, though a little immature in places showed originality and some sense of style. His literary powers in our opinion are fairly promising. [God, I hope so!]

"He is a friendly, talkative and open person who is obviously very sociable . . . and not afraid of the limelight; when he is more experienced he should be able to lead and organise the work of others. He has plenty of confidence and he is a co-operative and dependable person though he is perhaps a little self-centred at present.

"His chief ambition is for medicine. We certainly do not rule this profession out altogether though we do not feel we can regard it altogether with favour ... He also expresses an extreme interest in the theatre and has considered the possibility of becoming an actor.

"As he realises, this is very insecure even for those of exceptional talent. We do not feel we can give it our strong support."

So much for the vocational guidance ... Funnily enough, I was never in the school productions at Bootham. But I was now appearing for my mother in the holidays – Simon in *Hay Fever*, Danny in *Night Must Fall* – oh, yes, I was hooked. But at school my talents went unnoticed! However, twenty-five years later the President of Old York Scholars' Association referred to me in his inaugural address:

"Although it is a well established convention to claim John Bright as our most famous old scholar, I believe when the bicentenary comes to be celebrated, it may well be that Philip Noel-Baker, Olympic runner and Nobel Peace Prize winner, may lead the poll as our most distinguished old scholar, and besides the long list of famous historians and scientists, doctors, teachers and professors who were at Bootham we can also claim Brian Rix of the Whitehall Theatre."

I must say they were jolly good to me when I returned to the school to speak at a lunch in 1970. Quite a number of my old masters turned up to see me and it all seemed very pleasant. Perhaps it was totally *my* fault I was bullied so much. At least I made two great friends at Bootham. One was David Stross, whose cousin, Raymond, became a well-known film producer. The other is a close friend to this day – Bill Turvey. He's also my dentist, and Elspet and I go to visit Bill and Ann at their home in Saffron Walden for weekends and he then has a go at my teeth.

It's all very civilised. I'm a devout coward so he always gets me pissed before starting work. I don't think any of his other patients have a gin and tonic next to the mouth wash on the bracket table – but I have known Bill for a long time.

School, by 1940, was irksome to say the least. We had been evacuated from York to Ampleforth College and were herded into overcrowded conditions in the Junior School. I found the wind whistling off the Yorkshire Moors was freezing at all times and solidified my brain. I therefore failed my Latin Matric which put paid to any hope I had of going to Oxford. I only wanted to go there to get my Cricket Blue, so I persuaded my father to let me leave school to study Latin alone and, such was his love of cricket, he let me. I repaired to the Rector of Rise, Mr Read, to improve my Latin. All he succeeded in improving was my driving. I used to belt his old jalopy round and round the Rectory drive but Latin remained, at all times, in bottom gear.

So the months dragged on. Activated by adulthood and acne I found all of the shop girls eminently desirable. One worked in a cheap lending library and I read at least two books a day so that my visits could be frequent and noticeable. A fat lot of good it did me. Between the book covers I was highly active. Between the bed covers with this particular librarian – never. All I developed was a pain in the scrotum and a loathing for pulp literature.

All other activities, other than sex and amateur theatricals, had been forcibly curtailed by the war. I had been a "ham" – the youngest amateur transmitting licence-holder at the time – but licences had, of course, been withdrawn. Amateur photography, too, had gone. Films were needed for the war effort. True, I played cricket for Hull in the Yorkshire League, but cricket had also been pushed into the background by the war. It still offered many attractive opportunities, though. Once I went to play against York and was given bed and board by the father of another Bootham old boy. I'd always fancied the daughter of the house and this time all those nocturnal imaginings became reality. The next morning dawned hot and sunny. In those days I bowled fast off an eighteen-yard run so I opened the bowling

15

at 11.30. By 11.45 I was flat on my back in the pavilion. Heat exhaustion was the diagnosis. Ah, well. *Honi soit ...*

So 1942 approached rapidly. I suggested to my father that I'd probably be killed in the war anyway, so why shouldn't I spend my last months happily in the theatre?

By the spring of that year I had my first theatre contract with Donald Wolfit. I celebrated by eating egg on beans in Field's Café. It was a banquet I'll never forget.

Act II

It was really all Sheila's fault. In 1937 she'd gone to the newly formed College of Dramatic Art at Stratford-upon-Avon. The principal was that fine Shakespearean actor, Randle Ayrton, and when he'd been the lead at Stratford one of his juniors was Donald Wolfit. Since those days Donald had blossomed forth as an actor–manager but he still had the greatest respect for Randle and when he recommended Sheila to Donald she was offered a job immediately.

So we got to know the great man. He even visited our house in Hornsea when he was playing at the New Theatre in Hull. I nearly swooned when he arrived. Black Homburg hat and Teddy Bear coat, a beautifully modulated voice which performed sonorously at all times: my idea of what an actor–manager should be. I listened open-mouthed to all his stories and nearly burst with pride when I was able to recount to people that "Donald came over to see us yesterday".

"Donald?" they'd say.

"You know, old Wolfit. He's playing at the New." When I worked for him two years later I never called him "Donald" then. It was "sir".

Anyway, in the spring of 1942, I was appearing in Hornsea for my mum as the Stranger in Philip King's *Without The Prince*. This was a very funny farce but the Stranger had to be played straight for he was supposed to be a famous actor, suffering from amnesia, who became involved in a Parish Hall production of *Hamlet*. At one time I had to speak the whole of the "O, what a rogue and peasant slave am I" soliloquy, which was greeted with unbridled laughter as various members of the cast reacted to it. As we were *actually* playing in a Parish Hall I don't know how we had the nerve ...

Donald was once more on tour in a piece called *David Garrick*. Again he visited us in Hornsea and this time I plucked up courage to ask if I could audition for him.

"Have you any audition pieces?" he asked.

"Well, I know Robert Service's 'Bessie's Boil'." (I used to recite that at troop concerts and then assault the ears of the assembled soldiers with my impersonations of George Formby. I accompanied myself – fairly slowly – on the banjo.) "And ... 'O, what a rogue and peasant slave am I'," I said casually. Wolfit was suitably impressed.

"That should give me a fair idea of your comic and dramatic possibilities," he said, somewhat dryly. "Come and see me after the matinée this Thursday and I'll hear you."

So, I went, auditioned and landed the job in his autumn tour. This rehearsed in July and, joy-upon-joy, rehearsed in LONDON. I'd only been to the capital for half a day when I was fifteen so the thought of working there nearly blew my mind. That, plus an Equity contract which was going to pay me the fantastic sum of £3 per week – to perform as cast and to perform the duties of Assistant Stage Manager. Gosh! Can you wonder I had such a blow-out in Field's Café in King Edward Street. Incidentally, Wolfit thought I'd learnt "O, what a rogue and peasant slave am I" especially for him and he noted my keenness. I never disillusioned him ...

Mention of King Edward Street in Hull reminds me that my father's office was just up the road in George Street. My grandfather, Robert Rix, had been a ship's master and become a shipowner with a very small boat, the *R & M*, named after his first initial and that of my grandmother, Margaret. They had three sons, John Robert, Ernest Bertie and, my father, Herbert Dobson (Grandma, having married a Bert was determined to keep it in the family) and all three went into the business, via the sea. JR became a master, EB an engineer and my father went to Trinity House but because he was the youngest and good at Maths he was taken straight into the office – those days in "The Land of Green Ginger". If that strikes a chord, but you can't remember where you've heard it, look up Daniel Defoe's *Robinson Crusoe*.

Well the business prospered and eventually moved to Carmichael Chambers in George Street. These offices backed on to R. P. Carmichael & Co. Ltd, by then the biggest and smartest jewellers, leather goods and antique furniture dealers in the North East. R. P. Carmichael – Bob – was one of my father's closest friends and they lunched together daily at the Exchange for thirty years. They were so typically Yorkshire they never bought each other a drink in all that time. Anyway, occasionally, on high days and holidays, I was allowed to lunch with them and once I overheard the following:

"Arthur's lad's" (Arthur being Bob's brother) "got some bloody silly idea of drumming in a dance-band. Daft young bugger." The daft young bugger hasn't done too badly. He's Ian Carmichael.

My father was also mainly responsible for starting a highly successful company known by the splendid title: "The Dry-pool Dry Dock & Engineering Company Ltd", now known, typically, as "The Dry-pool Group". Most of my family were shareholders and once, when I was a "success" and my father, as Chairman, wished to show me off, I was wheeled along to the AGM. It was a rubber-stamp affair for the old man was supposed to read his report and that was, more or less, it. The meeting was attended by my uncles as Directors and JR was then a huge old Yorkshireman of eighty-seven supported on a tripod. His elder son, Kenneth, was sixty-two and sat beside me in the body of the hall. After my father had read his report he asked if there were any questions.

"Why is the dividend only twelve and a half per cent?" enquired sixty-two-year-old Kenneth.

"You bloody shut up, Ken," said his eighty-seven-year-old father, and Kenneth hurriedly sat down. That was the end of question time.

19

There is a marvellous North Country story told about one of my father's friends that is, perhaps, similar. The Chairman of the meeting was giving his annual report and it *has* to be read with a Yorkshire accent (Lancashire will do, if you must). "I'm very sorry to say we've 'ad a bad year and lost one 'undred thousand pounds." A voice at the back said, "Aye, but wot about shareholders?" "I'm coming to thee. The loss was due to strikes and lock-outs, as a result of which we 'ad to improve amenities and then put up workers' wages and this cost us the brass." A voice at the back, said, "Aye, but wot about shareholders?" "I'm coming to thee. Wot sort of shareholder are you?" "I'm a preferential shareholder." "I'm very glad to hear it – very glad indeed. You'll get bugger all two days afore rest of 'em."

I've always felt this could apply to my father, either of my uncles or *any* of their friends, for that matter. JR was once stopped for speeding when he was in his eighties.

"Are you aware," said the traffic cop, "that you were exceeding sixty miles per hour?"

"You'd exceed sixty miles a bloody hour if you wanted a bloody piss as much as I do," replied my uncle. The statement was read out in court and he was fined £2.

They don't make 'em like that any more. JR died and was succeeded by Kenneth who, in turn, died when only sixty-five and the business is now run by his son, my second-cousin, John. I'm sure he's as tough as his grandfather, but he's more subtle about it. My other cousin, Geoffrey, EB's son, as well as my brother and I are out of the business. It's all very sad really.

During the war JR's sons, Kenneth and Leslie, were not called up, no doubt for very good reasons. However, Malcolm, Sheila and I were and so was Geoffrey, EB's son. This rankled with EB and my father. There were endless fights in the office and JR went off with his sons, Kenneth and Leslie, to form J. R. Rix & Sons. They took over half the shipping and all the petrol business (in the East Riding you'd be well advised to buy Rix petrol: it's cheap, and I've *no* shares!) and now it's all John's, plus Leslie quietly in the background. EB and the old man went off to

Prince's Avenue like a dose of salts and, not unnaturally, the lot went down the pan in time. But more of that later . . .

So it was rehearsal time in London. No home-sickness now. Just the joy of doing the one job I wanted to do. We rehearsed at the Duke of Wellington in Great Windmill Street and every day I used to walk through the West End clutching my *Complete Works of Shakespeare* in an ostentatious position in the forlorn hope that someone would recognise me as an ACTOR and a Shakespearean one at that! No one ever did. The only girl who seemed to know me stopped me regularly when I was going home.

"Good evening," she'd say.

"Good evening," I'd reply and politely go on my way.

I was so naïve – I never realised this pretty little girl was a whore. We didn't have girls like *that* in Hornsea. Not ones who were paid, anyway. Fortunately, my father staked me for my first week and I stayed at the Howard Hotel along with my mother. Every night was theatre night – and it was at the Piccadilly Theatre I saw John Gielgud's *Macbeth*.

"There's a lot of superstition about this particular play in the profession," I announced to my mother in a loud voice during an interval. "Fortunately, the same nonsense doesn't apply to our *King Lear*." Oh God, I must have been nauseating. However, the reference to King Lear was genuine enough for Wolfit was rehearsing his first stab at the part. Directed by Donald himself and assisted by Nugent Monck (from the Norwich Maddermarket Theatre) with settings by Ernest Stern, the whole production was, to me, a knock-out. How could these actors be so certain in their inflections and interpretations? How erudite was Wolfit when discussing changes in the text or cuts or transpositions with Monck. Fortunately, my interpretation required little erudition *or* inflection. I played Curan, a courtier, who speaks three lines. Even so, throughout that long autumn tour and the subsequent season at the St James's Theatre I was always slightly miffed that my name was never mentioned in any paper whatsoever – except *The Stage* which said I gave "able support". I felt like a jock-strap.

21

Apart from *Lear* Wolfit was relying on three standards from his repertoire, *A Midsummer Night's Dream*, *Twelfth Night* and *Hamlet*. I loved the *Dream*. Not only for its poetry and Mendelssohn's music but because I had a small chance to be funny as Snout. In fact, that's how I lost my trousers – or rather my tights – for the first time. In the clown sequence, I had to duck down inside the wall and stand up to speak a line or to overdo a suitable facial reaction. Standing up, on one occasion, my tights fell straight down to my ankles, with suitable screams of laughter from a school audience. Wolfit called me to his dressing room at the end.

"I believe," he declared, "that you could become a comic actor." I tried to explain that my tights were very old and had been washed and darned hundreds of times and all the elasticity had gone out of them. Wolfit enquired why I did not keep them up with the traditional pennies put into the tops of the tights, which were then screwed round and tied off with string. I proffered the excuse that on £3 a week I was finding it hard to make ends meet and had *spent* my pennies. The bolt went home and when the ghost walked on on Friday my salary had been increased by fifty per cent to £4 10s 0d. There's inflation for you. But all the same it was generous of Wolfit, because I must have come near to being kicked out. Years later, Donald said he *meant* that statement about my becoming a comic actor. I wonder . . .?

Hamlet was a bit of a giggle. Wolfit had really put on too much weight to play the part convincingly and for every performance he strapped on an enormous pink corset in an effort to control his overflowing avoirdupois. He also wore a very white make-up with heavy shading to make his cheeks sink. The result was *not* convincing – but I loved hearing "O, what a rogue and peasant slave am I" spoken properly. How Donald must have winced at my version. I'm amazed I got the job. As you can gather, tights were in somewhat short supply during the war – but Donald had managed to buy a splendid new black silk pair for *Hamlet*. The first time he wore them he was dying to have a pee and pulled at the front seam to make the necessary aperture. Unfortunately his desperation overcame his prudence, the tights were irretrievably torn and he came back on stage with the pristine black tights a mass of white ladders all aiming, unerringly, at his crotch. We kept out of his way, that night.

Twelfth Night has never been my favourite piece. Wolfit was a splendid Malvolio, but it really is a pot-boiler and Belch and Feste have always reminded me of school pranksters and bullies – and that's enough for me. On tour I played a tiny part – Curio – but eventually in London at the now demolished St James's Theatre I was promoted to Sebastian. I was bloody dreadful. I have a long face with a thin hooked nose. I had to look like the twin of Rosalind Iden who has wide cheek-bones and a sweet, retroussé nose. I tried nose paste and I looked like an elephant. I tried shading and I just looked mucky. In the end I looked like an overpainted old pouf prancing around in a blonde page-boy wig and my performance matched the appearance. Not many actors can transcend their total miscasting in a part. I can't, anyway.

You will see that I have just mentioned Rosalind Iden for the first time. On this tour, she was in the middle of a tempestuous courtship with Wolfit and I often thought he was very tough on her. When she became his wife they were the most devoted couple. I loved Rosalind on that tour. She was always kind, always understanding and a great champion of us lesser mortals when the great man was on the rampage. I always thought she was much underestimated as an actress but unfortunately she suffered because of all the snide sniping that went on against Wolfit during a great deal of his career.

Anyway, rehearsals proceeded to put the repertoire into shape. My mum went back to Hornsea and I left the splendours of the Howard Hotel for the doubtful delights of a furnished room in Sussex Gardens. Even this had glamour for me. Breakfast of corn-flakes, lunch at a Milk Bar and supper at Joe Lyons. Oh yes, this was living and the four weeks sped by. Then we were off. My first train-call (oh God, Sunday wartime journeys) and into my first digs in Cardiff. A huge double bed, a po which one had to slop out into the outside loo and incessant bloody meals of Welsh Rarebit. This wasn't a nationalistic idiosyncrasy on the part of my landlady, simply a complete inability of mine to keep my big mouth shut. On the first night the Welsh Rarebit was there for supper. I enthused politely about its tastiness and that was that ... Every night from Sunday to Saturday ...

So to the theatre on Monday morning to hang all the sets for the repertoire. How the hell we did it in one day I'll never know; but we did *and* a dress rehearsal. The date: 24th August 1942. The theatre: Prince of Wales, Cardiff. Curtain up on *King Lear* at 6.30. I WAS A PRO!

Being a pro, I was also taught my first "pro" stories. They all have the same air of resignation. Actor to Landlady: "What are your lowest terms for actors?" "A thieving bunch of bastards." Actor seeing another actor with cigar box: "I see you've hit the big time, old man. Cigars!" "Cigars, be buggered, I'm moving." Method actor rehearsing Long John Silver in *Treasure Island* – his first job in years – is eagerly hunting for a parrot and finds the perfect one. "Come back on Friday," says the shopkeeper, "I'll have him ready for you." "No, I can't come on Friday," says the worried actor, "I'm having my leg amputated." Ancient actor runs across old flame in the Salisbury, the actors' pub. After a few gins the flame is rekindled and they repair to the actor-laddie's room in Sussex Gardens. On the job she is making a terrible noise, gasping and coughing and wheezing. "Enough, no more," booms the old actor, climbing off the creaking bed. "Oh please don't stop," says the old crone, "it's only my asthma." "In that case, back to the conjugal couch. I thought you were hissing my performance." Actor on seven days' trial at rehearsal, really worried that he isn't going to get the part, sees the manager approaching the director with a note in his hand and then sees them pointing at him. He sweats and sweats with fear but keeps on rehearsing. The director calls him over: "My God, this is it," thinks the actor as the director hands him the piece of paper. He glances at it and bursts into hysterical laughter. "It's all right, everyone," he yells. "It's only my mother – she's dead."

The above old jokes' almanac just about sums up our profession. Anyone care to join?

And so the tour went on. After Cardiff, Torquay. Here Wolfit hired a boat and went out rowing with two juniors – myself and

Bryan Johnson (the singer, not the commentator). The tide turned and we had to row like the devil to get back to the safety of the harbour. Wolfit exhorted us at the top of his voice and could hardly cope with *Lear* that night. Come to think of it, his performance in the boat was similar to Lear's. "Blow, winds, and crack your cheeks ..."

Exeter was next, and my first encounter with bed bugs. Our fairies were all in the same digs (I am referring to the dancing girls not the prancing boys) and one morning a very tearful one (Anne Rogers I think it was) rushed round to the digs I was sharing with an actor – subsequently TV director, Michael Blythe.

"Come quickly," she sobbed. "The landlady says we brought the beastly bugs in with us and won't let us leave." Michael and I had to bluster and threaten but eventually we succeeded in getting the girls out. Ugh! The place was crawling. One of the fairies was known as Fairy Dettol from then on. She soaked herself in that pungent disinfectant for weeks on end in an effort to guarantee it would never happen again. Poor love, she developed a dreadful skin rash instead.

Then followed the Coliseum, Harrow (prices 1s 6d to 6s), Cambridge (half the sets had to be left at the station – the stage at the Arts was so small), and then, my home town – Hull. Living at home was marvellous. Wolfit visited us, as usual. This time, however, it was different for I was a member of his company and had to be deferential. I found myself with this attitude still when Donald appeared on my "This Is Your Life" twenty years later. On that particular programme he was at his most garrulous – and went on for at least five minutes over his time, launching into a story about me which really concerned Bryan Johnson. Such were my feelings for the man that I didn't contradict him. It would have been like contradicting one's feared, respected and formidable ex-headmaster. Manchester next, where it *did* rain – every day – and the usual short trip across to Liverpool. That was where I saw my first meths drinker. It was very sad. He wore a bowler and tail coat, both green with age and looked like a travesty of Charlie Chaplin. It was a memory of Liverpool that will never leave me, along with the Cookery Nook Café whose theatrical teas were "a speciality". Back to Yorkshire and Leeds where I was arrested as a possible spy.

My old school friend, David Stross, lived in Leeds and, not unnaturally, I went to visit him. I found his parents' house, rang the bell, but there was no one at home. Rather stupidly I asked a passing neighbour if the Strosses were away, coming back or what? She mumbled that she didn't know and shot on by – straight to a phone box. Moments later a police car arrived and two large gentlemen climbed out. Whipped into the car, I was closely questioned as to my knowledge of Germany or as to the whereabouts of my housebreaking implements. Luckily I only knew "*Achtung*, Spitfire" and had one rather blunt nail-file about my person. Even my identity card didn't placate them and it wasn't until I persuaded them to take me to the Grand Theatre and pointed out my Angus McBean 10″ by 8″ photo outside that they began to believe me. Further enquiries to the company manager, Alexander Brownlow, convinced them and I was released. I never did see David Stross on that trip. I didn't dare risk all that again.

So on to Glasgow – and my first fight over a bird. I was shacked up with a girl in the company who was married. As her husband was shacked up with a girl elsewhere it seemed a perfectly reasonable *quid pro quo*. Unfortunately, Cecil Cross, who was sharing digs with us, didn't agree. He was very scathing about her morals and about my part in encouraging the lack of them and we argued furiously about the rights and wrongs of adultery every night until dawn was coming up. Unfortunately, it was the only thing that *was*, for I'd then stagger into my bed so exhausted, that the adultery part was quite out of the question. This really brought new meaning to "sleeping with a woman". However, the row between Cecil and me continued on to the Sunday train-call from Glasgow to Edinburgh – so much so that he called her a whore. It all ended in a perfunctory bout of fisticuffs and we both stepped off the train looking the worse for wear and to this day I have a small scar on the bridge of my nose to prove it really happened. To make matters trickier my mother and Dorothy Rymer decided to visit me in Edinburgh that week – with the result that I had to explain away the scar on my nose by saying I'd bumped into a wall in the black-out. This deception, plus staying with my mother, finally put paid to my relationship with the married lady and my possible trip to the divorce courts was avoided. Cecil Cross changed his name to Hugh Cross and is a very respected local politician with aspirations to become an MP. He may even *be* an MP. Who knows? I wonder where his vote went when it came to the new divorce laws?

Coming south again saw us in Newcastle and then at the Theatre Royal, Nottingham – and the only time I've ever been "off", which means missing an entrance, and is the actor's chief nightmare, apart from the worse one of being thrown on for a first night without knowing your lines! There's an old actor-laddie story about the days of the one-night stands where you were given an idea of the story and told to go on and do the best you could. This particular old man was sent for as a last-minute replacement – arrived and found the stage manager.

"All right, laddie, I'm here. Now where is the stage and what is the play?"

Oh, my God – can you imagine the horror of it. Actually, come to think of it, it did happen in a sort of way to Ronnie Shiner in the fifth year of *Worm's Eye View* at the Whitehall Theatre. He, Jack Hobbs and "Taffy" Davies dried up in the middle of a scene. The prompt came and no one took it. Again it came and again silence. A third time came the disembodied prompt. Ronnie looked at the corner.

"We know the bloody line," he said, "but who says it?"

Anyway, back to Nottingham. I was well and truly off. Next door to the Theatre Royal stage door stood the Empire stage door and during the Saturday matinée I whipped out to see all those lovely dancing girls in *Chu Chin Chow*. Fascinated by the difference backstage at the Empire I wondered at all the noise and colour and music and the fact that everyone seemed to continue talking as loudly off-stage as they did on. If you so much as breathe backstage in the "legitimate" theatre, you've had it. Anyway, I was so gob-smacked that I missed my entrance as Curan in *Lear*. They pushed on another hapless ASM to squeak my few lines and *Lear* proceeded. I had the worst bollocking of my life from Donald. Totally justifiable, but I resented the one I got from my fellow ASM, Dennis Fraser, for, after all, I gave him his first chance. Up to then, he'd never spoken a word on stage! I don't think he ever did again, either. He went into carpets.

Apart from being off for the first and last time, I also received my first fan letters in Nottingham. One was from a Miss Brenda MacGregor who sent her request for a photo along with a 2s Postal Order. Magnanimously, I returned this (I was *so* grateful to be asked) together with the photo. Miss MacGregor obviously told her nextdoor friend, a Miss Lucy Weight, who made a similar demand. I duly sent the photo but kept *her* 2s!

So, to our final date, Croydon, and back to Hornsea for Christmas. Wolfit, in the meantime, was due to open his third London season at the St James's Theatre with *David Garrick* but I'd never been in that so was glad to be out of work to enjoy all the strictly rationed Christmas festivities at home. However, I joined him for *King Lear* and then on my nineteenth birthday, 27th January 1943, came my ghastly opening as Sebastian in *Twelfth Night*. My mother and Sheila were in the audience to see my triumph. Afterwards there was a slightly strained silence.

"I thought that sniff you gave was very funny," offered Sheila. As my sniff was a family failing on my mother's side, I knew she was being kind. Still, London was London and I had made the West End within five months of being a pro. Pity I wasn't better.

Then came disaster. Wolfit had to do a certain number of weeks for ENSA. He decided to do – wait for it – *Twelfth Night*, mainly because it was light-hearted and required the minimum of sets. We merely pushed round Ernest Stern's gaily painted, many sided screens. You can imagine it, can't you? Uncouth soldiery seeing me walk on in my blonde wig.

"Get you, darling." "Don't bend over, will you. You might lose your virginity." "Who's taking you home tonight – after the ball is through?" (Little did *that* soldier know!) And so on and so on and so on.

It was even worse when we played to the American troops at Tidworth. Within five minutes of our first night only the officers were left. All the rest had, noisily, gone. The second night armed Military Police patrolled the aisles and any misguided GIs who inadvertently came to see us *had* to remain to the bitter end. No, *not* a runaway success. Even birds were out, for Wolfit marshalled the snoring males into one dormitory, the non-snorers into another and so on. As I snore prodigiously, I was with the snorers but soon realised I was a beginner. I didn't get a wink of sleep for the whole six weeks of the tour and I didn't get anything else either.

That was nearly the end for me as far as Wolfit was concerned. Immediately after the ENSA tour finished, on the 28th March 1943, I was enlisted at Doncaster for the RAF. This meant we had two days of aptitude tests which were rather similar to those I'd taken at Bootham a few years before. Only now the problems were military rather than academic. I couldn't see the difference but apparently I exuded the necessary aggressive tendencies for I was selected for PNB training and put on deferred service. In simple English I was considered possible cannon-fodder for future training as a Pilot, Navigator or Bomb-Aimer. Deferred service merely meant that not enough of the going cannon-fodder was, in fact, feeding the cannons and we lucky younger ones would have to wait our turn. My deferment was ten months, in theory. In practice, it turned out to be six months longer . . .

Wolfit immediately offered me a contract for the limited future. I decided that if I was going to live through the Holocaust (and I'd a good chance – I hadn't been picked for air-gunner and the war was going well), I ought to come out at the other end with some varied professional experience. Thoughts of Medicine or shipowning still eluded me. My future as an actor was set and I had to do all I could to further it and, therefore, repertory was the next logical step. So I wrote to Mrs Peacock who ran the White Rose Players in Harrogate. I must have picked the right time, for I got the job as juv char (juvenile character to you).

By a strange coincidence I last saw and spoke to Donald Wolfit outside the Garrick Theatre on the Twenty-fifth Anniversary of my becoming a professional actor – the 24th August 1967. I was then struggling to keep my repertoire of farce going at the Garrick. He was struggling to keep his life for he was a very sick man. For Donald the date must have been even more poignant for twenty-five years earlier he had been giving his first splendid performance as Lear and I'm sure one of his greatest disappointments was that he was never able to perform it at one of its natural homes – the Royal Shakespeare or the National Theatre.

I suppose I must thank, or curse (according to business) old Donald for the fact I became an actor-manager, for he set the pattern I was to follow. I even used his rehearsal rooms opposite Holloway Jail when *Reluctant Heroes* was taking shape early in 1950. He always encouraged me and predicted great things for it. He was right. It ran for 1,610 performances . . .

Act III

If I had to go back to weekly rep. now, I'd give it all up. But in those far-off days of 1943 I was nineteen, study came easily and here was a chance for me to learn how to speak up and not bump into the furniture. Actually, what to do with your *hands* is one of the first problems to overcome. In Shakespeare you hang on to your sword. In a suit it's different. Some young actors play pocket billiards with their hands thrust deeply into their trouser pockets. This causes only slight difficulties when opening or closing doors but gives a studied appearance of naturalness. Other young actors clutch, like drowning men, on to the backs of chairs. This can be very dramatic – especially if the hands are seen to tighten and the knuckles glisten white through the tautened skin. The major hazard of this particular business is when you are walking about the room clutching chair back after chair back and suddenly come across a low stool. The audience can be forgiven for wondering why you are doing press-ups in the middle of a tense scene. Yet a third ploy for the young hopeful is to become a "fag" actor. Not a queer actor but an actor who resorts to chain-smoking in an effort (a) to appear casual (b) to give his mouth something to do. This was very popular in the Thirties and Forties. Look at all the early films on TV and count up the number of fags that must have gone into the making of a picture. The major hazards of this particular form of acting are cancer, emphysema, bronchitis, heart disease and lighting up a cork tip at the wrong end. This will burn off your eyebrows and get a big laugh when you least want it.

All these tricks I learnt and perfected at Harrogate. Nowadays I *never* put my hands in my pockets, I *never* clutch furniture and I *never* light a fag. I'm a rabid non-smoker. In those days, however, I was learning and copying my elders and betters.

I arrived in Harrogate on Monday 10th May 1943, ready to start rehearsals the following day. I hadn't bothered to book digs as I was told the Stage Director, Colin Collins, would be able to fix me up. He wasn't exactly a mine of information but he was friendly and said he thought there were rooms in a house opposite the stage door. The lady of the house greeted me most warmly. I was shown a small, rather dirty room and agreed to take it for a week. I lasted one night.

It was *very* dirty I discovered as I climbed into bed. In fact, the sheets had clearly been slept in by quite a number of people with *extremely* dirty feet. There were also some rather obvious biological stains around the pubic area so I hurriedly climbed out, buttoned my pyjamas tightly to the neck, put on my socks and tucked in my pyjama bottoms so nothing could actually climb up my legs. I laid a handkerchief on the pillow and climbed back for what was clearly going to be a poorish night. I'd no idea how poor for as the night wore on I suddenly realised I was in the middle of a knocking shop doing a roaring trade. Harrogate was then full of members of the RAF and most of those members were on ops that night next door to me.

I was shagged when I arrived at rehearsals the following morning – but, unlike the RAF, through no efforts of my own. Mrs Peacock had a firm belief that actors should be phased in and out of the White Rose Players. Small parts at the beginning and small parts at the end – then the audience wouldn't hate you when you arrived or miss you when you went. So there I was rehearsing two lines in Chinese off a cue script for the Head Boy in Somerset Maugham's *The Letter*. It's a pity they couldn't have pushed me on to perform that first morning. Yellow with lack of sleep and little slit eyes that someone, charmingly, described as "piss holes in the snow" – I needed no make-up.

But the following Monday I had recovered and needed the full weight of the make-up box on my face. I even soaped my eyebrows out so that my own hairs would lie flat and I could draw on a suitable Chinese pair. I did the soaping bit so vigorously that parts of my eyebrows have remained bald to this day.

Before that first night of *The Letter* I had to appear, voluntarily, as a member of the company on Sunday 16th May in "Yorkshire Remembers – A Festival of Remembrance and Dedication". All part of the Harrogate "Wings for Victory" Week. My particular contribution was to recite verses by Andrew Marvell and my new landlady said she thought I had "a beautiful voice, dear". I'd moved from my bordello to a house further up the street and was sharing digs with several members of the company, including Honor Shepherd. Here everything was clean and tidy and splendid – for a time. Then the landlady appeared to be having a little menopausal trouble for she accused me of letting down my country by not being at the front. She then presented me with a white feather (she'd obviously got her wars mixed) and chased poor Honor round the house with a carving knife because Honor had suggested, very mildly, that I *was* a deferred service.

"He should have been killed by now," screamed our landlady. Clearly if I'd stayed there a moment longer I would have been. All of us left those digs very hurriedly.

I moved on to Mrs Richardson at 38 Dragon Parade. The mother of our scenic designer, Oliver Richardson, she was a dear soul and she and her daughter, Dorothy, looked after me magnificently. I had an enormous double feather-bed which I found had a secondary use, apart from comfort. A blonde, nubile, juvenile girl had just joined the company. She was clearly a splendid charver so I persuaded her to seek digs at No. 38 and she was duly installed. She was also duly installed in my featherbed the same night but exhaustion or comfort or both caused us to oversleep. Mrs Richardson walked in, as usual, the next morning with my breakfast and went to draw back the curtains. Quick as a flash, I rolled on top of my nubile blonde who immediately sank without trace into the all-embracing feather mattress. I was able to chat quite casually to Mrs R who never for one moment suspected that two into one *can* sometimes go. My

33

gorgeous blonde was, unfortunately, a lousy actress and didn't last long. A pity in one way – but perhaps just as well in the other. By now my parts were getting bigger (no pun intended) and required more attention to detail.

Learning *could* be a bit of a problem. Not because of feather-bedding but because of the dreaded cue script. In those wartime days, to save money and labour, actors in rep. were often presented with those diabolical, penny-pinching monstrosities. An entire part could be encompassed in a few pages. All you were given was your cue (the last few words of the previous speech) and then your speech. It looked like this:

JOANNA: . . . so, do you?

JOHN: That's a many-sided question which clearly demands a many-sided answer. The first part is the one that intrigues me, though. You did mean it rhetorically, of course?

FRED: . . . truth (*he exits*).

JOHN: You have the temerity to sit there having just destroyed all my belief in myself. I posed a simple question which you have seen fit to tear to shreds with your damned clever arguments, your smug self-satisfaction etc. etc. etc.

Not easy – as you can see. And remember, you were given your scripts on Monday nights, you rehearsed from 10 a.m. to 2 p.m. on Tuesday and Wednesday. Thursday was off for study and Friday and Saturday you ran through the play at least twice. Sunday: no rehearsal. Dress rehearsal on Monday at 2.30 p.m. and curtain up on the first night at 7.30 p.m. And we *did* learn *Man and Superman* – *all* of it in a week – and lots of others – God knows how – plus the show *every* night, except Sunday, and twice on Saturday.

The plays themselves at Harrogate were the normal run-of-the-mill repertory successes. But the standard was good and the houses were always packed. Ruling the roost was a very formidable pair: Addie Peacock and Marie Blanche. Mrs Peacock was the widow of William Peacock – a stalwart of the provincial theatre and the repertory movement. He had founded the White Rose Players many years before and when he died Addie continued the good work. Their most famous product was probably Trevor Howard – but Noel Johnson of *Dick Barton, Special Agent* fame didn't do too badly. Nor did Sonia Dresdel, nor yet another Beverley (near Hull) stalwart – Philip King – author of *Without The Prince, See How They Run, On Monday Next*, and co-author, with Falkland Cary of *Watch It Sailor, Sailor Beware* and *Big Bad Mouse* – to name but a few – the few I can remember without reference to the reference books!

Addie was ably assisted by her daughter, Marie Blanche, who had been a considerable name in musical comedy. They controlled the theatre with a rod of iron. Every Monday they were there on their special seats fitted to the back wall of the Dress Circle. Every Friday they were there too, in evening dress, even in wartime, to receive the patrons on what was the "posh" night. Honestly, Hitler never had a chance. They also wore white gloves to check the dirt around the dressing rooms and everything was always immaculate. They'd have wept if they had seen backstage in my dressing room nearly thirty years later when the theatre was struggling to keep alive and I went back for a charity show.

It was in that dressing room, Number 8, that I had my second and last bout of fisticuffs. A new young ASM had joined the company – Miles Manderson. He and I were not on the best of terms and on his first Monday in a play I whistled loudly from my corner in our shared dressing room. Now whistling, like *Macbeth*, is supposed to bring bad luck and Tim (for such is Miles' other name) politely asked me to stop. I whistled the louder and he came over and knocked me down. He wasn't the theatre's best actor but possibly one of its best heavyweights. However, he eventually joined the BBC, founded a chauffeur-driven car company (he was the chauffeur), left the BBC and now runs the best hire-car firm in London, Miles & Miles Limited. I should declare my interest – I'm a director of the company. Tim is godfather to my youngest, Jonathan, and has laid down a pipe of port for him – what a Twenty-first that promises to be – and is married to a vague relation of mine by marriage, Anne. She, by the way, is Louisa's godmother and Louisa is my second daughter. If you knock something down you never know what you may pick up.

My first leading part at the Opera House was in *Nothing But The Truth*. This old American farce will figure again in my story but for the moment let me remark that it was the *first* farce I had ever done and the audience *did* laugh.

"Brian Rix, in the lead, enhances the favourable impression he has already made since joining the company recently." So quoth the *Yorkshire Evening News*.

It was after I had been in the company for six months that my first big success came. Not, however, in a farce – but in Emlyn Williams' superb thriller *Night Must Fall*.

"We do not often get the chance of complimenting Brian Rix on his handling of a major part, but this week praise must not be stinted for his Danny. His keen appreciation of that prime factor in Danny's mentality, the need to be deemed clever and masterful, is especially admirable. He responds exactly as he should to the fluctuating opinions about him, he reaches his terrible climaxes of rapid staccato most effectively, and throughout he sheds his words with a fluency that proclaims a memory, unusual even in one whose business it is to remember easily and well."

I never let the critic on the *Harrogate Herald* know that I'd already played the part for my mother. Nor did I let the management into my guilty secret, for at the end of the week an extra fiver was tucked into my pay packet – a generous gesture from Addie and Marie and much appreciated by me. It went straight into my Post Office account along with my usual £4 a week.

My first appearance as Dan, as an amateur for my mum, took place entirely due to the kindness of the author, Emlyn Williams. Rather foolishly my mother and father had made all the plans for *Night Must Fall* without getting the final confirmation that the amateur rights were still obtainable. After all, the play was an old one, it was published and amateurs had been doing it for years. Apparently, however, Emlyn Williams had received a new offer for the play which meant withdrawing the rep. and amateur rights. This news came as a bombshell to us in Hornsea, two weeks before the appointed production date. My father wrote to Mr Williams, who was then appearing at the Globe Theatre, explaining our stupidity and also explaining that all the money raised would go to War Charities. Mr Williams was magnanimous. He would make an exception in our case and good luck to us. My first appearance as Dan was saved and War Charities benefited to the extent of £130. Thank you, Mr Williams. You allowed me my finest hour (and £5 extra for good work the second time around). Your letter was also published in our programme. Published? It practically *was* the programme. It's not every amateur company which hears from Mr Williams.

My performance as Dan raised my status in the company and I suddenly found myself playing bigger, better and *older* parts. I painted on more crow's feet, whitened more sideboards and stuck on more moustaches than hot dinners. I had plenty of those too. Mrs Richardson used up a lot of her own ration coupons to keep me fit and happy!

"Brian Rix gives a finely tempered performance as Robert Caplan in J. B. Priestley's *Dangerous Corner*."

I have the photograph and hardly recognise myself, looking like an aerial photo of Clapham Junction. I also note that I'm clutching the back of the chair with *all* knuckles glistening white. It must have been a *very* tense play. And so on, and so on, until my second ENSA tour. This time, thank God, with a play the audience would accept – *Suspect* by Edward Percy and Reginald Denham. Our six weeks was spent mainly at RAF camps. We gave many a performance and ate many a "breakfast" of bacon and eggs with air crews off on ops. It was a strange feeling, wondering how many of our audience wouldn't return ...

We returned to Harrogate with our "Grand Easter Attraction" – *Indoor Fireworks* by Arthur Macrae. I never liked the play very much, but I think the notice gives away why we weren't very good in it: "A series of family quarrels in which everyone shouts as loudly as possible." Generally the sign of inexperienced actors: if you don't think what you have to say is very good, speak up and say the lines as quickly as possible. I've seen very respected and well-known actors shout and mug their way through farce – the National Theatre's *A Flea in her Ear* was a classic example – simply because they were not experienced in the genre.

Man and Superman came next and the part of John Tanner was splendidly played by our director/producer, James E. Mills. Jimmy was a first-class organiser, a sound director and, occasionally, a brilliant actor. The West End never appreciated him and he went off to Australia unrequited. There, unhappily, he died. But Jimmy is typical of so many in the theatre. They can bring so much, but do not have that share of luck or spark of personality which makes all the difference. Perhaps the most interesting thing about *Man and Superman* was that it marked the introduction to the company of John Whiting – as an actor recently demobbed for health reasons. The writing came later. The strange thing is that my remarks about Jimmy Mills could, in the main, be applied to John Whiting. He had so much to offer as a writer, but in his lifetime it never really happened.

So it went on. Frederick Lonsdale's *Spring Cleaning*:

"Miles Manderson's make-up was decidedly unconvincing on Monday as a middle-aged butler, and would be improved by a less valiant attempt to assume years."

That'll teach him to knock me down ...

But, of course, it didn't. Fate plays strange tricks. I mentioned earlier how I was afflicted with a sniff – particularly at the first performance of *Twelfth Night*. This became worse over the months and was finally diagnosed as chronic sinusitis. The ENT specialist said an operation was necessary, so there was I admitted into hospital and there was Miles Manderson taking over all my parts ...

I went into hospital on Monday 5th June and on Tuesday 6th June as I was slipping into that delightful drowsiness that comes with the pre-med jab I heard the BBC announcement about the D-Day landings. The play I was missing was *French for Love*. Hardly appropriate when you consider what *was* going on in France.

I emerged from the anaesthetic feeling decidedly the worse for wear. The operation was an old-fashioned one by today's penicillin standards – but in 1944 it was the only way. Delightfully named a "double nasal anstrostomy" it consisted of chiselling permanent holes in the bones around the sinuses. The patient then inserted a cannula, twice a day, attached it to a Higginson syringe and pumped disinfectant into the offending cavities. For the uninitiated, a Higginson syringe is the same as one used to administer an enema, and for a long time all the old gags came trotting out: "Friend or Enema?". "If that's your arsehole, mate, what do you do when you blow your nose?". "Wouldn't like to tell you where that syringe was before you used it", and so on.

Within minutes of coming round I suddenly felt a "click" in my nose and blood poured from me. Panic set in. The surgeon had moved on to another hospital but was sent for and came rushing back. Blood transfusions were ordered and to stem the flow they packed my nose with ribbon gauze. Yards and yards of this stuff were pushed up my raw and bleeding proboscis, while I clutched on to the bed-head and cursed all doctors (and surgeons in particular) for being so fucking careless when it came to carving bits out of me. My language was so bad that the sister could hardly bring herself to speak to me – but I was past caring – for I slowly slid into half-consciousness and stayed like that for twenty-four hours. Then they were at me again. They *removed* the ribbon gauze this time and it was as bad being dragged out as it was being stuffed in. After *that* display of bad language there was *total* silence from the sister whenever she approached me.

Some years ago I mentioned in an article how my money stopped from the theatre as soon as I went into hospital and yet how generous Addie Peacock and Marie Blanche were with flowers, books and fruit – so much so that they spent almost as much on me as if they'd kept my weekly salary going. This was only meant as a jocular comment – but it brought forth a very angry letter from the Isle of Wight – for Marie Blanche lives there now – pointing out that it was all part of the old theatrical custom "no play, no pay". Absolutely. I make no further comment except to say that nowadays if you're ill whilst working in the theatre you *do* get paid and sometimes the management send you flowers, books and fruit as well – no raspberries though. Actors are sensitive about those.

Because of the haemorrhage my recovery was slower than anticipated – and it was hardly speeded up when my call-up arrived. I was to report to the ACRC (Air Crew Reception Centre) at Scarborough on Saturday 22nd July. My first long run was nearly over. Rather foolishly I decided to go back to the company, instead of taking a last look at liberty, and I found myself being "phased out" with two very small parts in *Drake's Drum* and St John Ervine's *Anthony and Anna*. The curtain fell for me, professionally, on Saturday 15th July 1944 and didn't rise again for nearly four years – and when it did, it didn't! Read on. You'll see what I mean in *Act V*.

But Harrogate and the White Rose Players provided me with a lot of work, a lot of experience and £200 in my Post Office account. Not bad, when you consider it was saved out of £8 a week (plus £5 for good work) earned over fourteen months. It also provided me with a girl with the biggest boobs in the business. They were so huge, you could dive into them just like my feather-bed. I have never seen their like again.

We will pause a while to accord them due respect.

Act IV

I joined the Royal Air Force on Saturday 22nd July 1944 with a
suitable theatrical flourish. My sister Sheila, by now a WAAF
officer, had a Free French Major in tow. It was just before he went
back to France to continue the fight on his own soil – but he was
very keen on Sheila and very keen to impress all the family that
his feelings were genuine. Once he got back to France that keenness rapidly evaporated but on Saturday 22nd July 1944 he was
still on the boil and volunteered to drive me to Scarborough
some thirty-odd miles from Hornsea. So there was I in a dirty
great Staff Car – chauffeured by a Free French Major, with a
WAAF Section Officer riding shotgun. I sat at the back in regal,
if somewhat car-sick, splendour. We duly arrived outside the
Prince of Wales Hotel, Scarborough where 34 Flight, E Squadron,
No. 36 R & C Wing was stationed. A squad of men was drilling
smartly on the promenade outside. Their instructor saw our Staff
Car slowing to a halt, two officers in front, and began to wonder
nervously who on earth was in the back. The rear offside door
opened. Corporal Collinson (for such was the Corporal's name)
decided discretion was the better part of valour, called his men
to a heel-stamping attention and brought up the most tremend-
ous salute. Out of the car stepped 1593333 AC2 Rix B.N.R. and
politely enquired from the Corporal where the guard room was.
Much suppressed laughter in the ranks and the Corporal told the
new recruit, in no uncertain terms, where he could find the bloody
place. Actually, he was a splendid chap and we became good
friends even though he was the Drill Instructor for our flight!

41

The motley collection of new arrivals settled themselves, uncertainly, on the appointed benches and waited for all the horrible things that were going to happen to us. They did – but not before I saw someone else with long hair sitting beside me. Long hair, in those days, denoted you were "arty" so I enquired if he was an actor. He turned out to be a pianist called Tommy Watt – newly departed from the superb Carl Barriteau band. We have remained friends ever since but then we were more preoccupied with the horrors of our first RAF haircut. It was *just* as ghastly as we had expected and even in July the wind whistled round our shaven necks. All the other delights came, too, in rapid succession. Kit issue and those lovely boots that not only blistered your feet but also blistered your ankles and shins as well. Buttons that had to be polished and polished – I wish I'd had shares in Duraglit – and vests and underpants I used to great comic effect when I finally returned to civvy street. One compensation. Because we were potential aircrew, we wore little white flashes at the front of our fore and aft caps. This gave us a great feeling of superiority over lesser mortals – although not one of our bunch ever qualified as a pilot. The war ended before we were needed, so everyone was made redundant. Even in those days, that ghastly word was in common usage.

For the moment, though, we wore our flashes proudly and clattered off to Sick Quarters for our FFI and jabs. For the ignorant among you FFI means "Free From Infection". You are all lined up, having first stripped off, and told to raise your arms above your head. The MO then walks up and down the serried ranks with a torch and a swagger stick. The torch is to illuminate the gloom of the armpits and the swagger stick is to lift up the beastly things hanging in the nether regions – it would never do for the MO to touch them – even with gloves on. This rigmarole is to make sure you haven't pox, clap, crabs, or some other sweet-sounding infection. Having assured himself on that point and having raised an enquiring eyebrow when it came to my turn ("RIH and Orchidectomy, aged eight, sir," I said smartly, to avoid any discussion on the subject, to which "Splendid," was his somewhat bemused answer), the MO then delivered a little homily on the dangers of promiscuous sexual activities.

"My advice to you fellows," he drawled, "if you MUST have it orf, is to put on one very thick French letter, pause, and then put on yet another French letter. This will make the whole affair as pleasurable as taking a shower with your clothes on. Consider this *slowly* and *carefully*, decide against the entire operation, remove the French letters and toss yourselves orf." He then turned to the Medical Sergeant: "Instruct them in the use of the ET room, Sarn't," and made his exit. The Sergeant was even more terse and to the point than the MO.

"Now, you men," he intoned, "if wankin' does not assuage the pangs of desire you may well find you've rogered the arse of some lovely lady without takin' suitable precautions. In that case repair immediately to the ET Room, to the rear of the guard room, urinate in short, sharp bursts in the receptacle provided and squeeze some prophylactic cream up your unclean hot-throbbing weapon." Frankly, I never heard of *anyone* using the ET Room. I think it was a diabolically clever psychological trick to make sex so unattractive it would put you off, if not for life, for at least as long as you were on that particular station. I never did discover what tricks they used to keep the WAAF celibate.

After the FFI – inoculations and vaccinations – your left arm was scrubbed clean with soap for that delicious scratching vaccination needle and your right arm was wiped clean with spirit for that delicious blunt TAB and ATT jab. You were then informed you were on forty-eight hours' light duty. As far as I could ascertain, light duty meant being doubled out into the road, doubled back to the billet and told to swing those arms as high as possible to keep the jabs going round. Several strong men fainted, several weaker men developed temperatures but it was only *then* that we were informed all inoculations and vaccinations were voluntary. This information was dropped in amongst all the other mass of knowledge we were supposed to assimilate at our first lectures. They also showed us an American Forces film, in glorious Technicolor, about – wait for it – the horrors of VD. Once again our ears and eyes were assailed with the problems of

43

Pox, Clap and a new one, Soft Chancre or Blue Balls. Clearly the RAF were determined to make their initials stand for "Rogering Almost Forgotten".

Of course, it wasn't. Hundreds of fresh young men scoured Scarborough looking for crumpet. I was lucky and fell in with an attractive nurse – although "fell in" is, on reflection, hardly the expression to sum up our relationship. She lived near that famous beauty spot, Oliver's Mount, and my friend Tommy Watt, always a wag, suggested that the trips to see my lady love were so frequent that it should be renamed Brian's Mount.

My off-duty hours may have been taken care of but my on-duty ones were certainly not. During my lengthy Medical Examination (as opposed to the FFI and jabs) it came out, not unnaturally, that recently I had suffered that operation for chronic sinusitis. My ears, nose and throat were sprayed, illuminated, X-rayed and examined from every possible angle and finally the doctors said I would have to be taken off training for a few weeks to see how things developed. If my sinuses did not clear . . . well, bad luck, but flying in unpressurised aircraft was completely out of the question and I would have to be re-employed.

I was re-employed. This meant being sent to the re-employment centre at RAF Eastchurch on the Isle of Sheppey and the nearest equivalent to a concentration camp we had in the RAF. It's now an "open" prison. In those days it was a closed one. You see we were the unwanted ones. Some redundant, some medically unfit or some, in the ghastly jargon of the day, LMF – Lacking Moral Fibre. My fibre had never been put to the test, thank God, but here were hundreds of aircrew, many decorated, stripped of all rank, brevets and dignity because they had, say, asked not to go on a particular mission. It was awful to see them with the faded sections of their uniforms showing clearly the badges that had recently been sewn there. Like the marks when you take a picture off the wall on moving day.

For me, moving day didn't take long. Being medically unfit I was offered alternative jobs which did not exactly ring any bells: cook, medical orderly and down the mines as a Bevin Boy. I chose the latter.

So there I was. Called up July 1944. Demobbed February 1945. However, during my last fortnight in the R A F (at least I *thought* it was my last fortnight, but more of that later) my father was admitted into hospital for an operation and chose to go to Harrogate. As it was a hernia operation and knowing what had happened to me in Hornsea Cottage Hospital, with the same operation, he may have decided that discretion was the better part of valour. I was granted compassionate leave on 26th January, the day before my twenty-first birthday, to see my dad, and travelled on a *very* slow train up to Harrogate. I arrived in the small hours of 27th January, on a cold and frosty morn, and had nowhere to sleep. I wandered round to the police station to ask their help and they very politely offered me a cell. I, equally politely, accepted but asked that they should not shut the door. The next morning, the prisoner ate a hearty breakfast, popped two bob into the Policemen's Benevolent Box and went on his way rejoicing. What you might call a *real* "coming-out" party!

A few days later, dressed in my lovely grey chalk-striped suit and green porkpie hat which clearly showed I had been in the forces, I was making my way for training at Askern Main Colliery near Doncaster. There we were given practical tuition underground or lectures on the surface. My first visit to the pit bottom was not, exactly, a success. We were all herded into the cage (the mining equivalent of a lift – but it has open sides with bars) and I was wearing all the regulation gear. Steel-capped boots, belt for my lamp, water bottle and snap-tin, all topped by a helmet, and, to complete the ensemble, pigskin gloves. Not that I thought I was going to the office – but as an actor I felt I should protect my hands from all that coal-dust. The cage jerked upwards and then plummeted into the depths. Down, down we rushed and suddenly we were going up again. Later I discovered that was an illusion and was caused when the wheelhouse applied the brake. Then, a splash and there we were at the bottom of one of the deepest pits in England – 960 yards – or so we were told. We stepped out into a version of the underground at Piccadilly Circus. Whitewashed walls, electric light, neat little arches leading to various parts of the mine. This happy similarity didn't last long as we soon discovered trudging along the roadways. For the moment, however, we were highly delighted. The instructor gathered us together and then looked at me:

"What the bloody 'ell's them things on your hands?" he enquired.

"Gloves," I said. "I'm an actor, you see, and I must protect them."

"The only protection you need is to be a bloody sight fastern'n me, lad," said he. And he held up one hand with the three middle fingers missing. "That's wheer t' bloody roof came down fast. Me hand wheer on top of a tub and me mates had to hack them fingers off." By now I felt distinctly sick. "You'll get them bloody pansy gloves stuck in machinery. Chuck 'em away, you silly sod." He turned to his mate. "By gum," he opined, "I sometimes think the best part of them Bevin Boy lads ran down their mothers' legs when they wheer born." And that's the way we really must have appeared to that unique and splendid body of pitmen. Ever since my brief encounter with them I have *never* had any hesitation about being "on their side". Put on your white overalls and your white pit helmet and inspect them by all means. You've no idea till you've worked there for a few weeks just what it's like. When I first went to Askern Main I came from a fairly sheltered background. I listened with amazement to the Socialist doctrines our instructors spouted on the surface. A short time underground and I was equally amazed at the restraint that had kept them away from the owners' throats. That's why, years later, I was delighted and proud to present for an all too short spell in London that superb entertainment *Close the Coalhouse Door*.

But we learnt a little at a time. No "new boy" was allowed near the coal-face. We were used for shovelling rubble – caused by ripping (the enlarging of the roadways to the face) – into moving tubs after the shot-firer had done his work. We learnt, too, about the construction and the "safety" in pits and the future envisaged for them. Nationalisation was just around the corner. Since that time I have met several ex-mine-owners. Their arrogance is incredible. "Our men loved us," they'll spout. "Even now they doff the old hat, you know." I *know* I'm making them sound like Bertie Woosters – but that's how they sound to me. Ugh! Those days made me a wishy-washy Conservative-cum-Liberal with dangerous Socialist tendencies.

I settled down and began to enjoy the shift life. Once, a crowd of us, off-duty, donned boots and helmets and tried to get a cup of coffee at the Danum Hotel during the time the ladies had their elevenses. We did succeed after much argument, and our little egos were satisfied.

We held our revelries, too, in the Danum on those evenings when we were off-duty and could afford the gins and orange or the ports and lemon. I remember the first time a girl asked me for a port and lemon. I was so embarrassed I could hardly bring myself to mention the drink to the barman. However it then occurred to me that any port in a storm might well apply here. "Get enough of those in her," I thought, "and she could be anybody's." So the ports and lemon flowed but, unfortunately, so did the gins and orange. I was drinking the latter (it's funny, isn't it, that in our youth we cover up our dislike of alcohol by sweeteners) and when we arrived back at her office, where in the daytime she worked as a secretary, she took everything down with *great* alacrity. I mumbled something about needing a pee – staggered to the loo and promptly came crashing down with my head resting on the basin. Very convenient to be sick in and there I rested fitfully till dawn dimly lit Doncaster's dwellings … Meanwhile my unrequited love had slept soundly in the office armchair and awoke completely refreshed – still ready for action. Unfortunately, I was a Fernet-Branca case and completely incapable of raising even a smile, so she swept out of the building and I tottered after her, suffering the most monumental hangover and too ill to notice that she'd carefully removed my cigarette case, lighter and money – for safe keeping no doubt – and failed to return them. I have never been drunk again … Doncaster and the pits taught me many a valuable lesson.

About the same time my old friend – oblique stroke – enemy, Tim Manderson, was called up and suffered a similar fate. His lavatory, however, was of the stalls variety which gushed forth water every few minutes. *He* awoke with his battledress top wringing wet. If *I* didn't get into port – he was hardly flushed with success. Come to think of it, neither was I. My medical papers arrived, incredibly slowly, from the RAF and I was told to report to the medical wallahs looking after the Bevin Boys. Again my nose was picked over, at considerable length, and this time it was decided that if altitude would hurt my ears – so would depth. I was hoofed out of a job I was not enjoying but, shall we say, appreciating. To make matters worse it was decided I was fit for ground duties. So, even though the war in Europe was over, back to the RAF for me and, strangely enough, I had a ball – in constant use, of course.

I had long longed to be a doctor but my stupidity at Latin, Chemistry and Physics overcame my desires. Now I was forced to become that *very* poor relation – the Nursing Orderly. We were even poor relations to the SRNs for our training was perfunctory and much shorter. I say "forced" because my particular alternatives were cook – I can still only boil an egg – or paratrooper. The latter was only for butch characters like Tim Manderson. Having become the heavyweight champion of Dressing Room 8, Opera House, Harrogate, he decided that the active life of a paratrooper was for him. He made his first jump, broke his back and returned to civilian life (with total mobility) while the rest of us slogged away for King and Country in the hell holes of deepest Hertfordshire.

I suffered my three months' course as Med/Ord U/T N/Ord at RAF Halton with consummate bravery. With only Tring and Halton to choose from as points of activity and only 2000 WAAFs to choose from for proclivity, life was a struggle. Somehow one managed and whilst I was there I joined the Station Dramatic Society and gave my well-known guest performances in *Nothing But The Truth* and *Night Must Fall*. This drew the authorities' notice to the fact that I'd been an actor in civvy street and someone decided I'd make a good instructor. So, one day, there was our squadron leader, a doctor, of course, bursting into our classroom and demanding that I give a lecture. Even then, my detractors would say, I went for the easy laugh and gave an hysterical turn concerning the use of bottles and bedpans. I say "hysterical" because my audience laughed a lot. Luckily the squadron leader was no Peter Black, dismissing the laughter as canned or merely sycophantic, and decided I'd make a good lecturer. All I had to do was three months "field" work in hospital or Sick Quarters and I could return as a full-blown Corporal Instructor. Would I accept? Would I accept?!! I'd have paid a premium.

Field work at R A F Hospital Cosford. This consisted of cleaning out the sluice rooms, emptying bottles and bedpans (where were my easy laughs now?) bumping floors and generally acting as anybody's dogsbody. But it could have been worse. Sometimes we were given medical work to do, but somehow it always ended up, literally, around the anal area. Shaving someone and cleaning them up for an operation in the groin or changing the dressings for someone who had just had their piles removed. One of my mates put it better than I:

"Ever since I became a Nursing Orderly," he groaned, "I've felt a right arsehole."

Occasionally we felt differently, for whilst I was at Cosford the war against Japan ended. We all repaired to the nearest town and there was much dancing in the streets of Wolverhampton *that* night. Those who weren't dancing were occupied in other pleasurable ways. At Cosford, however, things got a little out of hand. Many of the patients had been prisoners-of-war and when they heard the news they almost went berserk. Much of the furniture from the officers' mess was piled into a great pyre and the flames lit our unsteady way home as dawn was breaking. Accompanying this eerie scene was a recording of Glenn Miller's "When Johnnie Comes Marching Home" played again and again and again. I never hear it now without being transported back to those unreal days.

For they were unreal. The war was over – but the rigours of peace were about to descend on us. With no war to unite us I noticed an almost immediate change in our relationships, one with another. Politics became important again and friends who had been happily discussing women or gin or other normal

49

subjects suddenly became desperately involved about who was responsible, say, for the shortage of butter – the Conservatives before the war or the new Labour lot after the war. Bloody silly really ...

My three months at Cosford ended by my being posted to Sick Quarters at Croydon. Joy upon joy again. Just like my rehearsals for Wolfit – I was going to be in London. But I reckoned without the love of one man for another! Somewhere along the line my predecessor had been having what is euphemistically known as a "relationship" with another man – a sergeant. He was posted and I was to take his place. In the meantime, however, my predecessor had left his sergeant and concentrated on the postings clerk. I arrived at Croydon to find out that my predecessor was to stay and I was to take his posting to a far corner of Scotland – Milltown, near Lossiemouth. The journey took three days. First a slow train to Carlisle. Then a twenty-four hours' wait, because there were no further trains to Elgin, followed by the slowest of all trains to the north. I really do believe that train driver grew vegetables along the track and tended them every few yards. Ten hours later I arrived at my destination, to be greeted by a jovial Geordie MO, a cheerful Cockney corporal and an old sweat leading aircraftsman – "Pop" – who eventually became a Chelsea Pensioner, but even in those days he must have been eligible, so great was his age. The four of us were the Sick Quarters' staff of Milltown, but really there was nothing to do except go to the flicks in Elgin or to admire the beautiful russet tints which coloured the trees that autumn. Our MO was such a likeable chap it was difficult to remember to call him "sir" – but I once saw him in a rage that ended in a man getting fourteen days in the glasshouse for concealment of disease.

At sick parade one morning an Irishman wandered in and told me he'd got a "bit of an itch down below". I invited him to drop his trousers and when he did I nearly dropped "down below". He was, literally, red raw from ankle to crotch. A further invitation to remove his upper garments elicited the fact that he was red raw up to his neck, too. I asked the MO to pop out and see him.

"Jesus Christ, man, how long have you had that lot?" was his startled enquiry.

"T'ree months, sor."

"Three months. You've got bloody scabies from head to foot."

"I don't know about that, sor. But I do know I've got a bit of a flea."

It took a month to get him better. He was then wheeled in front of the CO and given his fourteen days. God knows how many men he infected during his three months with a "bit of a flea". Every blanket on the station was called in for fumigation.

Another very much cleaner person admitted to Sick Quarters was a certain AC2, Posner, G. He'd knocked himself out at rugger practice. Since those days he's knocked himself out with his law practice as well as sailing, hunting, and acting as my solicitor. Please refer all libel suits arising from this book to him . . .

Christmas was now approaching and the sick parades virtually ceased to exist – so much so that the MO told me I could take an extra four days' unofficial leave and go home for Christmas. I arrived at Elgin station to be greeted by a panting "Pop" who had cycled down to catch me.

"You're posted," he gloated, "that's cocked up your Christmas" – evincing the true Festive Spirit. Indeed, I thought it had, for my posting was to MTE & D RAF Halton as a trainee instructor. I arrived – two days later, smarting at my loss of leave – to be interviewed by the same squadron leader who'd been moved by my bedpan lecture.

"You do want to be an instructor, don't you?" he enquired.

"Yes please," I replied, "if I can go home for Christmas." I was lucky. He still remembered my lecture . . . I became a trainee instructor *and* was granted ten days' official leave for Christmas. It was the start of a very fruitful twenty-two months for very soon I was considered an ideal instructor for the WAAF. Tee-hee-hee!

How daft can you get? After my instructor's training (when I appeared in several more plays at Halton) I was given both my corporal's stripes *and* my first course – thirty-five, young, vibrant, nubile, bedworthy trainee members of the Women's Auxiliary Air Force. It was like asking a buck rabbit to take a vow of celibacy. *They* were recruits – *I* was a corporal! Within the first week I was already intimately aware of the potentialities of the front row and impatiently pawing the ground at the thoughts of the second one. I reckoned without woman's guile and man's inhumanity to man. Two of my front row reported sick. They claimed pregnancy. They also claimed me as the putative father. Fortunately the MO knew they had been with me for only one week and recognised that their respective pregnancies were of longer duration. I was absolved but my activities noted. The Station Warrant Officer sent for me.

"Corporal Rix," he mused, "it h'appears that you 'ave been h'intimate with approximately 25% of your course during the first week. As the course lasts twelve weeks – you'll be in for a second helping within a month. Par for a WAAF course is one. You'll be Pa for the *entire* WAAF course *in* one if you're not very careful. This is a Court Martial h'offence, you know, but we'll let that go. I suggest you tie a knot in it and concentrate on the permanent staff with wot h'appears to be *your* permanent staff. If I catch you co'abiting with anymore of your trainees I'll stuff your corporal's stripes straight up your h'arse and you'll be posted to the H'outer 'Ebrides. Do I make myself clear?"

Too clear! From now on permanent staff were the only targets for tonight. I grew quite fat through lack of exercise.

My SWO, Wally Everett, was a splendid chap. On two more occasions he saved me from certain Court Martial and if I over-write his accent I do it with great affection. It became posher every time he was promoted. When I last met him in 1959 he was a Squadron Leader and it was practically coming out from behind his ears. Another splendid Senior NCO was our Drill Sergeant, Jim Ivory. He had been a boxing booth fighter in pre-war days – but was much loved for all his rough manner and terrible jokes. On pay parades he'd call us all out in alphabetical order: "Fall in all the As, all the Bs, all the Cs, all the Ds, all the

Es, all the Fs – come on, Phillips, get fell in wiv the fuckin' Fs!"
When he and his wife came, years later, to see *Reluctant Heroes*
he was knocked out.

"I didn't know you could h'enjoy yourself in the f'eater,"
was his opening remark. "I f'ought it was like church."

A story, apocryphal I'm sure, was told about Jim. Once on
church parade, the men were marching into the hallowed pre-
cincts, hats off, of course. All except one – still with his side-cap
on. Jim sidled up to him.

"Take your 'at orf in the 'ouse of Gawd. Twat!" The offending
titfer was removed. I'm glad he'd didn't yell that at me from
the front row of the Whitehall – if he thought it was like
church!

So 1946 drew peacefully to a close. I was promoted from
instructor to Corporal in charge of medical staff postings. This
meant I worked one day a week – docketing all the movements
in and out of the station. I also sat on Medical Trade Test Boards,
asking simple questions about splints and first aid *and* bottles *and*
bedpans, and awarding marks to the hopeful candidates. Warrant
Officer Relph and the Squadron Leader asked the more difficult
questions. I was hardly overworked but fortunately our CO was
an Australian, mad on cricket and the Officer Commanding
Central Medical Trade Test Board was a Scot, mad on the
theatre. I came up from under my bottles and bedpans smelling
of roses. I was Captain of Cricket and ran the Station Dramatic
Society. As I noted all the postings, it was easy. If a good cricketer
or a good actor appeared on the books I reported this to the
SWO. He in turn reported it to our Australian Wing Commander or our Scottish Group Captain and the lucky airman was
on the permanent staff. We had the best cricket team and the
best amateur dramatic society in the RAF. All from a total of
eight hundred! I'll never forget visiting RAF Cardington to play
cricket. With ten times our number of men to choose from they
expected to annihilate us. We shot them out for sixty-three and
made the necessary runs for the loss of one wicket, a dubious
LBW. They didn't realise till then that all of us played or had
played County Cricket, Minor County Cricket or League

Cricket. Next to God, there's nothing like having the CO on your side.

1947 came in with a bang – or rather with a dull thud as far as I was concerned – my second hernia. This careless rupture has already been described, but an incident connected with it has not. The particular WAAF responsible for my incarceration had been a frequent visitor to my small bunk room. Two nights before the night in question she was with me till the small hours when she suddenly woke up and evinced a wish to pee. We were closeted in my tiny room at the end of a Lang Hut consisting of thirty lumpen, snoring, hoiking, farting erks. Not easy to get past them and return. All right when making the dawn escape – but that was a one-way procedure. Furthermore it was snowing outside and a squatting WAAF might well have had her ardour frozen. Necessity is the mother of invention. I removed the white porcelain lampshade, bunged up the centre hole with some rolled-up paper, offered the home-made po to my lady love and gallantly withdrew suggesting she emptied it out of the window when finished. I heard a muffled curse and rushed to investigate. My paper bung had come out, my room was flooded, I lost my footing, fell down with a dreadful clatter and smashed the porcelain lampshade *en route*. Thirty lumpen, snoring, hoiking, farting erks were aroused into instant life and there I was pleading for their understanding and help whilst a poor, shivering damp WAAF was banished into the snow never to darken my door again. Unfortunately she did, for two nights later she returned and was responsible for my second hernia. Well it was a joint effort, I suppose – if you'll pardon the pun. The resultant chaos on *that* occasion again awakened the gallant thirty but they remained faithful and quiet throughout – or so I thought. There *was* a Judas amongst them and next morning my conduct was being carried hot-foot to the SWO. Fortunately, I was being carried hot-foot to the RAF Hospital at Halton, this time as a patient, so a moratorium, as it were, was placed on my conduct. This time-lag was further helped by the weather. It was 1947, the year of the great fuel crises, the year it snowed and snowed –

so not only did I get my fortnight in hospital plus my month's sick leave but I was also told not to report back to Marsworth for a further fortnight as everyone had been sent home, the camp being uninhabitable.

By the time I reported back, two months had elapsed and my conduct was warmed-over potatoes. The S W O sent for me, yet again.

"Before you pissed h'off for two months," he said, using his usual old H'etonian accent, "h'it h'appears that you were mis-h'employin' your Hampton yet again. Fortunately for you, Corporal Rix, the h'airman who reported you has been posted – so the 'eat is h'off h'and h'I'll take no further h'action." I trem-blingly blurted out my thanks. "H'it beats me," he mused, "how you h'even managed to get a 'ard h'on in that cold weather. Talk h'about brass monkeys . . ."

That was the second Court Martial saved. I was, and am, very grateful. H'as h'I – oops sorry – as I walked back to my bunk I resolved never to run so close to the wind again. Within two weeks I was once more up the creek . . .

This time it wasn't a woman who caused my downfall but an insatiable desire to get back to civvy street and the theatre. A group of ex-service actors and actresses had banded together on demob and called themselves Reunion Theatre. They organised mass auditions and even put on two plays – *Exercise Bowler* and *Noose*. My sister, Sheila, now demobbed, was in *Exercise Bowler*, in the West End, on T V and on a Services tour of Germany. Through her I met the powers-that-be and one in particular, Campbell Singer – now a successful co-author of the "business" dramas, *Any Other Business, Guilty Party, Difference of Opinion* and the like – was very helpful. So much so that when I was on sick leave in February I attended one of the mass auditions which took place at the Duke of York's Theatre. We rehearsed a short play or extract for three days and then performed it, along with several other presentations, to an audience consisting of manage-ments, agents, film producers and so on. The effectiveness of these auditions could be quite startling. I was in a dramatic little piece by John Steinbeck – along with Gerald Campion. Gerald soon became very well known as TV's Billy Bunter but perhaps even better known to members of the profession as a marvellous club-owner. We must have made a good impression for I was invited to meet Sydney Box, then running Gainsborough Films at Lime Grove – with a view to a contract – and also offered a small part in an HM Tennent production by Daphne Rye – their formidable casting lady – who eventually went into the restaurant business and started a superb "Daphne's" in Draycott Avenue and another in Spain at San Pedro de Alcantara. I've often eaten at both – motivated by pleasure and gratitude.

Of course, neither chance could be taken for I was still in the Air Force. I resolved to get out. But how? My devious mind realised that if *deferred* service of sixteen months was added to my *actual* service my release group would come down with a thump from 69 to 60. I also knew that the posting and demob clerks were pretty confused by my papers – for I'd already been in and out of the Air Force – down the mines – and back again in the RAF. I suggested to one of them, a pretty WAAF that there appeared to be some mistake with my release number. I planted the necessary doubt, amongst other things, and asked her to look into the matter. She did and as if by magic, my number was reduced by nine and I was due for demob in March instead of October. Gleefully I roared round the station handing back all my gear and getting my clearance chitty signed. All that stood between me and freedom was my interview with the CO. I repaired to the SWO's office to be wheeled in to the Wing Commander.

One look at Wally Everett's face and I knew I'd been rumbled.

"Corporal Rix," he said, "h'I 'ave been h'examining your release papers most carefully. There h'appears to be some dis-crh'epancy. Now h'I know, and you know how the mistake arose. But it could be the postin' clerk's balls up so we'll say no more. No, come to think of it, it was probably your balls up that did it. She's a pretty little scrubber. One little thing, though. As you're so keen on prancin' around in front of people, h'I've got a little job for you. From now on, you're parade marker. Yew will be on the parade ground a quarter-hof-han-hour before any of the recruits and they will mark up to yew. I know you're fond of h'early risin', in a manner of speaking, so this should get you h'up in the mornin's throughout the summer until your real release number comes up. 69 isn't it? By the time I'm finished with yew, yew'll wish you'd never heard of *soixante-neuf*."

Court Martial number three avoided – and I had a *marvellous* summer. The weather was glorious, cricket abounded (Compton and Edrich went berserk) and frankly I *enjoyed* getting up early – the sun was always shining and to crown it all, I fell heavily for a pretty blonde WAAF who consented to spend a dirty weekend with me at the Kensington Palace Hotel. Dirty was hardly the word – for her guilt was so enormous that she spent the entire forty-eight hours in the bath, washing away her non-existent sins. I, too, was nervous – so much so that I signed my brother's name in the book when we registered. As he was a married man, I often wonder what would have happened if they'd had occasion to write to him – referring to his "wife" and the weekend in question. Funnily enough, I suggested this ploy to Michael Pertwee and it's woven into our new play *A Bit Between The Teeth*. In this, my partner always gives my name to his birds whenever he's having a bit on the side. Needless to say, it leads to complications ... The postscript to this tale is the story of the biter bit. Years later I was married – and visited a club theatre, the Watergate, with Elspet, my wife. An attractive brunette walked over to me.

"Hello, Brian," she said, "remember me?"

"No," said I, completely baffled by the brunette hair.

"Well you bloody well should," came the reply, "we spent a dirty weekend together in 1947." I was left blushing a deep crimson, trying to explain to Elspet that our *dirty* weekend was actually a *clean* weekend – but I don't think she believed me ...

It was now mid-summer 1947 and my genuine demob number was getting nearer and nearer. But all the time the jobs were going to actors pouring out of the forces. I became very depressed at my prospects of finding work easily, or even at all, but running the Station Dramatic Society, plus memories of Wolfit, had given me the idea that I might like to become an actor–manager.

I had one hundred pounds saved. I went to my father. "If I

put up a hundred quid – would you and Uncle Bert put up, say, another nine hundred. I can get a rep going for that." Much to my surprise, he agreed. I was in business.

The last rites of my RAF service took place in October. By November I had headed paper and an attic over a chemist's shop in Hornsea, which served as an office, but no theatre. But I was full of confidence. I wrote to everyone offering my non-existent company. Wally Everett's last words to me were prophetic:

"You'll bullshit your way through h'anything," he said, "as long as you remember not to put your balls where your brains h'are." I have, so far, kept them fairly well apart but occasionally I've noticed some strange bulges around my ears ...

Act V

Those bulges must have been very visible when I eventually found a theatre where no angels had trodden for a *very* long time. The *Ilkley Gazette* reported on 30th January 1948:

> "Yet another Repertory Company is anxious to come to Ilkley and attempt to succeed where others have failed. A new company, Rix Theatrical Productions, is negotiating with the Ilkley Council for the hire of the King's Hall. Two members of this Company have had considerable experience with the well known '*White Rose Players*' of Harrogate and they are confident they can provide Ilkley with first-class players and productions."

So we were, and so we did; but Ilkley was too small and also had a penchant for supporting their amateur societies better than their paid companies. I don't think they realised the difference! The two White Rose Players referred to were my business manager, Colin Collins and myself. Colin, the Stage Director who had directed me to the brothel, had been at Harrogate for many years and was glad to join my new company for it was both a challenge and, in a way, promotion. Unfortunately, he didn't last long. He became involved with a charming girl in Otley, got cold feet and six weeks after we'd opened he left me a farewell note and the keys to the safe, which he pushed through the Box Office letter-box. I've only seen him once since then – and he was walking across Putney Bridge. Unfortunately I was in a car

– so I never did find out the truth. My imagination has filled in many lurid details.

Still, we worked well together at the outset. We had our opening date fixed – Easter Monday – and came down to London to cast. Most of this was done through Reunion Theatre and the result was very curate's eggy. However, my Stage Director Peter Lait, and Jenny Webster, my set designer, were absolutely first-class and provided a magnificent stream of settings for nearly two years. So 29th March dawned and Britain's youngest actor-manager, *me*, came into being. That damned label stuck with me till middle-age for no one else seemed willing to go in for such a bloody silly job.

7.30 p.m. approached and the curtain went up on good old *Nothing But The Truth*. Unfortunately, half of it promptly came down again. You see, we had checked everything in the theatre: new lights, new dimmers, new lines - ropes to you – *but* we had failed to check one thing, or rather two things – the ropes taking up the curtains. The curtain was in two halves and each half was drawn up to either side of the proscenium arch. That was the theory. In practice the curtain on the audience's left came down with a sickening thud as the rotten old rope parted. There was a horrified silence all round and then everyone burst into activity.

"Fucking hell," imprecated Colin Collins – resplendent in a hired tail suit – and ran up the ladder leading to the flies.

"Bloody hell," swore the actors and proceeded to push all the furniture on to the side of the stage visible to the audience.

"Jesus Christ," blasphemed I as I tried to make an entrance. Unhappily all the furniture was now piled up against the door so I had to run round and enter through the window. The audience were at first stunned, then fascinated – for by now Colin Collins was leaning out of the flies, dangling a rope, which a stage hand proceeded to tie to the offending curtain. Meanwhile, back at the ranch, the play proceeded. By now Colin was hauling the curtain upwards. The audience was mesmerised. Would it reach the proscenium arch? Would this cliff-hanger be resolved? It was. The stage was now totally visible and the audience broke into uninhibited applause. The play might be forgotten – but this was THEATRE – the best entertainment they'd ever had. The *Ilkley Gazette* reported:

> "The new Ilkley Repertory Company were given a magnificent send-off on Monday evening when they opened to a capacity audience in the King's Hall with *Nothing But The Truth* by James Montgomery. There was an unfortunate incident at the start, when the cord of one of the stage curtains broke. The players were apparently unconcerned, however, and carried on to the end of the first act with half the stage hidden from view. From this point the play continued without a hitch."

Oh yes? Little did the *Ilkley Gazette* know. Colin Collins descended from the flies with his hired tails torn and filthy. The hire firm refused to take them back, so any profit we might have made in Easter Week went up the spout. However, I'm a careful man. Some might say a mean man. I kept those tails for ten years and Leo Franklyn eventually wore them for 1,200 performances in the first act of *Simple Spymen*. It's an ill wind ...

Strangely enough, there was an incident with the front of the house curtains, known as "the tabs" when we were doing *Simple Spymen*. Maybe those tails were haunted. The fly-man lowered in the tabs at the end of Act I. Unfortunately, he'd left his brake off and the tabs continued to be lowered in, till we were staring at the audience over the tops of them. The fly-man realised his mistake, panicked, and heaved the tabs upwards till they shot above the proscenium arch, revealing the spot bars, the grid, the fly floor, the works. They also revealed a demented fly-man tugging frantically at a couple of thick ropes. The audience was in ecstasies – believing it to be all part of the play. The fly-man took a deep breath and the curtain was lowered in, a few inches too far. It is a well-known fact that a few inches can often cause trouble – and here was no exception. In the interval, the set was changed and a very heavy pianola placed down right. On this occasion it was placed on those unwanted inches of curtain – anchoring them firmly to the stage.

The interval being over – up went the curtain for Act II. At least *most* of it went up – leaving a torn section clinging to the feet of the pianola – looking for all the world like a giant cobweb. Leo Franklyn and I made our entrance.

"My God," said Leo, "that must be a bloody big spider. Get the scissors." I obediently trotted off stage – collected a pair of scissors – ran on – stood on Leo's back and cut the offending remnants down. The audience fell about – the fly-man had hysterics and fled from the theatre, never to be seen again. Well – we've all had trouble with our flies, from time to time.

I had little trouble with them in Ilkley – for I was choosing the plays, directing the plays, playing in the plays, typing the letters, typing the publicity, typing the programme copy, attending Rotary luncheons, Women's Institute teas and Repertory Supporters' Balls. I helped strike the sets, set the sets and build the sets. And, furthermore, I had my lines to learn. There was very little time for coition. An occasional quick roll on the Cow and Calf, or a frolic on Ilkla' Moor were sometimes possible – but those were the exceptions – not the rule. For all that, the summer sped by. Our work was totally consuming and the fact that I was doing so much for so little – ten pounds a week – never worried me. We occasionally broke away from the typical weekly rep. mould of comedies and farces with such plays as *A Hundred Years Old, The Eagle Has Two Heads* or *Portrait in Black*. When these plays were presented we were always praised but good notices didn't pay the bills or bring in the audiences. On 24th September the *Ilkley Gazette* told the story:

"Once again a repertory company in Ilkley is faced with a crisis. Mr Rix announced this week that the sum total of the company losses is nothing less than disastrous and that it would be folly to go on suffering them. During an interview Mr Rix emphasised the heavy losses which had been sustained during the opening weeks and said there was a period afterwards when the Company was paying its way. Had that position continued, they could have carried on but last week there was a loss of £70 and another deficit was certain this week."

Blimey! Seventy pounds! What a piddling sum by today's inflated standards – but for us it was the end. A thousand pounds to capitalise the opening – scenery, lighting, furnishings and so on. Twenty-eight weeks losing seventy pounds a week and you have a loss of around three thousand pounds. In 1948 that was a *lot* of money and my father and uncle decided, quite rightly, that consanguinity had had its day – at least as far as Ilkley was concerned. The old man summed it all up in a letter to the local paper in reply to a Mr Appleton, who felt we would have done better if we had stuck to "drama".

"Our record over six months shows that what is known as drama has involved us in very considerable loss, and our highlights, so far as takings are concerned, have been the 'trivials'. Surely no further comment is necessary! Since finance is inexorably the final consideration you can well see, Mr Appleton, why more of your fine classics have not been presented. This is all very sad, but you will find it is the same up and down the country and apparently Ilkley is no exception. It is such a pity that the yearnings of our cultural minds should have to be subordinated to the implacable power of pounds, shillings and pence.

The writer, incidentally, is the unfortunate who has to foot the bill."

Not quite true. My Uncle Bert was involved, too – but it's near enough to the truth and still applies today – a quarter of a century later. More's the pity – but thank God I learnt the lesson early, for "trivials" have paid the mortgage, educated the kids and bought some Staffordshire china. I miss the "drama" though . . . occasionally . . .

Ilkley Repertory Co.
FAREWELL BALL
Winter Garden
Next Friday 15th October

★   ★   ★

Tickets 5/–

63

In spite of all the efforts of our enthusiastic and splendid supporters it was, in the end, rather pointless:

"These sort of boobies think that people come to balls to do nothing but dance; whereas everyone knows that the real business of a ball is either to look out for a wife, to look after a wife, or to look after somebody else's wife."

So wrote Robert Surtees in *Mr Facey Romford's Hounds*. He was right. Anyway, at least people *don't* come to resurrect a moribund repertory company. We closed on 16th October.

I'm an eternal optimist. Having flopped in a small town I promptly went to *another* small town – Bridlington. This time there was method in my madness – for I felt that if I could make the winter a success they might give me the summer season – up to then in the hands of the ubiquitous Harry Hanson. There were no promises, mind you, but I sensed the wind of change was blowing up a few Aldermanic robes. Thank God, I was right.

We opened at the Grand Pavilion, Bridlington, on 1st November with that splendid, albeit flawed, ghost story by Emlyn Williams – *Trespass*. The most influential critic in East Yorkshire, Katherine Yorke, was generous:

"I have nothing but sincere praise for the Viking Theatre Company. [We'd changed our name on leaving Ilkley. However, we had our printing blocks left. They were Spanish galleons – so, for some inexplicable reason we called ourselves Vikings.] Without doubt this is the most talented company we have seen here, for the production of Emlyn Williams' *Trespass* left no doubt whatever in our minds of their calibre. While each member was beyond criticism, the brilliant performance of Mr Brian Rix, as Saviello the medium, was remarkable for its interpretation."

At least we were off to a good start. And the letters went to the local papers:

"It is a long time since such a production as *Trespass* at the Grand Pavilion last week has been seen here. I can only echo what many were heard to say after the opening night: 'What a pity the Court Players are already engaged for next season!'."

These letters had the necessary effect and we were duly offered the summer season. This was a great relief to me, for I found that writing letters to the newspapers in a disguised hand was an additional strain I could ill-afford. We were now *expanding* and I was not only running Bridlington but negotiating for a winter season (with hopes of the summer to follow) at Margate. Both companies changed my life. Casting for Margate provided me with a wife. Looking for suitable plays to fill the summer at Bridlington provided me with *Reluctant Heroes*.

We were due to open at the Hippodrome, Margate on 24th January 1949, so casting had to be done just at the New Year. I went down to London to hold auditions and became involved in the traditional piss-ups which go on around that time. The result was that I attended the Interval Club at 10.30 on 2nd January feeling, frankly, bloody awful. I crouched over a gas fire whilst our Margate director, John Franklyn, interviewed the young hopefuls. Suddenly my hangover was forgotten. I sat bolt upright, scrubbed surreptitiously at my tongue with my handkerchief to remove the green fur coat, did up my tie and generally made an effort to look young, gay and dashing. The reason for this display of cock feathers? Into the room had walked the most gorgeous red-head; the most gorgeous girl I had ever seen. She was wearing a green tweed costume, which set off her eyes and hair to perfection. In fact I reacted in the traditional Peg's Paper way – including falling in love at first sight. John Franklyn was launching into his *Spiel* about Margate – but I hastily interrupted and suggested that I had a vacancy for an Assistant Stage Manager in Bridlington and I was only going to Margate for the opening play and wanted all the help I could get when I returned to Yorkshire. Miss Red-Head – Blue-Eyes – Green Costume – demurred. She *had* been a Rank Starlet, she *had* made films, she *had* been Edward's wife with Robert Morley in *Edward, My Son*. I was quite prepared to believe that she had starred *above* Robert

65

Morley – such was my infatuation – but I only had a vacancy for an ASM. My juvenile girl, Jeane Stenning, was very good and a great favourite. I was desperate, and as always when I'm desperate I become a great little chatter and often people give in just to shut me up. My ideal was no exception. After a continuous stream of nonsense suggesting that being an ASM at Bridlington was practically a passport to stardom and that to be with the parent company was important and that we would be doing new plays and that anyway I would be there and that I would try to give her a rise – in salary – as soon as possible etc. etc., Miss Elspet Gray accepted the job at £4 10s 0d a week. John Franklyn was furious, I was cock-a-hoop and sat smiling foolishly into space throughout the rest of the day. I cannot remember a single person interviewed after that time. As we left, my desire to see Elspet again was acute and so I rang her up and made some silly excuse to go round to Portland Court, where she lived with her mother and sister, Rhoda – father still being out in Pakistan with Lloyds Bank. Elspet was with a medical student boy friend and they were about to go out for the evening. I went with them – talking all the while. Eventually we ended up in the kitchen at three o'clock in the morning and I was still at it. Wally Everett was right, but on this occasion the bullshit was accompanied by definite swellings in the auricular area – and other areas as well . . .

So Elspet went up to Bridlington with another new member of the company, Clement Lister. On the train she announced to Clem that she'd had an offer from Chesterfield Rep. to be the juvenile lead – and felt like taking it. Clem lectured her on the ethics and loyalties inextricably woven into the "theatre". Elspet stayed, at least till I returned. That was enough. Thank you, Clem, wherever you are. The last I heard of you, you were hunting the Loch Ness Monster.

Three days before my twenty-fifth birthday we opened in Margate with John Patrick's *The Hasty Heart*. We were a success and I loved playing the part of Yank – who at one point has to recite the books of the Old Testament (once learned, never forgotten – I can still do it) – but all the time I was itching to get back to Bridlington. This desire was considerably increased by my landlady's five-year-old daughter, who did *not* fall into the water, but did the next best thing by producing her potty at every meal and filling it from every available orifice. Mummy thought this activity both endearing and hilarious. I thought the opposite. However, as the guest, I had to smile indulgently whilst the little darling relieved herself.

After our opening week I left Margate with indecent haste – leaving the company to battle on till the 18th June. Actually they did jolly well and if old Leslie Mason-Rogers, the Hippodrome's Managing Director, had had any sense we'd have continued. However, he asked us a ridiculous summer rent. So – we left and successful repertory died in Margate. I wonder if our landlady's daughter continued to void her bladder and bowels for the entertainment of holiday-makers? We may have no theatre, folks, but at least we have one for the pot.

Some interesting actors, too, played in the Margate Company. Julian Mitchell, repeating his success in *An Inspector Calls*; William Franklyn, that tonic to us all and son of Leo; Dennis Cannon, who made his name shortly afterwards, as the author of *Captain Carvallo*; Earl Cameron, again in *Deep Are The Roots*; and, last but not least, Peter Mercier who eventually married my sister, Sheila.

But I was back in Bridlington. I raced into the theatre on the Monday morning and there, performing her duties as ASM, was my beloved. Actually I could only see her bottom, clad in trousers, for she was up a step-ladder hanging a picture, but that was enough. My heart turned over, I blushed and stammered out that hoary old favourite:

"I'd recognise that face anywhere."

"Ha-Ha," went the back of the head.

"I feel a bit of an ass standing here," I went on, getting cornier with every sentence.

"Now you're getting cheeky," said the back of the head and turned. At least she was smiling. Hair awry, face smudged, old shirt on top of those trousers – she was just as beautiful as I remembered. My hangover *hadn't* played tricks with my optic nerves. So, as far as I was concerned, that was that. I was going

67

to marry her. Of course, I overdid it, as is my wont, and went too far too soon, but that's me. I asked her to the Young Farmers' Ball in the Spa Royal Hall that coming Wednesday. She came, we danced all evening, badly – we've always been elephants together on the dance floor – and I proposed as we left. I'll never learn. This definitely worried her and didn't really advance my cause. However, most of us had moved into the St Leonard's Hotel, so I was able to keep up the pressure from breakfast to bed-time. Eventually she reported my desires to her mother by phone. Her mother told her not to be silly and her sister burst out laughing. So I gave up asking. But I went on working underground just like a termite. First Elspet was promoted from ASM to Juvenile and her salary increased to £8 per week (I'd need the extra when we married). Next, I engaged her sister, Rhoda, to be the Assistant Scenic Designer (she's done my sets ever since). Then, as summer approached, we had to leave the St Leonard's Hotel and four of us took a house together. Elspet, Rhoda, Peter Mercier (who'd joined us from Margate) and, crafty devil, ME! After three months Elspet remarked that I hadn't pressed my suit for some considerable time and was getting all the perks with none of the problems. As we were sharing a bath at the time, she probably had a point. And so it was we became engaged. The *Scotsman* Edinburgh, Tuesday 24th May 1949 did *not* report the method *or* the location:

"The engagement is announced between Brian Norman Roger, younger son of Mr and Mrs H. D. Rix, Kirkdale, Hornsea, and Elspet Jeans, elder daughter of Mr and Mrs J. MacGregor-Gray, of Lloyds Bank, Rawalpindi, Pakistan, and 40 Portland Court, London."

Bet old Mac had a few chota-pegs that night. He didn't even *know* the son he was gaining.

By now we had moved the company from the Pavilion, with its ghastly forty-five-foot opening – safe from the winter gales – to the delightful little Spa Theatre. By now, too, we'd made our peace with "Tug" Wilson, Bridlington's Technical Manager, who hated our guts when we moved in – we'd disturbed his winter hibernation. He and a lovely fellah, Syd Temple the electrician, had even begun to accept our own carpenter, Charlie Bentley, who'd come with us from Ilkley (and before that from Hornsea – where he used to help my dad out when it came to building sets). You might well think, naïve fools, that presenting good productions of good plays is enough. You would be wrong. At all times the poor presenting manager (in my case, actor-manager) has to arse-crawl to everyone: theatre-owners, theatre back-stage staff, theatre front-of-house staff, theatre box-office staff, actors, authors, directors.

I suppose it's worth it? I sometimes wonder. Anyway, there we were in a proper theatre and business flourished. Not without its vicissitudes, however. During one performance of a brand-new drama Elspet and another young actress, Betty Lait, dried up completely. George Radford was on the book in the prompt corner – but no prompt came. Elspet and Betty looked at each other in growing horror. Neither had a clue. Then they heard "Psst! Psst!" from the direction of a large open fireplace down left. Both rushed over, believing succour to be close by. There was George, the script in his hand and his head stuck round the chimney backing. "I'm awfully sorry," he whispered, "but if you could give me the page I could give you the prompt." As the girls hardly knew the *play*, let alone the page, it was hardly surprising that both made a grab for the script and in full view of the audience found the place and their lines. They then solemnly handed the script back into the fireplace – where an unseen hand removed it – and proceeded with the play. The author, who was in front and prone to hysterics, collapsed into floods of tears. This at least distracted the audience from the activity on stage and I think they went out that night convinced they had seen an early attempt at "Free Theatre". Judging by the number of complimentary tickets we had to give away that week – they practically had.

A similar incident took place when a rather dramatic actress, Appaline Yale, was playing a scene with an actor by the name of James Haggett. Both dried, both panicked and Jimmy rushed off – leaving poor Appaline alone with nothing to say – and nobody to say it to either.

"Jimmy, come back," she screamed, "come back you rotten sod. It's my best scene." Hardly, I would have thought. *My* best scene, however, was close at hand, as one day I sent for a reading copy of a play by Colin Morris called *Reluctant Heroes*. I only did this because he'd written an army play – *Desert Rats* – and I thought *Heroes* might be similar. WRONG. But at least it was about the army. When it arrived I was able to read the play quickly between shows on a Saturday. I rolled around the place with helpless laughter and hurriedly asked Peter Lait to type a letter to Colin Morris' agents to see if the rights of the piece were available. They were. And so I grabbed an option with both hands – hopefully hoping to do *something* with the play even if it was only a tour. Then we put it on as a high season production in Bridlington. It played to more business than *See How They Run* and in those days that was equivalent to saying the Archbishop of Canterbury commanded a bigger flock than the Pope. I was delighted and the feeling that this play was going to bring me to London grew and grew – but, as yet, I'd no idea how. All I know is that I took a recording and photos of our production to Colin Morris, to show how funny we were. He was horrified. He'd described my part, Gregory, as a huge, slow Lancastrian. I am five foot ten, scraggy (in those days) and a Yorkshireman. So I played Gregory with a false nose, a red wig and the speed of a leaden-footed tortoise. There was nothing Colin could do – the option was mine – but the play was his and when it came to the actual production out went the false nose, the red hair and the masterly inactivity. In its place came a centre parting, George Robey eyebrows and a high-pitched falsetto. *Plus ça change* . . .

In the play at Bridlington was George Radford – the son of Basil Radford – and the fact that he had Basil for a father was to prove our saving when we were on tour months later. George is now a highly respected business man in Canada. I mention this at this juncture in the hope of bolstering the Canadian sales – but Canadians will have to wait till the next chapter before all is revealed. Once, when I was on holiday in Italy, I met some Canadians named McKay.

"Where do you come from?" I enquired.

"Canada," was the reply.

"No," I said. "Where do you come from *originally*?"

"Canada."

"Yes, I know – but with the name McKay, surely you're from Scotland?"

"We are from Canada," came the steely reply. "Are you taking the God-damn piss out of us?" I wasn't – but I now realise all ex-colonials are sensitive. I apologise profusely and I won't even mention convicts and the Antipodes. But I digress.

Reluctant Heroes safely proven to be very funny, it was now time to get a different kind of horse laugh. Elspet and I set the date of our wedding. We were to hold it at my local Hornsea Parish Church because Elspet's dad was still in Pakistan and it was a long way to go for a wedding. So, instead, we decided to record the ceremony and the speeches and post the acetates to him. It was cheaper. Elspet's Uncle Jack was to give her away and her mum was to act as hostess in my parents' house. She and my father met the night before the wedding. They hated each other on sight. For the sake of propriety it was also hinted that Elspet and I should occupy separate beds before the ceremony – so she moved in with Rhoda. As I had a severe throat infection at the time and a roaring temperature the decision to move wasn't hard to take. A sweaty husband is one thing. A sweaty husband-to-be is quite another. We were supposed to be playing together in *The Hasty Heart* that week, but I had to drop out of the first four performances and only came in for the end of the week. What we egocentric actors will do for applause. I was determined to take a curtain call with Elspet the night before our wedding, just to hear our loyal supporters' response.

We were to be married on the Sunday – for this was the only day the entire company could come along. To make this possible we had to apply to the Bishop for dispensation. As he'd admired my cricket twelve years before, the necessary permission came through by return of post. Then we hit another snag. Our vicar, Walter Hollis, was to marry us. Unfortunately, when the time came, he was unable to perform the ceremony. His son, Gerry, recently qualified to perform marriages, offered to stand in as understudy. We gratefully accepted. All the same, it was odd, and strangely moving, being lectured by a man I'd grown up with and played against at rugger, cricket and tennis. Gerry played rugger for Oxford and England. He had, and has, hands like bunches of bananas. They never missed a pass that day. So, we were married. Katherine Yorke brought her critical faculties to bear for the *Bridlington Chronicle*:

"And now I am sure many admirers of the Rix Company will want to know all about 'The Wedding', which came up to all our expectations in letting us see the most beautiful bride imaginable in Miss Elspet Gray, who became Mrs Brian Rix last Sunday 14th August, at St Nicholas' Church, Hornsea. The day was fine and sunny, and quite early many people assembled outside the Church, which was filled with guests and other well wishers ... Later the very happy pair left by car for the South, the bride looked equally beautiful in her travelling suit of grey, with grey overcheck, and a very pretty grey hat of the beret type with a plumage mount.'

Elspet actually wore her hat back to front by mistake.

I made a mistake too. Our nuptial night was spent in the Cock Inn. Only farce actors could go for such obvious laughs.

So we returned, to the early chills of autumn and the early chills of marriage. We moved into a furnished flat with our presents, including a golden spaniel, Noggin. Noggin developed meningitis and that was that. We were heart-broken – but rehearsing for our first pantomime, *Babes In The Wood*. I played one of the robbers; George Radford, the other. A far cry from his performance with his father, Basil, who'd visited us as a guest for *The Blind Goddess* several weeks before. A far cry for us all, too, after our varied successes and failures of the past fourteen months. Unfortunately, the spectre of hunger was once again stalking the dressing-room corridors and once again I was writing impassioned letters to the local papers, pleading for support. This seemed to be a hardy annual – I could almost have dusted down the same correspondence used at Ilkley a year before, but I didn't. However, Mafeking was about to be relieved: *Reluctant Heroes* and 1950 were just around the corner. In the meantime – Christmas. I bought a replacement for Noggin to give to Elspet. He was a huge golden labrador puppy who came from Beverley – he always talked with a Yorkshire accent – and we called him Bastien. Elspet and I first appeared together in *By Candle Light*. She played Lulu Keck. I played Bastien. It seemed a suitably commemorative name for our golden bundle of fun. It was. The commemorative bundles of fun he dropped around our flat on Christmas morning did *not* enhance the Christmas Spirit. A Happy New Year to all our readers . . .

Act VI

Reluctant Heroes

Rix Theatrical Productions are sending out a short tour of this new farce by Colin Morris, opening at the White Rock Pavilion, Hastings, on Monday next. The cast includes Dermot Walsh, Wally Patch, Elspet Gray, Brian Rix, Larry Noble, Marie Germaine, Janet Butler, Allan Scott, George Radford and Colin Morris. John Cleaver is Stage Director and Production Manager is William E. Raynor. The farce is being produced by Frank Dermody.

So ran *The Stage* advance notice – written, incidentally by me. In those days I couldn't afford a press representative and every night, during rehearsals, I was up till the small hours typing out all the publicity. I had only a portable machine which did few carbon copies so I became the fastest two-finger typist in the country – but didn't sleep much. Elspet was *very* restless.

We duly opened at the White Rock Pavilion on Monday 27th March 1950. After a "short tour" we finally berthed at the Whitehall Theatre, London, six months later. Quite a lot happened in between ...

The Stage reported from Hastings:

"There was delighted appreciation from a moderately full house [I love the qualification] and so Mr Morris may feel that his piece has been successfully launched. At the same time one could wish that the capable company had better material to handle. Even in farce – or rather, especially in farce, which depends so much on situation for its interest – there is scope for more originality of invention than is to be discerned in *Reluctant Heroes*. [I have read that notice in different guises THOUSANDS of times since then – frankly I'm amazed I've ever earned a living!] But thanks to the massive personality of Wally Patch, who plays a sergeant of the old school for all he is worth and receives excellent support in particular from Dermot Walsh, Larry Noble and Brian Rix, as three newly joined National Servicemen – of contrasting types and from the author, who gives us an amusing caricature of a certain type of officer, the piece proves far more entertaining than at first appeared likely. For decoration we have the charming personality of Elspet Gray, who as a WRAC officer, has nothing much to do. In this agreeable task she is ably assisted by two attractive young ladies . . ." etc. etc. etc.

After that you might be excused for thinking that *Reluctant Heroes* would never reach the West End. Of course, you would be wrong for it was probably, in a very simple way, the funniest army farce ever written. There were over five hundred laughs – and those don't grow on trees. It also had that indefinable quality of identification. EVERYONE who had ever been called to attention by a bawling NCO recognised something of their own lives – and as most of the male population (and much of the female too) had served in the war or been called up for National Service – we had a ready-made audience of millions. But first we had problems to overcome. I'll list them in chronological order.

February 1950
I contracted Dermot Walsh "by permission of The J. Arthur Rank Organisation" and paid accordingly. The week we opened his contract with Rank was *not* renewed. His agent had known this would happen all along but we were stuck with the inflated price. Still Dermot was a pleasant bloke and we argued about the world's problems until many a crack of dawn. However in those days he had one failing. He'd get to the theatre at least one hour

before the curtain went up but he could *never* get on stage on time. Night after night we'd have to hold the curtain for him until in the end I had to have his understudy, George Radford, dressed and ready. The ultimatum went out to his agent: "If he's late again his understudy goes on and he'll be suspended." The ruse worked well until one night George fell down the steps leading to the stage and knocked his front teeth out. This meant his enforced absence for a few days and in that time Dermot slipped back into his late habits . . .

March 1950

Our "short tour" was booked by a respected agent, Leslie Bloom. He obviously saw me coming, for the contract I signed for Hastings was for our share to be fifty-five per cent, the normal share being sixty-five per cent. He also arranged for the money to be paid direct to him and he would then pay us. Unfortunately for him the Hastings Director of Entertainments, Kenneth Day, made a mistake and paid us some of our share direct on the Friday so we could have cash for salaries. It was then I realised that our share was larger than expected. I queried the amount and found our contracted percentage *was* the normal sixty-five per cent and Leslie Bloom had planned to pocket the extra ten per cent plus a booking fee. Mr Day and I requested his presence on a matter of some urgency. He arrived, to be confronted by two very angry and impolite managers. His avarice cost him all his bookings with the Hastings Corporation and his booking agency for me. I moved over to an ex-secretary of Bernard Delfont's – a Miss Renee Stepham – who had just started up as a booking agent for tours. She was, and is, super and I've used her good offices ever since. So has practically everyone else in the business. I was very proud and happy to act as Master of Ceremonies at the party she gave to celebrate her Twenty-fifth Anniversary as Renee Stepham Limited. Ours is a small business and news travels fast. I imagine Leslie Bloom lost more business to Renee by his stupidity than by any other means. I wonder if his ghost was around gnashing his teeth that anniversary night twenty-five years later?

April 1950

A further "bloomer" from Leslie Bloom came to light and forced us to have a "week out" after only three weeks on tour. He had booked our first six dates before the Hastings débâcle and the fourth of these was at Stoke Newington. The management sent for me and told me that the last play to visit the theatre had grossed under £100 on the week, less entertainment tax. This meant our share would not have paid our leading man's salary – let alone anything else. They pointed out it would be much cheaper for us not to play and would gladly release us from our contract. I gratefully accepted but notched up another black mark against Mr Bloom.

April, too, presented us with an even greater problem. At the end of six weeks we were to lose, for a period, our Sergeant Bell, Wally Patch, for he had been pre-contracted to appear in a tour of *The Magic Cupboard*. So along with my difficulties over bookings came the all-important loss of our lead. I was desperate – but an idea came to me. George Radford's father, Basil, was due to film *The Galloping Major* in the early summer – but was available till then. Although he was quite wrong for the part I asked him if he could help us out of a hole so that we could keep the tour going. Such was his good nature (and his regard for his son) that he agreed. I'll never forget concluding arrangements with his agent, a Mr Vere Barker, in the back bar of the Café Royal, off Regent Street, one Monday morning. Vere Barker was with Connies – a very well-known theatrical agency and his partner was Connie herself – a Mrs Constance Chapman. When I arrived at midday – there was Vere with his client, Basil Radford, and Basil well into his third or fourth large scotch. There, also, was Connie, well into her third or fourth large gin, awaiting a client of hers. Uproar outside in the street and Connie's client arrived: Robert Newton bibulously loud and booming good-naturedly to all concerned, and dressed in vest, pyjama bottoms, slippers and jacket. *Much* was revealed that day – for his pyjama trousers were not too securely fastened . . . I was completely taken aback – remember I was new to the London scene with its grand theatrical names and their agents – but the barman and any other drinkers who could stand the din and the sight appeared to be totally unmoved. Apparently, such goings-on were a regular feature of the day's events. However, Vere Barker sensed my bewilderment and took me back to his office to conclude the deal for Basil. Actually, it was quite a good one for me considering I couldn't go on without him. When, finally, he *did* play the Sergeant he practically made sure I couldn't go on at all . . .

May 1950

We were in Torquay rehearsing Basil in his last week before opening, when I began to sense that all was not well. Basil insisted on playing the Sergeant as an English gentleman complete with silver-topped walking stick and officer's battle dress – and *this* for a character whose opening speech goes:

"Now, you lucky people, pay attention! This 'ut'll be yer luxury 'otel for the next ten weeks. From terday you're in the Royal Armoured Corps and it'll take more 'n the prayers of your wives and sweethearts ter get yer out of it. Yer in the Army and – tho' anybody but me would think twice before sayin' it – yer going to be soldiers. Every one of yer." (*To Gregory*) "Even you! It's up to you whether yer become a soldier the 'ard way or the easy way. The easy way's not easy and the 'ard way's bloody 'ard . . ."

Somehow this speech, delivered in a well-modulated public school accent, didn't sound right. On top of this, Basil was clearly having trouble learning his lines and was very nervy and jumpy. We went back with him to his room at the Imperial Hotel in order to help him study. There he opened a cupboard and the *real* problem was revealed. Lined up like the soldiers we were playing, were half a dozen bottles of scotch. They would all be gone by the weekend. Basil developed the taste during the First World War – he was flying – and it never left him. When he was nervous, in doubt or worried, his intake would increase alarmingly – but he never once ceased to be the gentle, kindly creature he was. A great pity – for he was a very good actor along his own chosen path – and he and Naunton Wayne made

78

a wonderfully funny pair. So he opened – *twice nightly* – at the Palace Theatre, Plymouth on 8th May. The experience nearly killed him *and* us. All confidence left him and he forgot, virtually, every single line – to such an extent that Dermot Walsh, Larry Noble and myself were literally saying *his* lines first and then answering *ourselves*. We stood beside him, behind him and in front of him in an effort to give him his prompts – but he just couldn't take them and so we had to act like ventriloquists. The *Western Morning News* was kind to Basil. "One could at times sense in his performance a struggle with this strenuous and exacting role." You can say that again! Hey Diddle-de-dee – an actor's life for me? "The easy way's not easy and the 'ard way's bloody 'ard ..."

Somehow we got through that week of purgatory. It was so bad that three years later when we'd been on at the Whitehall for over a thousand performances, the Mayor of Plymouth popped into the Silver Cross, the pub opposite the theatre and said to the publican, George Hoiles:

"I see you have got *Reluctant Heroes* opposite. Has it opened yet? It won't last. I saw it in Plymouth some time back. It was bloody dreadful!"

George told him the facts – but that story does illustrate two points. Firstly, you can't fool the people all of the time *in* the theatre – but you can sure fool them *out* of it. We actors are inclined to think the sun shines out of our bottoms and that *everyone* knows what we're doing. In fact, hardly anyone does – as the Mayor of Plymouth illustrated. "Has it opened yet?" I ask you!

The next week was an important one for me – for we were paying my first visit back to Hull since I'd become an actor-manager. I dreaded the opening night – but over the weekend a miracle happened. Basil had learnt his lines and although he was still wrong for the part at least he could get through it. The *Hull Daily Mail* was ecstatic – "a packed house rocked in helpless laughter" – so my return home was not the misery I'd expected. Nor were the remaining five weeks Basil helped us to keep going and it was during his term of office that I sowed the seeds which eventually brought *Reluctant Heroes* to the Whitehall.

June 1950

Week commencing 5th June saw us playing, in boiling hot weather, at the Theatre Royal, Birmingham. Now, at that time, the man who had the lease of the Whitehall (and who was presenting *Worm's Eye View*) was a Mr H. J. Barlow – who actually owned a nuts and bolts factory in Wolverhampton and lived near by. Here was my chance to impress him. *Worm's Eye View* had already been on for nearly five years and must, surely, be coming to an end – or so I thought – and therefore I invited him to see us in Brum. He came along on a sweltering night; it was a poor house but he loved the show and invited me to have lunch with him the next day. Shining and newly pressed I duly presented myself at his house and he was kindness itself. One bombshell, though, came along fairly early and this turned the lunch, excellent though it was, into ashes. Mr Barlow told me he was giving up the lease of the Whitehall when it expired in July and transferring *Worm's Eye View* to the Comedy Theatre, where he hoped to run it for a further year. If I cared to wait till 1951 he'd be delighted to find a place for me. I was, shall we say, crestfallen. In fact, I doubt if my crests had ever fallen as far as they did at that lunch. I left, after the usual courtesies, and rushed back to my dressing room and typed out a letter to the Whitehall offering my play as the *Worm's* successor. I found typing very difficult for my two fingers were firmly crossed as I worked away. All to no avail. A polite note came back from the Whitehall. They had fixed up the play to open in July. It was called *The Dish Ran Away* ...

So there I was. No chance of the Whitehall. Basil Radford leaving to make his film. Wally Patch still touring *The Magic Cupboard* and no dates to keep going. Straight on the phone to Renee Stepham.

"Please get me some more dates," I begged.

"All right," said Renee. She did and we plodded on – with yet a *third* Sergeant Bell. On this occasion the author, Colin Morirs, stepped into the breach – but merely as a stop-gap until Wally Patch could rejoin us. George Radford moved up, temporarily, from the Medical Orderly to the part of Captain Percy and a young actor called John Chapman took over the Orderly. More about *him* later . . .

July 1950

The impossible happened. *The Dish Ran Away* . . . opened to the worst notices imaginable at the Whitehall and they wrote to me at the Theatre Royal, Nottingham, asking if I'd be interested in opening there in September. Would I be *interested*? Bloody hell! I drove down to London as fast as my Standard Vanguard would take me and met the management in the offices I was to get to know so well over the next sixteen years. There was the owner of the lease, Louis Cooper, his general manager and MP for Goole, George Jeger, and the front-of-house manager, Vincent Lawson. It was Vincent who made the whole thing happen. He'd been H. J. Barlow's front-of-house man and when HJ had seen us in Birmingham he'd told Vincent what a funny play it was. Vincent didn't move with the *Worm* to the Comedy and when *The Dish Ran Away* . . . was an instant disaster, he remembered Barlow's opinion of our piece – hence the letter to me in Nottingham. For hours that Wednesday morning, we negotiated in the Whitehall offices and then suddenly all was agreed, provided the management liked the play when they saw it. That evening I had two performances, one at 5 p.m. and one at 8 p.m., so I suggested that Vincent Lawson could drive back with me and see both. This was considered a splendid idea and so we raced back to Nottingham. Remember this was in the days before the motorways – and such was my agitation, excitement and stupidity that I found myself in Leicester instead of Nottingham! A kindly speed cop put us on the right road and, hot and dishevelled, we arrived at the stage door of the Theatre Royal two minutes before the curtain was due to go up. The entire cast was gathered outside waiting for my return – nerves torn to shreds. Vincent Lawson was in a similar state, having been thrown around the car like a shuttlecock in my demented efforts to get back to the theatre in time. Hardly an auspicious beginning to the performance that indeed *could* be the beginning . . .

Without make-up I was shouted on to my first entrance by Colin Morris:

> SERGEANT: When I say "'alt" yer stop. You don't break into a trot! By the front, quick march. Left, right, left, right, left, right, left, right, 'ALT!!!
> (*He speeds up the rate of marching to an impossible pitch, howling the last word after* GREGORY *as he runs in, trying desperately to keep time.* GREGORY *is twenty-four, an awkward, slow-thinking Lancashire working man. He wears an old suit, cap, mackintosh, scarf, carries a small, cheap suitcase tied with string, and is quite obviously unhappy in his new role. He finishes up against the table with a slide.*)
> SERGEANT: Fall out!
> GREGORY: 'Ow do ah do that?
> SERGEANT: 'Ow do ah do that? Gawd Almighty!

It was a *very* small house that early evening in Nottingham. But – they *laughed*! So did Vincent Lawson. And they all went *on* laughing. Vincent came round afterwards beaming.

"It'll be a smash," he said.

We were IN! Thank you, Nottingham, for making it all possible – or, rather, thank you that *handful* who made it all possible. In case any of you read this book and have *very* long memories – the date was 5th July 1950.

There were still problems of course. The Whitehall management insisted on a few cast changes and this caused a certain amount of misery and we had to wait till Wally Patch became available, which was not until September – so the tour went on for a further six weeks – not without incident . . .

We arrived at the Grand Theatre, Swansea, on Monday 17th July to find chaos. Apparently the electrician had drunk more than was good for him on the previous Saturday night – had been sacked and proceeded to avenge himself by smashing up the switchboard with a five-pound hammer. So there we were: two sets, eleven actors and actresses, a few advance bookings but *no* lights. But, as always seemed to happen in those days, a good Samaritan was there to give us a hand – this time in the person of Archie Pipe. He'd looked after the lighting for a number of amateur shows and offered his services – which were gratefully received. He slaved away all day trying to create some order out of chaos and at 7.30 up went the curtain on a stage lit in what can best be described as Stygian gloom. But that Swansea audience is one of the warmest in Britain. They peered through the murk and laughed and laughed. Perhaps they were all miners and found our lighting positively dazzling! At any rate, Archie Pipe decided to stay in the business and eventually became a big success in America – in the production side of religious programmes. Lead, kindly light . . .

Where was our golden labrador puppy amidst all those to-ings and fro-ings? With us, of course. He was now huge and for most of the tour he had been suffering from a disease called hard pad. One conventional vet said he would have to be destroyed – so we took him to a vet who believed in homoeopathic treatment. Each day Bastien was given various pills and potions, fed on a diet of fish and clad in a little green woollen jacket. He survived – but not before he had been sick over Elspet and me in the car during an inter-city journey (even our best friends wouldn't come near us for a time after that – a pretty kettle of fish!) and had caused tumult by twice tearing open pillow cases, when left alone in our bedroom, because he was too ill to be taken to the theatre. The first time he did this was in Blackpool. The landlady was an horrendous creature who terrified us all and rationed her hot baths as though the war was still on. "*One* bath per week *each*" read the notice – hard by "God Bless This House". "*One* bath per week *each*. No more than *five inches* must be run. *6d extra per bath*. DO NOT use the bath before permission has been obtained. Vim is provided at no extra charge. LEAVE THE BATH AS YOU WOULD EXPECT TO FIND IT". So you paid your sixpence – entered the freezing cold bathroom to be confronted by a chipped, stained bath and a geyser which could have doubled for a Wurlitzer Organ. You turned on an assortment of taps, the mighty machine groaned and wheezed into life and out came a dribble of tepid, rusty water. Five inches? You couldn't get in *three* before the damned water was stone cold anyway. It's the only time I've ever tried to bath in cold iron-filings. At least my bottom was scoured clean by bits of enamel and old Vim.

By this, you will gather that we were somewhat in awe of our gorgon landlady. She'd looked askance when we'd taken Bastien along – but we persuaded her that his green jacket and need for smelly fish made him quiet and docile and really he was just a lovable lap-dog. Grudgingly she admitted us and him – with dire warnings of immediate ejection if so much as one dog hair mucked up her already filthy house. We meekly concurred – and Bastien was duly installed with his bed made in our large suitcase, and off we went to the theatre. On our return for our joyless supper, we first looked upstairs to check on Bastien. Horror upon horror. As we entered the room feathers floated and billowed up from all corners. Bastien greeted us wildly – certainly he'd done a good job – and the threshing of his tail adding to the chaos already abounding. We slammed the door – all thoughts of our cold cod and chips downstairs forgotten, and spent the entire night catching and collecting feathers, then stuffing them back into the torn pillow case. As dawn came up over Blackpool's treeless streets, we were completing the Herculean task. Elspet was reinforced in her belief that Bastien should go (she'd already tried to give him away – but I sulked so much he was brought back) or our marriage might well be in jeopardy. Fourteen years later we were still together and Elspet lovingly held poor old Bastien's head as he was put to sleep.

The second occasion Bastien chose to do his Augean Stable bit – with feathers – was in Elspet's mother's flat at Portland Court. There we were staying on Sundays – for we had no flat of our own – and off we went to the cinema. We returned to find an apoplectic mother oblique stroke mother-in-law and a flat full of feathers. This time it was out in the open – there was no need for secret stuffing – and the vacuum cleaner and carpet sweeper were pressed into service. Unfortunately, such feathers as these machines did succeed in picking up, clogged up the works and whilst Elspet proceeded with a hand job I had to unravel rollers and brushes inextricably tangled up with yards and yards of finest down. Then I went to empty the vacuum bag in the dustbin outside the flat's back door. The wind promptly blew them all back again into the kitchen. That was a *very* restful Sunday.

Another restful Sunday, which has passed into our family folk-lore as the "great trouser-press row", was spent on that tour when Elspet and I tried to go and see the film *Bitter Rice*. We'd tried on two previous occasions to get along, but had failed, so on this particular Sunday a determined effort was to be made. We were on the point of leaving when George Radford turned up with some scenery problem concerning our forthcoming entry into the Whitehall. We continued the debate in the car on the way to the cinema and it became clear that I'd have to go with George to the Whitehall where the carpenter was waiting to see us. Elspet was livid.

"This is the third time you've broken your promise to see this film."

"Well, darling, you can see I'm in a fix."

"No I can't. It's Sunday – your one day off. I'll go on my own."

"All right, bloody well go on your own . . ." etc. etc. With that Elspet demanded that I stop the car. I did and she stormed out. I stormed on to the Whitehall and the scene was set for our first big marital row. All over a film! I only wanted to see it, anyway, because of the poster showing Silvana Mangano looking absolutely splendid, with tits bursting out of her sweater and ankle deep in rice water.

Eventually I returned to Portland Court to find a tight-lipped Elspet already in bed. I slammed into the room and the row started. Within minutes it boiled up into that classic where the young husband packs and storms out. There was one difference, however. The hapless George was still in the sitting-room – rather like an expectant father listening to the off-stage noises caused by his wife's labour pains – simply waiting to be told that the day's work was over. As he was my stage manager, it seemed stupid not to avail myself of his services – so there he was lugging suitcases and tennis racquets and cricket bats down to the waiting Vanguard. Eventually, we were packed and George and I sat gloomily looking at each other from the corners of the car's front bench-seat. All I had to do now was press the starter and go. George would put me up for the night at his parents' flat. But it did seem a daft way to finish a marriage.

"Good God, George," I said, "I've forgotten my trouser press!" My parents had given me a Corby Portable Stretcher Press for school and I still had it (I still have, as a matter of fact) and it was upstairs in our bedroom. I bounded up those stairs two at a time, entered the flat and then the bedroom. Elspet and I stared icily at one another.

"I've come back for my trouser press," I explained. Elspet burst into tears and that was that. Twenty minutes later a somewhat dishevelled, red-faced, near ex-husband stumbled down to the Vanguard and asked George to help carry the luggage back again. George, a good friend and stage manager, dutifully obeyed and I never *did* see *Bitter Rice* – come to think of it.

September 1950

The company destined to open in London came together for the week commencing 4th September at the Opera House, Leicester. Wally Patch returned to the fold – and it was marvellous to have the old boy with us again. But just before our entry into the capital I became involved in an interesting little storm in a teacup. Two journalist friends of mine, Michael and Peggy Walsh, had written a play called *The Baker's Daughter* and we had planned to try it out at the Rep. in Bridlington. However, the Lord Chamberlain stepped in and banned the play for "it was obviously based on the marriage of Seretse Khama and Ruth Williams". The authors were bitterly disappointed.

"We submitted the play for counsel's opinion and were told it was legally okay. There are similarities to the Seretse Khama case, but primarily the play is one of ideas – seeking to show two sides of the colour bar. I can only think the Government wants the question of inter-racial marriages to be shelved." So quoth Peggy

Walsh – quoted by the *Daily Mail*. Actually, I have always believed the Foreign Office *did* have something to do with the play's banning. They certainly had two years later when we submitted a new farce by Roland and Michael Pertwee, *Tell the Marines*, for the Chamberlain's approval. On that occasion Michael Pertwee and I were summoned to St James's Palace, to be met by the Chamberlain's representative and a member of the Foreign Office who told us that the play was totally unacceptable in its present form – for it depicted British soldiers and Russian soldiers apparently fighting for some useless island, but, in fact, stage-managing all the fighting for the benefit of their respective High Commands. It was a funny, harmless piece of nonsense – but the Chamberlain's rep. and the man from the FO were adamant. Under no circumstances could the British be shown to be fighting the Russians, even though no fighting actually took place and the soldiers fraternised quite happily throughout. In that form the play would never get a licence – and it didn't. Roland and Michael rewrote it, but the damage was done and although the play toured in 1953, it was never the same again. Michael and Peggy Walsh couldn't rewrite their play – so it *never* saw the light of day.

Interesting really, isn't it? Here am I, with a reputation for putting on mindless bits of nonsense and yet, as a manager, I have twice run up against the Chamberlain for submitting plays that could cause us embarrassment abroad. No wonder the Chamberlain's censorship became a joke and finally disappeared. But not before it had twice taken me very seriously.

September, too, introduced me to my father-in-law, James MacGregor-Gray, for the first time. He had retired from Pakistan and Lloyds Bank at fifty-five. (All Eastern executives were retired early – the climate was supposed to be bad for them – and in his case it was, for he was dead before he was sixty.) So we met at his flat in Portland Court and it was pretty nerve-racking for both of us. He was faced with a son-in-law he'd only heard on a recording and I was faced by a father-in-law I'd never even heard. He turned out to be gentle, courteous and given to a little over-indulgence in both smoking and drinking. He had a soft Scots accent and bristling red moustache. We had a large drink together and hit it off straight away. He never gave me the impression he resented my marrying his daughter before he could get home. Maybe he didn't but I know I would have done . . .

So to the get-in at the Whitehall Theatre and the dress rehearsal of *Reluctant Heroes* at seven o'clock on Monday 11th September. At least that was the time it was supposed to begin – but it didn't. Early on the tour relations had become somewhat strained between the actors, on the one hand, and our director, Frank Dermody, on the other. In the early days he had been splendid – and certainly quietened down my performance – but since then seemed to have gone off into flights of fancy about certain sections of the play, and had been discouraged from seeing us too often. He was, after all, Irish, fey and from the Abbey Theatre, Dublin – which makes his original appointment as a Director even more incomprehensible when you consider we were doing a rumbustious British Army farce. However, he returned to conduct the London dress-rehearsal. By eight o'clock the company were beginning to get restless. Why hadn't we started? I went down to investigate. Frank was busy lighting a piece of sacking with some baby spots hidden in the floats. Elspet and Dermot played an amusing love scene on this sacking, interspersed with some even more amusing lines shouted by me from a doorway off left. *They* were to have special lighting – *I* was to be lit in darkness. Frank had always loved this scene and had spent many hours trying to create a thing of beauty out of it. Of course it couldn't be done – and it was eventually cut to the big laughs. However, now we were to open in the West End he was determined to make one more valiant attempt to re-establish his ideas for it – hence the special lighting.

Much tapping of feet went on and eventually, at eleven o'clock I went down and demanded that Frank stop "farting about and let's get on with the bloody play. Good God, we've been doing it with practically no lighting at all for nearly twenty weeks. Just turn everything up open white and let's bloody well go" – or words to that effect. So, we went through the motions of the

Brian's mother, Fanny Rix, aged 29

Brian's father, Herbert Rix, aged 45 in 1930

The Rix children in 1924, *left to right* Sheila, Brian (aged 6 months), Malcolm and Nora

Brian aged 11 as Giglio in *The Rose and the Ring*, 1935

Brian at 11 as Hercules the Page
in *The Sorcerer*, 1935

His son Jonty in 1971, aged 11,
wearing the same hat and cloak
as his father above

The first photograph of Brian Rix as a professional actor, 1942

Brian and Elspet Rix cutting the wedding cake, 14 August 1949

At the Air Crew Reception Centre,
November 1944

An audience at the Whitehall
Theatre watching *Reluctant
Heroes*

FRONTAL ATTACK!

Tone ... MR DERMOT WALSH * Gregory ... MR BRIAN RIX * Sergeant Bell ... MR WALLY PATCH

Reluctant Heroes

from PUNCH Sept 27 1950

original drawing loaned by the artist

Reluctant Heroes as seen by Ronald Searle in *Punch*, 27 September 1950

The televised version of *Love in a Mist*, 1956, *left to right* Diana Calderwood, Basil Lord, Elspet Gray and Brian Rix

Brian Rix, Elspet Gray and Patrick Cargill in *Round the Bend*

Brian and Elspet outside Buckingham Palace after their first Royal Garden Party, 1951

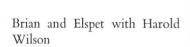

Brian and Elspet with Harold Wilson

At the christening of their younger son, Jonathan Mac-Gregor Rix, with Dickie Henderson, one of the godfathers

"This Is Your Life", September 1961, *left to right* Eamonn Andrews, Brian's mother, Brian's father Herbert Rix, Brian and Elspet

play – mainly for the benefit of the stage staff – with Frank muttering darkly in a corner about his lighting. At 1 a.m. it was all over – the actors were sent home by taxi and Frank and I remained to battle it out. Either he would have his way or *go*. I was tired, nervous and *certain* that actors in farce had to be seen to be believed. I was also an actor–manager and *certain* I should be lit! Frank *went* and we never saw him again – not in his official capacity as director, anyhow. From time to time he'd pop in and see the play and then write me a long letter afterwards with all his notes and observations. Often they were perceptive and useful – but throughout the many cast changes during the run of the play rehearsals were conducted by me or Colin Morris or both. Frank went on drawing his percentage for nearly four years but I suppose, on reflection, he must have been worth it – if only to side with Colin and stop me playing Gregory with a false nose, red wig and the speed of a leaden-footed tortoise. He allowed me, however, my centre parting, George Robey eyebrows and high-pitched falsetto.

Anyway, at 3 a.m. I started to light the play, with much help from Jack Ashman, the resident Stage Manager/Electrician. Even with his help, though, it was 7 a.m. before I got home and this on the morning of the first night. By midday I was back at the theatre, so you could say I had virtually no sleep at all before our London opening. Adrenalin is a marvellous help, though ...

So, at 7 p.m. Tuesday 12th September 1950 the curtain went up on the first Whitehall Theatre performance of *Reluctant Heroes*. I say 7 p.m. – but, more accurately, it was 7.20 p.m. In those days there was a free bar for members of the press and, frankly, it was difficult to get some of them out of it. Some *never* came out of it – but managed, all the same, to concoct their notices. Whatever the cause, the press were quite kind that night. Actually, they probably enjoyed themselves, for the audience laughed heartily and we took the unbelievable number of fourteen curtain calls. We had been warned that making a speech was a risky thing to do – but such was the applause that Colin Morris, as the author, stepped forward and gave an enormous hostage to fortune by thanking everyone for enjoying his elongated music-hall sketch of army life. Of course, that remark was bound to be picked up by the critics – we didn't realise just how *many* would use it, though.

Then, buoyed up by hope and excitement, we all went off to a party at Quaglino's. The reason for this choice of venue was quite simple. Colin's lovely wife, Viera, was appearing there in cabaret and Colin was able to arrange "favourable terms". So table-loads of family and friends streamed in to enjoy being favoured. We ate, drank, and were merry. Eventually, though, tiredness claimed many – but we younger ones went on till the early editions of the papers appeared on the streets. We toured Fleet Street and the railway stations ending up at a coffee stall in Covent Garden. There, we read our fate . . .

"Mr Morris, who joins breezily in this romp as a Fred Karno captain, disarmingly dismisses his khaki charade as 'a long-drawn-out music hall sketch bearing little relation to the British Army'. But farce or sketch, it is great fun in patches – and they are mostly Wally Patch's . . . And his recruits, Dermot Walsh, Larry Noble and Brian Rix, wilt most amusingly with some decorative WRAC aid."

So wrote Cecil Wilson of the *Daily Mail*. The others were in like vein.

"Colin Morris has strung together just about all the old music hall jokes about sergeants, recruits and female soldiers. Wally Patch is once again a sergeant of the music hall brigade and Brian Rix, the young Yorkshireman who brought the company to London, gives a well-turned performance as the dim recruit. The play, for all its deficiencies, certainly made the first-night audience laugh."

This from Walter Hayes of the *Daily Graphic* (do you remember, we had lots of newspapers in those days).

P. L. Mannock of the *Daily Herald* continued the theme:

"Well sustained, broad fun, but hardly a play. The author,

ex-Army officer Colin Morris, referred to it at curtain-call as an expanded music hall sketch. A gallery voice said, 'Hear, hear!'." (*I* never heard that voice – and there is no gallery at the Whitehall!)

He ended:

"Laughs were as constant as they were clean."

Even RPMG (whoever he was) of the *Daily Telegraph* fell into the trap:

"What was intriguing at the Whitehall last night was to see the sort of material one expects to find taking up 10 minutes in a music hall programme being expanded to make an evening's entertainment."

The totally anonymous critic (in those days) of *The Times* followed the same line of thought, but Elizabeth Frank of the *News Chronicle* became the first exception:

"That successful theatrical worm that found a cosy home for so long at the Whitehall Theatre has now moved to the Comedy, leaving the ground free for another of its kind – this time wearing the uniform of the British Army. Possessing so many of the same ingredients, I can see no reason why *Reluctant Heroes* should not have an equally long stay in the shadow of the war office ... The first-night audience found it highly diverting and laughed uproariously."

The evening papers, too, were definitely on our side – as were most of the Sundays. James Pettigrew, of the *Evening Standard*:

"Blunt-edged as a tin of bully-beef, Colin Morris's second Army play to see West End footlights, *Reluctant Heroes*, kept the Whitehall Theatre first-nighters amused for two and a half hours last night. Biggest triumph was 26-year-old actor-manager Brian Rix's performance as a 'dumb' Lancashire recruit. Helping him is his wife, Elspet Gray. As an officer of the new Women's Army, she wears on the stage the

Hartnell designed bottle-green WRAC uniform which will be issued to the Services next April."

Bill Boorne (a man who became friends with practically everyone in the theatre during his many years with the *Evening News* – he and his wife, Peg, are lovely people*) was even more specific:

"As for newcomer Elspet Gray, if these are the sort of officers they are having in the new Army . . . Shinwell here we come!"

Beverley Baxter MP had a weekly column in the *Evening Standard* and a good notice from him was highly desirable:

"There are some plays, like *Hamlet*, which are above criticism, and there are others, like *Reluctant Heroes* at the Whitehall, which are beyond criticism. A deferred public school boy, a deferred married man from Lancashire and a Cockney lad report to the Army for National Service. That is all. But I swear the equipping of them with uniforms and the vaccination of them by the medical orderly are two of the funniest episodes in the London Theatre. There isn't a neurotic in the lot. None of them is sex-starved despite a lively interest in the other half. When he writes a letter to his loving wife the Lancashire lad ends it, 'If closet gives any more trouble fetch plumber. Yours truly, Horace . . .'
    "Of course, there are bad stretches and even some dull ones. but if it's laughter you're after, here it is."

The *Daily Worker* ascribed more sinister motives to us in our efforts to raise laughter:

"One of the inevitable minor products of the rearmament drive and the build-up towards a third war is the re-appearance of comic conscripts in army life farces."

Frankly, that thought had never occurred to us before and it never occurred to us again but it does go to show how careful you have to be not to give offence. Oh dear, perhaps I shouldn't have used the word "offence". Sorry! I never thought I'd see the

* Since I wrote this he, alas, has died.

92

Lord Chamberlain and the *Daily Worker* in accord, as it were, but their respective reactions to *Tell The Marines* and *Reluctant Heroes* were very similar ...

Now to the Sundays. John Drummond of the *Sunday Chronicle* said he "laughed until it hurt", Dick Richards of the *Sunday Pictorial* rated us "a mirthquake", but it was left to the "heavies" to give us the Good Theatre Keeping Seal of Approval. Harold Hobson of the *Sunday Times* found us "entertaining in an uncomplicated way", but Ivor Brown in the *Observer* had no doubts at all. Since it is my first good notice from a highly respected critic, I make no apologies for quoting it in full:

"In the playhouse there are many partners – and a constant collision. One of the collisions is between the Art of the Theatre and the Industry of Entertainment. There is no reason why the two should not be happily entwined. But there is one party, small, which is horrified at the prospect of a single laugh and prefers the kind of play that befogs, baffles and bewilders and another party, large, which seeks only a bright spectacle and a hearty chortle. Both sides have a right to their own appetite. Such a piece of clowning as *Reluctant Heroes* is to be judged as Chortlers' Joy and nothing else. It makes no sort of pretences: it is full of rough fun in such rough houses as a conscripts' hutment and a farm during some oddly bisexual manoeuvres. There are three separate sketches rather than three acts of a play; there is fun with a stentorian sergeant and his assorted victims, there is fun with undressing and girls under beds, fun with mimic warfare and high explosives. All is audible, visible and as easily comprehended as a kick in the pants.

"Since the actor–author, Colin Morris, has not tried to write a play or to conceive the miseries of compulsory soldiering as anything but an excuse for antics and uproar, he is not to be faulted for omitting to be a dramatist. He and his team have knocked up some good old music-hall gags and goings-on; in the performance of this they confront us with an abounding will to please. Sergeant Wally Patch and Brian Rix as a woe-begone Blackpuddlian private have the best chances and take them. The ladies in uniform jump smartly to it – or under it, in the case of beds. So the myriad chortlers have their bliss and the few anti-chortlers will prudently stay away. The management will have a good, possibly an immense, run for its money."

Ivor Brown was quite right. We did.

Act VII

Shakespeare appears to have provided quotations and titles for every event and every writer. They all use him. So, when in Rome I intend to do as the Romans did and turn, naturally enough, to *Julius Caesar*: "Fortune is merry and in this mood will give us anything." Now, housed at the Whitehall and with those notices to sustain us, you might think fortune *would* be merry. You would be wrong. We struggled. One week a loss, one week a minuscule profit, one week a break-even figure achieved: it looked as though we would never get our money back. The total production had cost us only £1,800 – and that included refurbishing for London. Nowadays, the same production would cost ten times as much – and seat prices have only multiplied by three – so you can see the tightrope has become even more difficult to negotiate. My father wrote to me in great indignation about the various percentages we had to pay out every week to Dermot Walsh, Frank Dermody and Colin Morris.

"It's a case of heads you lose, tails I win. Yet it is *we* who have to take the great risks."

I love the expression "great risks". He must turn in his grave when he considers today's inflated costs. He couldn't grumble at the money Elspet and I were getting each week. £15 for me and £12 for Elspet. Hardly breathtaking and frankly not too easy to live on – even in those days – for London has always been an expensive place. We found a pleasant enough furnished flat in Queensborough Terrace off the Bayswater Road. At least it seemed pleasant enough ... till we discovered we had vast hordes of mice runnng all over the place and they seemed to *thrive* on poison. I remember one evening my sister Sheila had come round for supper after the show. We were experimenting with kebab and the meal was proceeding well when suddenly out of the dish popped one of our verminous friends. Elspet was straight up on the seat, I looked round for a suitable blunt instrument. Sheila, on the other hand, sprang immediately into action. Seizing an umbrella she unerringly speared the poor little brute with the ferrule. One look at our mouse kebab was enough. Supper was *not* a success that night.

We were also next door to a hard-working brothel. At least half a dozen girls seemed to be on active duty there, picking up their clientele in Kensington Gardens. They never bothered us – but some of their callers could be a bit difficult to circumvent, especially when they'd had a drink or two. We garaged the car up the road – so we always had to walk the length of the Terrace to get to our flat – and many nights saw us holding Bastien on a short lead and pretending he was a *very* fierce dog, ready to pounce on any attacker. Actually, he was so soft it was laughable. Once Elspet arrived home and in his excitement he jumped up at the front door before she could open it and knocked down the yale lock with his paw. Elspet's key was useless, so she found the caretaker's son-in-law, who volunteered to climb in through the window. Bastien knocked him down, too, through sheer exuberance – and wouldn't stop licking his face to show how pleased he was to see him. No, definitely not a watch-dog. He used to stay in Elspet's dressing room at the theatre during the performances and would never move a muscle until he heard "God Save The King" playing at the end of the show (we still played the National Anthem in those days). Immediately, he would be on his feet stretching and yawning and waiting to go home. Maybe he was no watch-dog but he was a true dog of the theatre!

However, in spite of our financial struggles, we were in the London Theatre and we had some illustrious companions to prove it: *Ring Round the Moon, The Cocktail Party, Seagulls over*

Sorrento, Top of the Ladder, Accolade, Mister Roberts, The Second Mrs Tanqueray, The Little Hut, Who is Sylvia?, Home and Beauty, Captain Carvallo, His Excellency, Home at Seven, Will Any Gentleman?, King's Rhapsody, Carousel, Ace of Clubs, Knights of Madness, Take it from Us, The Holly and the Ivy, Worm's Eye View, Dear Miss Phoebe and *Touch and Go.* In all a varied, even a distinguished, theatrical scene. It was fun to be part of it and it was fun to be a West End actor. We felt the stamp of approval was given to us when we were invited to take part in a charity matinée, *Yesterday and Today*, which was held for the Irene Vanbrugh Memorial Fund at Drury Lane on Tuesday 7th November 1950. In the Royal Box was the Queen, with the two Princesses, Elizabeth and Margaret. All *we* had to do was line up with the other shows at the end and take a bow as our titles were called out. Hardly a world-shattering first appearance at Drury Lane – but all day we rubbed shoulders with the theatrical greats and it was *marvellous.* Robert Morley, Eileen Herlie, Robert Donat, Eric Portman, John Clements, Michael Redgrave, Marie Ney, Paul Scofield, Margaret Leighton, Emlyn Williams, Diana Churchill, Binnie Hale, Dorothy Ward, Marie Burke, Anthony Quayle, Diana Wynyard, Esmond Knight, Claire Bloom, Robertson Hare, Alicia Markova, Anton Dolin, Beatrice Lillie, Cyril Maude, George Robey, Noël Coward – all were there and many, many more besides. I was knocked out. Nine months before that I was a young hopeful rehearsing in a draughty church hall opposite Holloway Jail. My gestation period had gone according to my wildest dreams. *Reluctant Heroes* might be a slightly unwell baby, but it was going to get better. On that point I was determined. But how? The answer was provided by the BBC six months later. In the meantime another exciting oyster was being opened ... revealing the pearl of FILMS.

A small company, Byron Productions, had made a killing with their film of *Worm's Eye View* and Ronald Shiner repeating his stage performance. Now they were looking round for a successor to provide Ronnie with another vehicle, and their eyes lighted upon the Sergeant in *Heroes*. They also saw that my part, too, was a very good one and offered it to George Formby. But luck, in the shape of ill-luck, was on my side. Christmas week came and we added extra matinées. Along with these I also added my annual Christmas cold and, as usual, my voice faltered and petered out altogether by the Friday afternoon matinée. My understudy was thrust on at short notice. His name? John Chapman. I told you he'd crop up again but this was the first time he did me a great favour. Quite simply he didn't get the laughs that afternoon. He was under-rehearsed, the house was poor and John hadn't, then, the experience to overcome those obstacles. It happened to be the afternoon George Formby elected to come along and see the play. He was unimpressed by both the play and the part – so turned it down and the film company eventually offered it to me. It must be the only time an actor has actually been offered a part by *not* appearing.

That Christmas week also saw another great piece of luck for me. I gave up smoking. It seemed daft to be damaging the only instrument that kept me earning money, my voice. So, with no regrets, I stopped and have never smoked since. Nowadays, I actively campaign against it. All converts are supposed to be the same. Ask my friends: I think they'll bear this out. But you must admit it's a mucky, smelly, stupid, damaging habit and the way it's advertised and the way successive governments have turned a blind eye to the whole problem, so they can lay their hands on the revenue, is downright immoral. That's it! I promise not to say another word on the subject . . .

Anyway, although the play was still running at the Whitehall, we sold the film rights of *Heroes* (its eventual early release did nothing to harm our theatre business) and waited, with bated breath, for the casting to be completed. Poor Wally Patch was the first to go – but then that was pre-ordained, for the film company was only looking for a film for Ronnie Shiner. Dermot Walsh, too, was side-stepped and Derek Farr was preferred. To be fair, he and Ronnie had film names which were better than Wally's or Dermot's; but it did seem hard. Elspet, too, was out, for Christine Norden was thought to have a film name and was moved into the part. I know it sounds like nepotism but in my view Elspet in the part was ten times better than

Christine. Helen Jessop, too, was out and an actress, whose name escapes me and who was at that time little known, was cast. But that's the film business!

Anyway, the rest of us were in and shooting started at Riverside Studios on 11th June 1951. It was the most incredible film I have ever known. Directing was Jack Raymond (responsible for most of the George Formby films) and he galloped through the whole thing in five weeks.

"Print it! Over here," he'd say after every shot. The camera would whizz over, the lighting cameraman, Jimmy Watson, would bang up his bashers, his bulbs and his pups, and the next scene would be shot – warts and all. Ronnie never knew his long speeches – but rendered a sort of synopsis, whilst I actually fluffed in one scene, mumbled, "Oh Christ," and sat down.

"Print it! Over here," said Jack.

"But Jack," I protested, "I actually said 'Oh Christ' at the end of that take."

"Not to worry, Brian," was his reply. "You were on edge of frame. No one'll notice." He was right, of course. No one did and my little burst of blasphemy is still in the film to this day.

Jack Raymond may have pushed through the film when he was on the floor, but filming was strictly limited when it came to actual working hours. We started a bit later in the mornings because Ronnie was in *Seagulls over Sorrento* and was, reasonably enough, tired. He and Jack used to have a further break at around eleven o'clock when they'd have a glass or two of champagne in Ronnie's dressing room. The morning's work would again break off a little early because Ronnie, Jack and the film's producer, Henry Halsted, would repair to the Clarendon (a posh pub in Hammersmith Broadway) for lunch – this meant at least an hour and a half – then came rushes and at about 2.45 work would start again. Because of Ronnie's theatre commitment he would leave around 5.15 and that would be that: a total working time of around five and a half hours in a possible eight-hour day. Can you wonder it was "Print it! Over here!" All for a total sum of £45,000 – even in those days an incredibly low budget – and when it was released it took more than ten times that amount at the Box Office; in fact it was the top British film money-maker of 1952. I, personally, was paid the handsome sum of £600, but luckily we, as a management, had a share of the author's royalties and he, thank goodness, was on a percentage – so we did all right!

So that was my introduction to the strange world of films, and even stranger world of "quickie" films. I was to make three more with Ronnie before he died, but none was made for that money nor in that extraordinarily haphazard manner. None of them took as much at the Box Office though. There must be a moral somewhere.

As some sort of compensation, Elspet had been written into the film, in a tiny part, but by then there was another "tiny" on the horizon – the patter of tiny feet – for we were expecting our first baby – due around the beginning of December. It would be pointless to go into our excitement and anticipation, for every parent must know this. However, Elspet was determined to keep working as long as possible, so that she could contribute to our new flat and all the usual baby expenses. The £600 from the film had enabled us to pay for "furniture and fittings" and we moved to a very pleasant two-bedroomed third-floor flat in Holland Park. In more spacious days these flats had been part of some town houses, but over-population and economic necessity had watered down their grandeur. There was one snag – no lift – and Elspet was to curse those stairs as she got larger and larger and the shopping became heavier and heavier.

With fatherhood a few months away the need to bolster up *Reluctant Heroes* became a matter of some urgency – and then a Fairy Godmother in the shape of Auntie BBC came to the rescue. They offered us a live fifteen-minute sound excerpt from the theatre. This was part of a series they were doing called "Around the Shows" and they proposed to split the half hour's allocation between us and a comedy, *The Happy Family*. Anything was better than nothing so we eagerly accepted. It proved to be the turning point for our play.

The date for the broadcast was Thursday 28th June 1951, right in the middle of the Festival of Britain and, frankly, the festival had put the mockers on West End theatre business. Everyone had expected a boom. Of course, the town was full, but people used to gawp at all the free entertainment and were so exhausted by nightfall they just wanted to put their feet up. It was a ridiculous situation. There were thousands of people jostling past the theatre doors and only a handful coming into the Box Office.

We made sure there was a splendid complimentary house out front, though, on that fateful Thursday. John Ellison, of "In Town Tonight" fame, introduced the play and we were off. All we did was the first scene, no more – but it was enough. The audience roared their heads off and many people must have been listening that night, for next day the phones started ringing, people started queuing and by nightfall we had a packed house. It was to be like that for many months. Sergeant Bell's last lines in that first scene had proved strangely prophetic for the man who roared them: Wally Patch. He'd suffered, with dignity, his loss of the part in the film. Every night he had bellowed his head off for the benefit of half-empty houses in the theatre and, suddenly, bingo, we'd hit the jackpot. His lines? "An' when yer say yer prayers ask Gawd to give me patience." He had, and it paid off.

We must have hit the British funny bone, though, just on the right spot. The other half of that radio programme, *The Happy Family*, had a happy cast, headed by Henry Kendall, Thora Hird and Dandy Nichols and was introduced by no less a happy voice than Brian Johnston. The result was *far* from happy, though. Their business slumped like a lead balloon and the play was off in a matter of weeks. Extraordinary, isn't it?

Our first year at the Whitehall was celebrated by the first of many super parties – in those days you could get them off expenses. Nowadays you need a cast of foreigners to obtain the same income tax concessions, but unfortunately they don't fit too happily into British farce! Arthur Helliwell in his *People* column reported:

"Nicest party of the week ... on the stage with the company and staff of the Whitehall Theatre celebrating the first birthday of that rollicking farce *Reluctant Heroes*."

The *Evening Standard* carried the following:

"Telegram to the author for the birthday performance: 'Congratulations on beating my London record – Mischa Auer'. I'm glad Mr Auer has a sense of humour; his farcical debut lasted for three nights ..."

My favourite quote, though, comes from *What's On*:

"Most fertile play in Town. *Reluctant Heroes*? Larry Noble's wife, Pamela Plant, had a baby a couple of weeks back. Elspet Gray, wife of actor–producer Brian Rix and originally in the cast herself, now expects one of those same happy events. And author Colin Morris, also in the play, says his wife, cabaret star Viera, is now knitting small garments. So far, however, no male member of the cast has asked for a transfer."

Actually we *were* a fertile lot. Over the next fifteen years dozens of babies were born to the various casts at the Whitehall. But then, we were all young, newly married, virile and heterosexual. The latter does help.

Elspet had, in fact, left the play at the beginning of August and her place was taken, for a time, by a very talented actress, Gene Anderson. Several years later Gene died, tragically, during an asthma attack just when she was beginning to establish her acting reputation.

When Elspet left, Colin had arranged a farewell gift and a message signed by all the company. It reads:

Whitehall Theatre
4th August 1951

Our dearest Elspet,

The men and women of the 1st Bn Whitehall Regiment (Rix's Reluctant Rifles) offer this token of their love and regard on your temporary retirement to raise another recruit.

They hope you will look in on them frequently prior to the

event when they en masse will look in on you both. All our good wishes, with maybe an odd tear and a sigh here and there, go with you! Good luck always,

From,

Wally Patch, Larry Noble, Dermot Walsh, Antony Baird, Philip Levene, George Radford, Gene Anderson, Richard Saunders, Clive Parkhurst, Helen Jessop, Colin Morris, Betty Impey, John R. Chapman, Emily Casey, William E. Raynor, Frank Dermody.

An ironical little note, really, in the light of future events . . . but more of that later. In the meantime may I point out a few of the signatories. One new to these pages, Antony Baird was reputed to be the greatest Don Juan in the business, but managed to stagger on for every performance as the Scots P T Sergeant. He also owned a very fierce bull terrier bitch who tore a gaping hole in Bastien's ear and spawned a bunch of puppies who ate all the furniture in his dressing room. Dogs were banned forthwith from backstage at the Whitehall. I ignored the whole thing and still took Bastien in when it was necessary. He, on the other hand wasn't keen. Having been bitten on the ear at the stage door – by a bitch, too – he was, not unnaturally, hesitant.

Philip Levene developed a highly successful writing style whilst at the Whitehall. He started as an understudy and this gave him time for his writing. Eventually George Radford left and Philip took over the Medical Orderly. When the play finished he went on to write a number of stage thrillers and many of "The Avengers" episodes. He died, suddenly in 1973. Helen Jessop and Betty Impey played our two WRAC Privates. Helen appeared in many subsequent plays at the Whitehall and Garrick but Betty married John Chapman and bore him four strapping sons. John, already mentioned as having given me a rather useful Christmas present in the shape of my film part, played a Scots soldier as well as understudying. This meant he had time on his hands too and, like Philip Levene, he started to write. His first effort was to be my next play at the Whitehall, *Dry Rot*. It didn't do quite as well as *Heroes*. It only ran for 1,475 performances!

So the "firsts" of 1951 rolled on. Our first year at the Whitehall. My first film. Our first broadcast excerpt. Elspet and I invited to our first Garden Party at Buckingham Palace. Our first baby.

She was born, after a forty-eight hour labour, at 2.30 a.m. on Monday 3rd December in the Westminster Hospital. She was a funny little thing, like all newly born babies, but she seemed beautiful to us. We were in raptures. Elspet's father roared with laughter as she stuck her tongue out at him. She seemed to stick her tongue out rather a lot . . .

Elspet was a little worried.

"They don't bring her to me as much as I'd like," she complained. "Do you think there's something wrong with her?"

"Don't be silly,' I said, "all the babies seem to be kept away from their mums, except at feeding times."

But the early warnings had been sounded. Elspet remembered her strange feelings during pregnancy. Often she thought the child she was carrying was not a normal child. She was, in the event, correct; but everyone was loath to tell us. It was the maternity sister, Sister Gilbert, who finally persuaded the gynae-cologist, Mr Searle, to reveal the facts.

"He'd like to see you in Harley Street at six o'clock tomorrow evening."

My reaction was understandably nervous. "What for? And why Harley Street? Why can't he see me here?"

She calmed me down: "It's just a routine interview he likes to have with all new fathers – away from the hurly-burly of the hospital."

So I reported this to Elspet and her fears multiplied, but I battened down my own feelings and attempted to encourage her. My fears, however, dragged side by side with hers and as I stepped into Mr Searle's consulting room I had only to look at his face to know the worst.

It's laughable really. Actors perform these parts better than their actual counterparts. Mr Searle behaved like the newest drama student.

"Do come in . . . Do sit down . . . Do have a cigarette."

I came in – but I neither sat down nor had a cigarette. I was a non-sitter and a non-smoker in those situations. A non-smoker at all times, anyway.

"Have you heard of mongolism?" was his first question. Well, that was one way of putting it. Direct and to the point. Our daughter was a mongol. My stomach went through his consulting room floor and has never, really, recovered its rightful place. "Have you heard of mongolism?" "I have to tell you your son has been killed in a car accident." "Your husband was a brave man." Jesus Christ! It's only in moments such as these when you realise the inadequacy of the spoken word. Afterwards you recognise that the poor devil stumbling and stuttering before you is as mortified and horrified at explaining the disaster as you are at receiving it. But that's the way we do it and what other way is there?

"Please tell your wife," he said.

It was now one hour before the curtain went up at the White-hall. I had promised to ring Elspet and tell her why Mr Searle had wanted to see me. I rang the Sister instead.

"I don't have to tell you, do I?" was my first question.

"No," was her answer.

"Please tell Elspet that all is well and I'll be round in the morning. Don't let her suspect the worst."

"Of course not. She'll sleep tonight. We'll see to that."

I drove back to the Whitehall. Colin was in his dressing room, knowing something was wrong. It wasn't long before he found out. His was a lovely shoulder to cry on, especially as Viera had given birth to a strapping son, Julian, only forty-eight hours before our daughter arrived. He filled me up with brandy and somehow I stumbled on. Our funny play now appeared to be full of poignant lines:

"Any children?"

"Aye."

"'Ow many?"

"One 'ere and another on t'way."

Somehow that didn't seem quite as funny as it had done before and the Sergeant's vehement "They're burnin' yer 'omes, they're carryin' off yer women and children." (*To Gregory*) "I daresay they'd leave your kids after a second look at 'em," caused Wally Patch considerable embarrassment that horrible night. Poor man, he went purple and could hardly bring himself to look at me. That was one speech definitely not spoken trippingly on the tongue.

As soon as it was over, I raced to the hospital to make sure that Elspet was all right and to make those ridiculous enquiries that one does make on those occasions: "Are you *sure*? How? Why? What can be done?" The Night Sister was kind. Yes, Elspet was asleep. No, nothing could be done. Mongolism was indiscriminate in its choice of parent. She gave me a large sleeping pill and sent me on my way. Actually I was staying with my in-laws who had, at that time, a flat in Baron's Keep. I was determined not to tell them until I had told Elspet – so their excited enquiries about mother and child were all the harder to bear.

It must have been a very powerful pill, for I slept like a log and when I woke up it was some time before I realised my vague memories of a nightmare were in fact actual and that this particular nightmare was here for keeps. With a heavy heart I drove to the hospital. The Day Sister gave me an encouraging pat on the shoulder and I was on. Elspet looked at me as I walked in. It was enough. She burst into tears. I burst into tears and throughout that morning we sobbed our unhappy way through to a state of realisation and recognition of the fact that we had a mongol daughter: Elspet Shelley.

The next questions: "What now?" "What of the future?" were not easily answered. It was suggested that as a first step she should be christened in the hospital chapel. That didn't seem to do much good – so the medical staff were consulted. The Resident Paediatrician chose his words rather badly.

"I am happy to tell you," he pontificated, "that your daughter is a mongol." Happy? "My advice to you would be to put her in a home and forget all about her. You're both young, you'll have other children, and there's no chance of it happening again." There is, of course, a chance of it happening again and Elspet and

I now believe him to be wrong with the other half of his advice –
but as all the other senior medical staff backed him up and as we
had no outside agency to turn to we, as young, disturbed,
ashamed, frightened parents, acquiesced. Shelley went into a
private home run by a wonderfully kind woman, Dr Sherwood,
and we went miserably back to our empty flat. Bastien was a poor
substitute that day.

Some good can always come out of the worst of situations.
We were fortunate on a number of counts. Firstly, it forged our
friendship with Johnnie Slater. John and I had played cricket
together for the Stage Cricket Club all through the summer of
1951 and he was an ebullient extrovert who provided the energy
we needed. None of "you poor things" and weeping with us for
John. It was breeze into the hospital, chat, chat, chat and breeze
out again. He even provided Elspet with some rare Japanese
buttons which he had made into cuff-links. They depicted,
appropriately, storks and were quite beautiful. I wear them to this
day. But John had known life's problems. Five years before he
and his wife, Betty, had crashed on a plane flying to Paris. Betty
was trapped and John crawled back into the burning wreckage and
carried her out. Betty was badly burned and spent years in the
East Grinstead burns unit. Johnnie was burnt too, but the amazing
thing is that when he struggled out of the plane with Betty the
plane blew up and he managed the last few yards on a broken leg.
Years later John and Betty were to lose their younger son, Simon,
at the age of eighteen, through cancer. Elspet and I then tried to
repay, as best we could, the great kindness that John and Betty
had always shown us. They're a lovely couple.*

Secondly, our problem over Shelley introduced us to the world
of charity. Charity is a ghastly word nowadays, because of its
Victorian connotation; but it's only the *word* that is ghastly.
The objectives and those involved in charities are anything but
ghastly. It never ceases to amaze me how many people do such

---

* Shortly after I had finished writing this book my mother and Johnnie
Slater died. Both had contracted rheumatic fever in their younger days and both
had completely ignored their subsequent heart conditions for all their lives. I
have made no attempt to change any reference to them – for they will always
be alive in my memory.

marvellous work, voluntarily, for charity. I often wonder if we'd have become so involved if it hadn't been for Shelley, but many, many kind folk have no personal reasons to help at all – except for an innate goodness. Shelley is now twenty-two and lives in Normansfield, a National Health Hospital, at Teddington. Their League of Friends was started seventeen years ago to provide a few extra comforts. The "comforts" are a school, a hydro-therapy pool, a clubhouse and shop, plus a magnificent holiday home in Selsey Bill, which is open also for mentally handicapped children from other hospitals. Most of the money for these wonderful additions has been provided by voluntary effort, sheer hard work and fantastic kindness. "Tall oaks from little acorns grow."

A far bigger organisation is the Spastics Society. Affiliated to this is the Stars Organisation for Spastics. This society, like so many, was started by a group of parents headed by Ian Dawson-Shepherd and he thought it would be a good idea if well-known actors and actresses could be persuaded to help – hence the formation of the SOS. The first Chairman was Wilfred Pickles, followed by Vera Lynn, me, Harry Secombe, David Jacobs, Leslie Crowther, Dickie Henderson and Roger Moore. But the Chairman represents the tip of the iceberg. There are, literally, hundreds of household names who have gladly given their time for the benefit of spastics and the SOS, with no thoughts of payment. Then there are the actors and sportsmen who help in so many ways with the Lord's Taverners, SPARKS, the National Society for Mentally Handicapped Children, Variety, etc. The list is practically endless and most of us overlap in our efforts, but they say if you want a staunch charity helper, ask an overworked person to give a helping hand!

Occasionally we are taken a little too much for granted. For instance – waiting in the wings for a Midnight Charity Perform-ance for three and a half hours can be a bit of a chore, to say the least. When you finally stagger on at 3.30 a.m. to face an audience fast asleep or fast disappearing you need either to be full of alcohol to anaesthetise you against the wave of boredom, or desperate to get on the boards at any cost. I've never been able to take either attitude – so now I tactfully decline and leave it to some other poor unfortunate.

Most of the new charities have been formed in the last twenty-five years, so that when Shelley was born the NSMHC was only a few years old and practically unknown. Therefore, no one in the hospital suggested we consult them, nor did the Health Visitor who came to see us. She was very kind but fairly useless. However, she did one great thing by putting Shelley's name down for Normansfield. It was five years before Shelley entered the hospital and then only because I made a fuss through my good friend George Jeger. As he was an MP and an ex-member of the LCC he knew which strings to pull and Shelley was admitted, but not before she had gone through a most upsetting medical at County Hall. One doctor was kind; the other was awful. She bludgeoned away at Shelley with her questions and as the poor girl neither walked nor talked at that age, Elspet and I could have hit the silly bitch. However, she was eventually satisfied with Shelley's condition and Shelley was able to go to Normansfield.

I'm writing this section on the eve of our Seventeenth Annual Ball: every year the League holds a ball at the Dorchester. It's my fiftieth birthday, I'm surrounded by table plans and Shelley has just come home for tea. So much water has flowed under the bridge of understanding and help since she was born. But funnily enough the founder of Normansfield led the way over a century ago.

A certain Dr Langdon-Down was interested in the phenomenon of these children with charming personalities, double-joints, foreshortened limbs, funny squashed noses and slightly Chinese eyes – in other words, the classic village idiot. He called them "mongols" and started a small fee-paying home for them where they could receive regular care and attention and some tuition. The home was, of course, Normansfield and it remained fee-paying till the Health Service took over the place in 1949.

Now the Russians had, of course, Mongols as a race of people – so they called mongolism the "Langdon-Down disease" and that is its official world health name today. Dr Langdon-Down had two sons; both became doctors and joint medical superintendents of their father's hospital. They, in turn, had sons: one became the last Langdon-Down to run the hospital (he was there when Shelley moved in), and the other suffered from the Langdon-Down disease and was housed in Normansfield. Even the most naïve punter wouldn't have had a bet on that. But a lot of us have cause to be grateful to the Langdon-Down family.

I had less cause to be grateful to Mr Enoch Powell when he was Minister of Health. Lady Salmon arranged with the NSMHC for a member of the Society – me – to go along with a specific request. It seemed simple enough – but it wasn't. The NSMHC wished to inform all doctors, midwives, maternity units, etc., of their existence, local addresses, the aid and advice they could give and so on. They hoped to disseminate their information through the good offices of the Health Service, for they felt that if all medical personnel knew about the local aid available it would be the greatest possible use to unfortunate parents when they first discovered they had a mentally handicapped child.

Mr Powell listened politely to this request and turned it down. He thumbed through various white papers and official reports and said according to the statistics available nearly every member of the Health Service now knew what to do in this situation and it was totally under control. Furthermore, if he agreed to our request he would be inundated with similar ones from other societies. The Health Service was not a postal service, etc. etc. All perfectly reasonable when looked at in statistical terms.

We argued statistically, too. The proportion of mentally handicapped born was far higher than any other handicap. This carried no weight. Neither did a thick file of letters I had brought, all written to me during the past year by distraught parents who did *not* know where to turn for help. If a mere actor received so many letters, what about the hundreds more that were never written because the writers were at a total loss to know where to send them? Mr Powell stuck to his facts and figures. I produced my ace. I explained that one of the principal teaching hospitals in London, Westminster, had been incapable of giving us any constructive advice and help when Shelley was born. My ace was trumped by Mr Powell pointing out that our daughter had been born several years before and things had changed a lot since then.

We left empty-handed, after a pleasant cup of coffee and an insight into the mind of Mr Powell. Ever since that day I have understood a little more his political ethos. Statistics do not always make it easier for human beings to help and understand one another.

So 1951 – which had started full of promise – ended on a very dismal note. Christmas and New Year celebrations became hollow mockeries for us. I had £300 saved up to pay my income tax. I decided to blow the lot, take a holiday and go to Madeira with Elspet. That almost ended in disaster too . . .

Act VIII

Our passport photos reflected our grim mood for the next ten years. Elspet's was taken in hospital and showed her looking very sad, in bed and clad in a bed-jacket. Mine was taken, glowering darkly, in the corner of my dressing room. We only had to look at them, whilst they were in use, to be reminded instantly of Shelley and those unhappy days, but their purpose was to enable us to escape reality for a little while. Quite impossible, of course.

We caught the train from Waterloo to Southampton at nine o'clock on Friday 11th January 1952. It was a freezing cold evening and as we climbed on board the Aquila seaplane on Southampton water it seemed even colder. Rugs were issued, for there was no heat in the cabin – not till we took off, anyway, and even then there wasn't.

For the uninitiated amongst you, Aquila Airways had acquired a few old Coastal Command Sunderlands, which lumbered through the skies at about two hundred knots and at an altitude of about seven thousand feet. Not exactly speedy and not exactly comfortable on the old ears, for the cabins were not pressurised. Furthermore, the flight to Madeira took eight hours, so one had to suffer this discomfort for a long time. All right, I suppose, if you were warmly clad in flying boots and jackets, with the adrenalin keeping up the body temperature as you chased Nazi submarines; but not so good for supine peacetime passengers.

Suddenly we were moving, being towed out to our start mark. The engines spluttered into life and we all waited whilst the captain and crew carried out the usual pre-flight checks. Then, a surge forward and we were off. At least that was obviously the intention. It was all very exciting. The cabin portholes were completely obscured by flying spray and one felt as though one was in a diving submarine. We practically were, for as we thundered up the waterway it was quite clear that the Sunderland had no intention of taking off on that run. We stayed firmly splashing about in the water and slowly gurgled to a halt. A long pause. Then, movement. Up chugged our tender and we were towed back to the start mark.

Again we beat up the water. Again we came to a shuddering, splashing halt. Again we were towed back.

I'll give that captain an alpha for effort. Either that, or he was a bloody fool, for he made that run yet a third time – with as fruitless a result as ever.

"Hello everyone. This is your captain speaking. I'm afraid we're experiencing a little technical trouble which may take a little time to sort out. You'll all be transferred to a hotel near by, where you will be given coffee and sandwiches and we will send for you as soon as possible." All air travellers will have heard those words, or some very similar, and any with experience will know the hours of waiting that will take place. We were different. We still had the light of innocence in our eyes. But seven hours later, unshaven (in my case), unkempt, unwashed and uncomfortable, the innocence was no longer shining out of our red-rimmed, bloodshot peepers. You might say that the scales had well and truly fallen from our eyes: in fact Madeira seemed a hell of a long way away; and was it all worth while in the first place?

But the bus arrived to take us back to our Sunderland and we dutifully and docilely climbed on board both bus and plane. We made urgent enquiries as to why we had failed to take off at 00.45 hours to be told that the ailerons had iced up, due to the freezing weather, but they had now been thawed out. What with? A blow lamp? Anyway, something had been done for we *did* take off this time and start the long bumpy journey to our Paradise Isle.

You effete modern air travellers probably think these brown paper bags in front of you are for sandwiches. We older hands know better. They are sick bags – and they were in short supply *that* day. Every passenger except one, me, was using them continually throughout that awful trip. I was determined to be the odd man out and sat with clenched jaw below my greenish cheeks for the entire journey. At last we landed in Funchal harbour and relief burst over everyone: just like the sun warming the island. Unfortunately there was a considerable swell and we were on the water for at least three-quarters of an hour, waiting for the boat to take us to dry land. Now I might not be air-sick but I'm easily sea-sick. As everyone scrambled out to the boat all cares and tiredness and sickness forgotten, I sat rooted to my seat. It was no good. Clenched jaw and stiff upper lip not withstanding, I just had to use that brown paper bag. I did feel sorry for the hostesses. They'd spent all day cleaning up the mess and now I had to complete the full house.

Exactly a year later the wing of an Aquila Airways seaplane sank and the passengers had to scramble out on to the other wing to balance the plane and stop it going under. If that had happened to us we could have sat back and used our sick bags for ballast. What a way to run an airline. But nearly a quarter of a century later and with hundreds of miserable hours spent hanging around for Scheduled Flights and Charter Flights and Cheap Weekend Flights and Package Flights – and with intimate knowledge of Heathrow Airport, Gatwick Airport, Luton Airport, Malaga Airport, Moscow Airport and all stations after – we know things haven't changed much!

But Reid's Hotel *was* worth the journey. The sun shone every day and two dear people, Celia and Jack Waller, cheered us up at all times. Jack was the theatrical manager who had originally presented that smash hit musical *No, No, Nanette!* and had made a fortune out of it. When we met him he was presenting another huge success *Sailor, Beware!* by Philip King and Falkland Cary – the play that brought Peggy Mount instant stardom – but in between times he'd been pretty successful, too. He'd started life as a fiddler and every afternoon he'd stand on his balcony, serenading the world at large with his violin.

There were only two snags with that Madeira holiday. One

was the constant begging that took place as you walked through the streets of Funchal and the utter degradation and poverty we saw as we toured around the hilly areas of the island. Maybe things have changed since then – but it was the first time I'd ever been abroad and the sight of people living in sopping wet grass huts and nailed-up packing cases came as a nasty shock. Elspet had seen it all before, in India, but for me it was a revelation.

The second snag was a purely selfish one. About a week before our holiday ended we began to dread the flight back. In the event, it wasn't too bad and the captain let me spend most of the time on the flight deck where interest in all that was going on kept me from going bright green yet again. Behind us, though, the sick bags were once more fully operational. However, all the passengers were now glad it was only an eight-hour flight. Whilst on Madeira we'd learnt that the unfortunates who came out by boat fared even worse and *their* discomfiture went on for several days as they staggered across the Bay of Biscay. Oh yes, we took our pleasures the hard way in the early fifties . . .

So back to the Whitehall and the fact that business was once more beginning to drop. In those days I was unaware of the tidal pattern that affected, and still affects, the popular type of light play. The best time to start a new production is around August – when London fills with vast numbers of holiday-makers, mainly from the provinces. Business reaches its peak during the motor show but tails off a bit during November. Back it comes with the Smithfield Show at the beginning of December (all except December 1952, when the great and final smog hit London: this didn't do anyone any good!) and keeps up with minor variations until the schools go back in January. Then people have paid their income tax, and there's generally a rail strike or a tube strike or a miners' strike or a power strike or a bus strike, so business is inclined to drop. It recovers a little with the onset of the *Daily Mail* Ideal Home Exhibition, then peaks again with the Easter holidays. After that you've had it till August, unless you've the type of show that appeals to the Americans. I never have, so I've generally done lousy summers.

But in 1952 I was only dimly aware of this pattern, so I began to worry. It so happened that I had met Cecil Madden, the assistant controller of BBC Television and we had vaguely touched on the idea of showing excerpts from current West End plays. Cecil was longing to get inside a theatre with the cameras for he was convinced the move would be popular with viewers and good for the theatres, too. The theatre managers thought differently. They felt exposure on television would ruin a show, so excerpts were out. However, I was young and inexperienced. All I knew was that my production was running down and needed another injection rather like our sound excerpt of a year before. I also guessed that the first play to let the cameras into a theatre would receive a lot of publicity. We did: handled expertly by my PRO, Torrington Douglas, and his BBC opposite number, Huw Wheldon. A far cry from PRO to Managing Director of BBC Television, but Huw has made the transition with apparent ease and grace, talking fluently the while – as only the Welsh can! On the 15th March, I made my decision and rang Cecil Madden to offer him our show as the sacrifice. He was delighted and within forty-eight hours he was back with a pencilled date for two months later, the 14th May. I eagerly accepted and then the battle was on. Agreement had to be reached with the West End Theatre Managers and Equity, the Actors' Union. The agreements stand in much the same form today as they did then but, unfortunately, the idea of excerpts has fallen into disfavour, for the idea spread that only ailing shows were televised. This was not so: in fact, many productions signed up for excerpts before they opened or when they were smash-hits. But, throw enough mud and it sticks. The purist television critics hated the "plugs" for the theatre, as did the purist television controllers, and so one of the theatre's best public relations exercises in years fell by the wayside.

However, we wangled and argued our way to agreement with the various bodies concerned. The managers insisted that the excerpt could not exceed forty minutes and must not come from the last act of a play. Equity insisted that the excerpt had to be in front of an invited audience and so when it came to the night we had to take the curtain up for the paying audience at 6.30 p.m. The auditorium was then cleared at about a quarter to nine and everything was set-up for the television to take place, live, at 9.20. We'd rehearsed standing closer to each other (or further apart) during the day for the benefit of the three cameras stuck in the auditorium under the benevolent eye of our television director, Michael Henderson, who sat in the scanner – the Outside Broadcasts van – which was stuck in the street behind the stage door. This pattern was to be repeated on many other occasions, but we were not to know it then.

So we nervously waited for 9.20. The cameras showed the audience settling down in the theatre, cut to Brian Johnston who introduced the proceedings and then cut to the curtain which went up on the first act of our well-oiled production. The audience, too, were well-oiled. Many a member of the Honourable Artillery Company was out front – arranged by my solicitor, Geoffrey Posner – as well as members of the Armed Forces invited from the Nuffield Centre. Most had whiled away the hours of waiting in the near-by clubs and pubs. The Silver Cross had never done such big business in an evening for years. The result was a pleasantly pissed audience, prepared to roll about at every available opportunity. And they did. It was marvellous. I think only the Swansea audience and a captive one at Wormwood Scrubs had ever given us such a reception. (We took our play to the Scrubs and played in the mess hall there. They were a fantastic lot – with fifteen murderers in the front row!) As soon as ten o'clock came and the excerpt was over, the phones started ringing in the Box Office. We had asked our super Box Office Manageress, Mrs Helen Foster, to hang around in case of any reaction. She, George Jeger and the lessee, Alice Cooper, were kept busy until midnight, although the Box Office had been officially closed for hours.

If we thought our sound excerpt of a year before had had an effect we were to learn that the telly was even more startling. Next morning queues stretched out of the theatre and right down Whitehall and it went on like that for months. The press, too, were tickled pink by the whole thing. Let Jonah Barrington, writing in the *Daily Graphic* and *Daily Sketch*, summarise the general reaction:

"Thank you, Mr Brian Rix! This far-sighted 28-year-old actor–manager has broken down years of prejudice and suspicion by allowing, for the first time since the war, a West End play to be televised from a West End theatre.

"And what fun *Reluctant Heroes* was, and how splendidly photographed and how Mr Rix has cashed in since, through overwhelming box office takings.

"No viewer, I suggest, minds only seeing *part* of the play; that adds to the excitement. A play excerpt has exactly the same sort of curiosity appeal as that which we experience in the TV film–trailer programme 'Current Release'. The appetite is whetted and both sides, viewer and promoter, benefit.

"So what about it, Messrs Jack Hylton, Emile Littler, Bernard Delfont, Val Parnell and other members of our TV-shy West End Managers' Association?"

What about it, indeed? That shyness disappeared overnight and managements pestered the life out of Cecil Madden to get their excerpts on the screens. Many succeeded, and it became a regular viewing pattern for years to come. How sad it is that now, when the theatre needs all the help it can get, only the high-brow productions seem to have programmes devoted to them. The rest of us, middle- and low-brow, hope to get in on a chat show or achieve a plug through "This Is Your Life" or "The Golden Shot". Yet the new films continue to have much programme time. Could it be that the television moguls want to make their care and attention known to the film companies so they can buy up the old films without let or hindrance? I suspect the worst. Old films are cheap and can be re-run and re-run. Plays need authors and actors and sets and costumes and, what is more, they need money. Let's have a film, chaps. It's more popular than a play and, better still, it saves us a fortune ...

The success of our television gave me an idea. If an *excerpt* from a farce could be so popular – how about a *full length* one, especially presented for television from a theatre? The actors would gain by being paid a fee for their television work. The theatre would gain not only a fee, but also all the attendant publicity. The BBC viewers would gain the feeling of a night out at the West End theatre. And I would gain all round. I suggested this to Cecil Madden who was overjoyed at the thought. Sunday was the obvious day to transmit, for in 1952 recording techniques were very crude and a show had to be live. I mooted a Philip King farce, *Postman's Knock* and, of course, the Whitehall Theatre as the venue. Cecil Madden took the idea to his boss, Cecil MacGivern, who was horrified. Never on Sunday, was his considered opinion. A farce was only fit for a weekday. I'm not sure how he came to that convoluted conclusion and he was to change his mind rapidly a few years later when Independent Television came along and brought with them "Sunday Night at the London Palladium". Then I became very welcome; but in 1952 Sundays were for straight plays, religious programmes and "What's My Line?".

However, Cecil Madden and I were not daunted. If we couldn't do it on a Sunday we'd choose a weekday instead and adopt a similar schedule to the one we'd used for *Heroes*: that is, to go up earlier for the paying audience and then start the new play, live on telly, at 9.15 p.m. There was one major difference. When we'd done the excerpt from *Heroes* it was the same play being presented twice, but on Tuesday 28th October, it was *Heroes* at 6.30, finishing at 8.45. Then we had to get the audience out, the invited audience in, strike the *Heroes* sets, put up the *Postman's Knock* set, change make-up, costumes, etc. etc. – all in half an hour – and, panting and perspiring, start acting a new play as though it was all lovely. Thanks to our Outside Broadcasts producer, Alan Chivers, the television end went smoothly; thanks to the stage staff, the set stayed up; thanks to our director, Alan Bromly, the play went on at all. Elspet was cast and was rehearsing the part of my fiancée. She had just had the glad tidings that we were expecting another baby, but it was early days and the television work didn't seem to be too onerous. We were wrong and during the last week of rehearsal Elspet was carted off to Westminster Hospital, where she proceeded to lose the baby.

(After that we changed our hospital, and our luck, for any forthcoming happy events.)

In rehearsal we were not only miserable for Elspet but also miserable for ourselves. How could we continue? Alan Bromly produced the answer. The play had been done in rep. at an earlier date, so he rang up the leading lady who had played Elspet's part and in four days she was on and succeeding magnificently. Her name was Joan Forrest and I shall always be very grateful to her, and Alan Bromly, for keeping us on the air, for *Postman's Knock* was the blueprint for all the successful farces I started to present on BBC Television four years later. Not only that, but it introduced me to Alan Chivers, one of the nicest blokes you could possibly meet, and he was to be a very great help to me when it came to our regular television productions.

Anyway, *Postman's Knock* was a success, and its success did no harm to *Heroes*. The Whitehall was becoming associated with my name, and laughter was the name of the game – hence the Box Office continued to tick along very merrily. There was one fly in the ointment. Wally Patch was finding the strain of shouting his way through Sergeant Bell a recurring problem for his voice. By the beginning of November it had failed completely and Wally had to ask to be released. It was a very sad day for all of us – but especially for Wally. Never again did he achieve a starring role in the West End and he'd come to look on Sergeant Bell as his favourite child.

But, as always, when one door closes another one opens. My friendship with John Slater had led me to believe that here was a splendid actor and one who could give Sergeant Bell a totally new rendering. I rang him up and offered him the part. He accepted, started rehearsals on 3rd November and five days later went on. How's that for study? Not only did he learn the part in that time but he seemed to do it without the benefit of a script. In those days, Johnnie had a weakness for mislaying his scripts. He'd leave rehearsal with a script, arrive home without a script, rush back and borrow a script, often lose that too, and so on. How he learnt his lines, I'll never know. Not only did he have a script security problem, but he also used the blank backs of the pages on which to write his TV short stories. The whole thing was an indecipherable mess, but somehow the mess was sorted out and Johnnie happily sailed through Sergeant Bell *and* his short stories . . .

We'd lost other actors during 1952, apart from Wally. John Chapman had asked to be released to get some repertory experience at Folkestone and it was whilst he was there he gained the courage to finish *Dry Rot*. He appeared in so many bad farces, he felt his own couldn't be much worse, so he pressed on whenever he had a spare moment. Dermot Walsh, too, left. His part was taken for a short time by Peter Hammond, but he was unhappy in such rumbustious farce and asked to be released. So in came Darcy Conyers – which was a strange quirk of fate.

Long before I knew Elspet, Darcy had been around as a boyfriend. In those days he had ambitions to be a film director and when eventually Elspet had decided to marry me, Darcy turned up and offered her the lead in his first film *Halfpenny Breeze*. The budget was practically a halfpenny, too, but it was a *film* and it all sounded very impressive. Elspet demurred.

"I'm marrying Brian in August," she said. "It would cut right across the film."

"What are you marrying him for, anyway?" asked Darcy. "He only runs that tin-pot little rep. in Bridlington."

Elspet was indignant. "It may be tin-pot," was her reply, "but he's got another one in Margate." *There's* loyalty for you. Anyway, Elspet *didn't* make the film and she *did* marry me, tin-pot reps and all. Darcy directed *Halfpenny Breeze*: it was a good little film but it made no money and two years later, when he was literally on his uppers, I was able to offer him a job as understudy in *Reluctant Heroes*. Tin-pots were not mentioned then. However, Darcy was jolly good – in the fullness of time he took over the part of Tone – and years later he and I were to make three films together. You can't carry grudges in our business. What goes up . . .

So 1952 drew peacefully to a close and meandered into 1953 which was, for me anyway, a year full of sound and fury signifying very little. My main preoccupation was to find a successor to *Reluctant Heroes*, for I felt we were the natural heirs to the Aldwych farces, and therefore spent much time and effort and money to ensure that the action would be continuous.

First, though, came the party on 4th February, thrown by Colin Morris at Quaglino's, to celebrate his *Heroes* thousandth performance. A long march for his troops since the White Rock Pavilion, Hastings. He decided to invest some of his money in another army play he had written, called, appropriately, *The Long March*, and he asked me to act as the management. It was a rewritten version of his first play *Desert Rats* which Henry Sherek had put on at the Adelphi Theatre with Richard Greene. It was a bad risk and although the play was well done by Dermot Walsh and William Sylvester in the leads, with three very striking sets designed by my sister-in-law, Rhoda Gray, to provide the background for the action, it was clear that the audience might want army farce, but they didn't want army drama. So the tour fizzled out. A very short march, I fear.

But my try-outs were all geared to a possible future at the Whitehall. A tour of *Tell the Marines* began in April, but the Lord Chamberlain's alterations had emasculated the play, and it never stood a chance. It stood even less after its visit to the Grand Theatre, Halifax. We were on a guarantee, but in spite of that we received absolutely no money at the end of the week. One used to hear of this behaviour in the bad old days – but this was 1953. It didn't make any difference. Eventually the theatre-owners went bankrupt with that particular company (they had some very rich ones elsewhere) and we received about four bob in the pound. As we did not get those four bobs until about three years later, they did little to revive the fortunes of Roland and Michael Pertwee's farce. However, we were working on another one of theirs, *In The Bag*, which first saw the light of day at the Theatre Royal, Windsor. A very funny play, but not right for my team – I was besotted by the "team" idea, following slavishly in the Aldwych Master's footsteps – so *In The Bag* too stayed away from the West End. Elspet was in that try-out, as she was in another Windsor production for me, *Spring Model*. Written by Alex Atkinson, of *Punch* fame, it had a surprisingly good cast of unknowns including Patrick McGoohan and Gerald Harper. Directing was Hugh Cruttwell, now the Director of the Royal Academy of Dramatic Art. The general effect was splendid, but my blasted "team" got in the way, so Spring Model too remained unveiled.

I had long conversations with Talbot Rothwell, Arthur Swinson, Roy Plomley, Norman Lee, Colin Morris – all respected authors – but nothing transpired. Bill Ward took Colin and me to lunch and tried to persuade Colin to write an army farce series for BBC Television. Colin dismissed the idea as old hat and, for him, regurgitation. Rather ironic when you consider the success of those that followed from other pens and with other casts: "The Army Game", "Dad's Army", "Sergeant Bilko", "It Ain't 'Arf 'Ot, Mum", not to mention the film M.A.S.H. The list is endless – but life is full of lost opportunities. And, by the way, Bill Ward was no slouch. He went on to become ATV's Director of Programmes . . .

What else happened in 1953? The Queen was crowned on 2nd June. We had a marvellous view from the roof of the Whitehall and I filmed the entire procession hanging out of the ladies' lavatory window in the front of the theatre. As it was a very cold day, the loo was in constant use but, as I was in the end cubicle, nobody seemed to mind my presence. You could say, with a groan, that I was flushed with success at the end of my filming session. I was, until the film was processed. There was a fault in my camera and the carriages and dignitaries and troops all seem to be marching along at midnight. When the darker-skinned troops go by, all you can see is the occasional flash of teeth.

Ken Tynan gave us a good notice, revisiting long-running successes for the Evening Standard. Elspet and I made two ghastly, unmemorable films. Hers was made at Bushey studios and was called Johnny's On The Spot. Mine was made at Walton and called What Every Woman Wants. The only thing memorable about Elspet's is that she had just bought her first car – a very old Morris – and promptly hit the studio gatepost at Bushey, bringing it crashing to the ground. It cost practically all her film salary to repair the damage. The only thing memorable about my epic was the fact I met Bransby Williams, who played my grandfather. Brenda de Banzie and Prunella Scales were also in the film. I bet they wouldn't like to be reminded of that fact now.

We moved into our first house in Roehampton Gate, hard by Richmond Park, and for the first time in three years in London I felt we were living again. No longer cooped up in a flat, but with a *garden*. Fantastic.

I became Secretary of the Stage Cricket Club. Tony Huntley-Gordon asked me to take over the job, for he was about to become company manager for a new Agatha Christie thriller starring Dickie Attenborough and his wife, Sheila Sim. He'd had a fairly rough time of late and felt he must devote all his energies to this new piece. It might run for a bit and he needed a success. He needn't have worried. The name of the play was, of course *The Mousetrap* and Tony's still with it to this very day. I notice he never asked me to hand back the Secretary's job. Who can blame him? Voluntary work of that description seems to carry *all* the brickbats!

No, the most important event of the year, for me anyway, was a tentative knock on my door in November. There was John Chapman smiling diffidently and holding a script.

"I finished this farce at Folkestone," he said, "and everyone says I should show it to you. Would you glance through it, please?" And so it was I took delivery of the first draft of *Dry Rot*. I *did* read it, with a mixture of both pleasure and disquiet: for John had written a very funny play, but had omitted to write a decent part for me! However, I suggested he rewrite the piece, running two parts together and generally giving me a chance. This he did and by the end of the year we were ready to offer John Counsell at Windsor yet another try-out. This one was to hit the jackpot for him, but not quite in the way he had hoped . . .

Act IX

John Counsell had the customary arrangement when it came to trying out plays for managements. That is, his company would take a small percentage of the takings if, and when, the play transferred to the West End. However, with *Dry Rot* John wanted to make sure of a more personal percentage and insisted on directing the play both at Windsor and if it came to London. He reckoned without the problems of a family. For years he had promised to take them on a summer holiday and 1954 was going to be *the* year. When the Whitehall production date was fixed it clashed with his dates, the family won and John did *not* direct the play. It cost him thousands. In his place came Wallace Douglas – the man I'd always wanted from the moment I had seen the sheer speed and efficiency of his production of *Seagulls over Sorrento* – and Wally and I have been together, with one or two exceptions, ever since. John admits, in his autobiography, that *Dry Rot* and John Chapman's subsequent farce *Simple Spymen* made more money for the Theatre Royal, Windsor, than all their other try-outs and transfers put together. What would he have made, in addition, if he'd directed them? The mind boggles. Being a family man myself, I understand, only too well, his dilemma. Promises can be expensive, though, at times.

But before the Windsor try-out of *Dry Rot* there were other fish to fry. I had formed a small film company, Nordic Films, with a bloke called Robert Davis. I believe he is now known as Robert Hartford-Davis and has made some impact in the world of films, but in those days he was a fast talker and an even faster cameraman. We decided to produce a two-reeler together, believing that there might be a market for a number of them instead of dreary travelogues. We were too early – for the market opened up later – but it was a brave try. I put up the money, naturally; the film was to be made in our new house, naturally; the unpaid leads were to be Elspet and me, naturally; everyone else was to get paid something, naturally. Fortunately, there weren't many others involved. A very small crew; a very small cast: I know Bill Franklyn, Leo's son, was in it and Larry Noble, but I can't remember who else. We shot the film in a week, dubbed it in half a day, added the cast list and title, *Traveller's Tale*, showed it to the distributors, who clearly thought we were mad, and it has remained, gathering dust, on my office shelves ever since. One thousand pounds straight down the pan.

The Rank Organisation spent much more than that on my next film. It was a Ronnie Shiner epic, called *Up To His Neck* and shot at Pinewood. Personally, I thought it was a very forced affair, but it made money and can still be seen, from time to time, on the telly. The cast have, in the main, outlived any short-comings in the film, but I bet Bryan Forbes, Anthony Newley, Harry Fowler, Laya Raki, Hattie Jacques and Gerald Campion – to mention but a few – still wince when it comes up on the screens. Probably one of the authors does, too, for Lord Ted Willis was responsible for the script, along with the director, the late John Paddy Carstairs.

But those were happy days. We were all glad to be working and we were all glad to be making films. None of us was in a position to be choosy about the scripts and, frankly, we didn't want to be. Take the money, enjoy yourselves as much as possible and be grateful: that was our attitude. I had one great worry though. I put on so much weight, it wasn't true. You see, when you're filming you get up early, grab a quick cuppa at home and afterwards eat sausage rolls, or something equally fattening, whilst you're being made up at the studios. Then comes the mid-morning break – more rolls – followed, at one o'clock by a large lunch. Tea and rolls mid-afternoon and a whacking great meal after the show at night. No wonder I reached my heaviest ever, thirteen stone. Apart from the discomfort of being over-weight, I had an additional problem, for if we were to do *Dry Rot* later in the year, I would be appearing as Fred Phipps, a jockey. Any poor nag would automatically have become sway-backed with such a rider – so slimming was the order of the day. I now knew how poor Fred Archer must have felt, although he had to do it *all* the time.

And, of course, we *were* going to do *Dry Rot*, for its Windsor try-out in April was greeted with gales of laughter, particularly the last scene. It was this last scene which was to cause so much trouble when *our* production went on the road in August . . .

In the meantime, a marvellous holiday with Elspet in Majorca. We didn't know it, but we were expecting yet again. *Had* we known, we certainly wouldn't have scooted all over the island, riding tandem on a bumpy Lambretta. With Elspet's propensity for losing things, we'd have stayed stock still in the hotel! But we didn't know: all went well and nine months later, our second daughter, Louisa, was born. I know Majorca may be considered common. We consider it a very *un*common place.

Reluctant Heroes finished its record-breaking run at the White-hall on 24th July, but as a money-spinner it went on and on. It was a smash-hit in Australia, where it ran for years. In the UK one tour had started back in March and was still going strong. A post-London tour followed, too, going round the "local" theatres. All but one are now closed and forgotten, but in 1955 our touring company, headed by unknown Antony Baird as Sergeant Bell, did enormous business. Amazing, isn't it, how quickly that business drifted away as television increased its stranglehold? I'll remind you of those theatres: Hippodrome, Aldershot; Hippodrome, Golders Green; Streatham Hill Theatre; Empire, Chiswick; Empire, Hackney; Coliseum, Harrow; Empire, Wood Green; and the only one now left open, the Richmond Theatre. That tour was followed by one for the forces in Ger-many. I don't think any actor in that company drew a sober breath for five weeks – such was the hospitality of their army hosts. Come to think of it, we must have had a blooming big army sitting on the banks of the Rhine in those days. Imagine being able to tour camps for that length of time. No wonder our unemployment figures were down.

Meanwhile, those of us not tasting the fruits of victory were rehearsing *Dry Rot* and the Whitehall was being redecorated inside and out. As a non-smoker (oops, sorry!) I must tell you that for years everyone thought the proscenium arch of the Whitehall stage was painted gold. Wrong! When they cleaned it, they found it was actually painted in silver and the gold was nicotine tar from countless fags lit up since the theatre opened in 1930. "NO SMOKING" notices were posted immediately. That proscenium arch was going to stay silver after 1954.

We opened at the New Theatre, Oxford on the 9th August. Our reception was something less than enthusiastic – but *The Stage* notice says it all for me:

"John Chapman, author of this romp, for that is the best term to apply to it, clearly believes that there is no joke like an old joke. He clearly believes, too, that the greater the number of years which bow the back of an elderly quip, the greater the guarantee that it does not suffer from the pernicious affliction from which he draws the title of his fast and furious tale. The tale is about the machinations of several questionable characters intent on 'switching' two racehorses, who use for their purposes a country inn run by an exasperated ex-Indian Army Colonel and his family.

The author is fortunate to have John Slater in the part of Alfred Tubbe, the crooked bookie whose shadiness is positively Stygian and who is as 'wide' as the checks of his suit are loud. Mr Slater, a very clever actor deserving of much more rewarding material than he is here assigned, projects his nonsense with immense gusto and attack. His timing of lines, which are often woefully slender in their humorous content, and his rich gamut of facial expression, are used at all times in the vigorous and effective service of the preposterous plot. Perhaps when Mr Slater gets to the smaller Whitehall Theatre he will not find it necessary to shout quite so much.

As his partner in perfidy, Brian Rix, that frozen-faced moon-calf whose Broad-Acred gormlessness never fails to register, is again very funny and far superior to his material. So much so, in fact, that one looks forward to seeing him in some of the great broad comedy parts of Shakespeare, Ben Jonson and the Restoration dramatists. What a delightful Abel Drugger he would make!

Charles Cameron speaks with choleric conviction for the Anglo-India that is no more; Cecily Paget-Bowman as his wife makes a commendably charming effort to introduce a note of sweet sanity into the lunatic proceedings; Basil Lord's Flash Harry is well in character; Larry Noble works nobly as the French jockey; Wynne Clark strives prodigiously to make her Gorgon of a policewoman funny as well as horrific; and Diana Calderwood and John Chapman supply the intermittent love interest.

Wallace Douglas' direction, apart from encouraging too much shouting among the players, whips the nonsense along at a spanking pace."

The shouting was easily explained. After years of roaring our heads off in army farce we'd forgotten that we'd changed plays. But a far more serious matter was the lukewarm reception given to the end of the play. Acts I and II were speedily cut and reshaped where necessary, but the Thursday night saw us still struggling for laughs in the last vital twenty minutes which had been rapturously received at Windsor. After dinner, Wally Douglas, John Slater and John Chapman, repaired with Elspet and me to our bedroom in the Mitre Hotel to discuss this vexing problem of few laughs. It was a bizarre sight. There was Elspet – now needing to take the weight off her feet – lying on her bed, sleeping fitfully. There was I, sprawled on my bed but definitely not sleeping. John Chapman pacing the floor, John Slater sitting on a wooden chair back to front and Wally Douglas looking magisterial on the only comfy seat in the room. Endless cups of coffee kept us awake and endless balloons of brandy loosened tongues and shortened tempers. Eventually the climax was reached.

"That last scene went like a bomb at Windsor," complained

the author. "Surely it should go just as well here with better-known actors." That did it.

Johnnie Slater burst like a boil. "If you're so keen on your bloody Windsor production and your bloody Windsor actors you bloody well get them and see what sort of bloody business you do."

John Chapman flared up: "Well, they deserve to do better business than you bloody lot."

Wally Douglas was next to join in: "I trust you're not including my production in your indictment, because you're a new author and have an awful lot to learn. Humility is one attribute which never did any of us any harm." This from a man who has never been renowned for his humility!

By now the fat was in the fire. Elspet was sitting bolt upright in bed, staring at four plethoric pink faces all glowering at one another, all breathing heavily through distended nostrils and a miasma of brandy fumes. The discussion broke up in some disorder, with Wally making his exit first and swearing to leave next morning, for, clearly, there was nothing that could be done with such a mulish, pig-headed author. That strange cross-bred dogmatist stumped off to his room, John Slater slammed out to his, and suddenly Elspet and I were looking at each other and wondering how we could breach a gap a mile wide and then think of something to save the end of the play. Oh, it *was* a restless night . . .

Discreet phone calls and surreptitious visits to bedrooms, with no libidinous motives in mind, gradually brought the worrying parties together and it was agreed that we should all congregate at our house in Roehampton, early on Sunday evening.

We met in a slightly stiff, but reasonably friendly, manner. I recounted a story that had happened between shows at the Mitre Hotel on the Saturday. Elspet and I had ordered tea and sandwiches to be ready at 5.30, when I returned from the matinée. We sat down in the lounge to enjoy the egg and cress and buttered scones when a French family entered and sat down opposite us. When the waiter went over they looked at our loaded tray and ordered a similar repast.

"I'm sorry, sir," intoned the waiter, "but no teas are served after 5.30. That lady and gentleman had ordered 'theirs earlier."

"Very well," shrugged the Frenchman, "we will have a drink instead."

"I'm afraid you won't, sir," triumphed the waiter, "The bar does not open to non-residents till six." No wonder funny foreigners think *we're* funny foreigners.

Anyway, I told this story with suitable embellishments and it broke the ice. It also sparked off a thought in John Chapman's mind. We started to discuss, yet again, why the last scene didn't work. John Slater hit the nail on the head.

"Look," he said, "we're listening to a race commentary on the radio. You have one leading actor off stage – Fred – riding the horse, and two leading actors on stage just sitting on their backsides listening to a wireless and an off-stage voice. The audience want to see them do something as well as just flapping their ears. Then comes a tie-up scene at the end, with all the funny business given to a comparatively minor character, Sergeant Fire. The audience have paid to see *us* be funny, not a loud-speaker and a policewoman."

He had a point: on this we all agreed. In the meantime our author grew pensive and suddenly burst into creative light.

"You know a tea scene wouldn't be a bad idea," he said. "If Alf [the bookmaker] and Flash [his runner] were made to be polite over tea when they've just lost everything, it could prolong their agony. Any ideas?"

I was enthusiastic. "The Colonel's wearing Wellington boots from the garden. Wouldn't it be funny if Flash had to tip his tea down the boots and the Colonel thought he'd wet himself?" was my first lavatorial suggestion. This was seized on with avidity. "If Flash had a cream puff in one hand and a cup of tea in the other," I went on, "he'd be in a jam if he was then offered sugar. Surely we can capitalise on that. He'd have to bung the cake in his mouth to free his hand. Then he takes the sugar bowl and is lumbered again." By now everyone was in full flight. Ideas came thick and fast and John said he would assemble them into a scene as he sat in the train on his way to our next date, Nottingham. He did and the result was an hilarious tea scene that sparked all that was needed to finish the play at a rip-roaring accelerando. Here's how it looks in cold print. Not much for nearly ten minutes of continuous laughter. Actors can work wonders.

FLASH *comes tearing through the front door.*

FLASH: Alf, Alf – the bloody foo ... (*Sees the* WAGSTAFFS.)

MRS W: Hullo, Mr Harold.

FLASH: 'Ow do.

MRS W: I don't think you know my husband. This is Mr Harold, Henry.

WAGSTAFF: How do you do, Mr Henry?

FLASH: Pleased to meet you, Mr Harold. (*Lifts his hat*). *Both look confused and* FLASH *backs to behind sofa, L. of* ALF.)

MRS W: Sit down. Have a cup of tea.

FLASH: No, no, I don't think I ...

ALF: He'd be delighted. (*Pulls* FLASH *over the back of settee into a sitting position.*) Behave yourself. What happened?

COL. WAGSTAFF *closes the front door, then crosses behind the sofa and sets a small table from the fireplace by the right side of the sofa for* ALF.

FLASH: He won!

ALF: I know he won, but how?

FLASH: He just hung on, the 'orse did the rest, but that ain't all ...

MRS W: Tea (*handing him cup of tea*).

FLASH: Ta (*takes cup*).

COL. WAGSTAFF *crosses back behind the sofa and collects his tea from the tray on the centre table. He pours his own milk in his cup.*

ALF (*to* FLASH): What do you mean that ain't all?

FLASH: Well, just as I got to the corner ...

MRS W: Sugar? (*offers bowl with cubes of sugar and tongs*).

FLASH: Ta.

MRS WAGSTAFF *returns to the table and pours another cup of tea.*

He hasn't stopped yet!!

132

FLASH *takes bowl with hand not holding cup of tea and then finds that he has both hands full and he can't pick out a lump of sugar. He changes hands and then when that fails, picks up tongs in mouth and tries to pick up sugar, can't, so when he sees the* WAGSTAFFS *aren't looking he tips all the sugar into his cup at once and puts empty bowl between his feet.*

ALF *takes tongs from* FLASH's *mouth and picks a lump of sugar out of the tea, puts it into his cup, stirs it, licks tongs dry and then puts them in his top pocket. They are both grinning at the* WAGSTAFFS *all the time.*

FLASH: He never pulled up!

ALF: Where is he now?

FLASH: Gawd knows, he jumped the rails, went through the crowd, over the 'edge and on to the main road, more like the Grand National it was.

MRS W: Cake? (*Offers a plate of cakes to* FLASH, *one of the cakes is a cream horn*).

FLASH: Ta.

FLASH *keeps on looking at* MRS WAGSTAFF *and puts his hand flat on top of the cake. Goes to wipe it on the frill of the sofa cover but sees* MRS WAGSTAFF *watching and licks each finger separately. He then takes a cream horn from the plate, can't think how to tackle it and finally licks it like an ice-cream cone.*

FLASH: He must've been doing sixty.

ALF: Why didn't you go after him?

FLASH: I couldn't, the cops were on his tail.

MRS W: Napkin?

FLASH: Ta.

FLASH *has both hands full so sticks cream horn straight in his mouth, takes napkin, wipes his brow with it.*

ALF *sees he is doing this and takes it from him and puts it into his top pocket as though it is a hanky.*

FLASH *takes cream horn out of his mouth but doesn't want to finish it so drops it into sugar basin.*

MRS WAGSTAFF *crosses back to the right side of the centre table and takes up her cup of tea and continues drinking same.*

FLASH: They must have rumbled something was up.

FLASH *pours his tea into his saucer and starts blowing it to cool it.* COLONEL *crosses and sits on L. arm of sofa.* FLASH *catches the* COLONEL'S *eye and takes off his hat to fan it cool. His grin slowly fades and he puts his hat back on then turns to* ALF.

FLASH: What we goin' to do, Alf, what we goin' to do?

ALF: Don't sound so worried.

ALF *sees* FLASH *drinking from his saucer, shakes his head and demonstrates how to do it with fingers crooked 'politely'.*

FLASH *crooks his and after several attempts, drinks from his saucer. Turns to the* COLONEL *and says:*

FLASH: Smashin' char.

WAGSTAFF: Yes (*to* MRS WAGSTAFF). It is a bit strong though, dear.

MRS W: Oh, I've forgotten the hot water, I'll go and get some. *She puts her cup and saucer back on the tray and exits through the kitchen.*

FLASH *pours his tea from the saucer into the* COLONEL'S *wellington boot. It soaks through his sock and he rises, looks puzzled, then places his cup and saucer on the centre table and makes his way up the stairs, shaking his foot at frequent intervals. He then exits off landing.*

But before that scene – plus all the rewrites – could go in at the mid-week matinée, fate, as they say, struck again. It was my custom to phone home after the show, but on the Monday night I rang up to be answered by Kitty, our new Irish housekeeper (we were moving up the social scale), and was told that Elspet had rushed down to Farnham where her parents now lived. Further questioning and I suddenly realised that Kitty was trying to break the news to me gently. Elspet's father had died earlier in the evening. For months he'd been looking unwell and losing weight, but everyone said it was all the gardening in his new house that was causing a shock to his system, after years of bearers and *ayahs* in India and Pakistan. They were wrong. He *was* unwell as they discovered at his post-mortem. Poor Greggy. He'd enjoyed four years of retirement and Lloyds Bank could once again afford a wry smile. They retired all their Far East representatives at fifty-five. Statistics showed that many were dead by normal retirement age and statistics proved, yet again, that they could be unfeelingly right. I drove to Farnham at the crack of dawn to be met by two desperately upset sisters, Elspet and Rhoda, who had rushed down to comfort their mother. It was the first time I'd met death in the family: and there's no doubt about the misery of it. I did all I could to arrange matters regarding the funeral, but it was no easy task rushing back and forth between Farnham and Nottingham. The worries about the new scene and the nearness of our London opening paled into insignificance – but "the show must go on". Sometimes you can't help wondering why. Anyway, Greggy reached his last resting place in Farnham cemetery; and, via the Pleasure Gardens, Folkstone, we reached our final resting place – for the next three and a half years, anyway – at the Whitehall.

We opened on a boiling hot evening on 31st August, having come straight from Earl's Court, where we had broadcast an excerpt from *Dry Rot* on "Henry Hall's Guest Night", which was at the stadium as part of the radio show. An appearance on "Henry Hall's Guest Night" was always a valuable plug, and we were on a number of them during the next few years. These, in turn, led to a friendship with Henry which had us contending together for a commercial television station a few years later. But more of that anon . . .

Our first night at the Whitehall was really rather like Oxford all over again. To begin with the audience were sweltering away in a temperature of about ninety degrees. Then again there was a smell of fresh paint everywhere, because of the redecoration, and that makes a lot of people feel sick. I felt even sicker when I broke a glass in the middle of Act II, purely by chance, just before the entire cast had to assemble on stage in night attire and bare feet. There was glass everywhere. Sweating with nerves and heat, Johnnie, Basil and I did our best to pick up the pieces. I even went offstage to get a dustpan and brush – but such extraneous activity in the middle of a farce is hardly conducive to fun and laughter. The audience cringed into absolute silence, and it was at least ten minutes before they dared breathe again, let alone laugh. So we came, lamely you could say, to the end and repaired to a party in the circle bar, which was more like a wake than a celebration. A message came that I was wanted on the phone. Rather grimly I picked up the receiver and was greeted by an excessively cheerful voice: excessive, I thought anyway, considering the black mood I was in.

"Hello, Brian," boomed excessively cheerful, "David Lewin here. Just thought you'd like to know I enjoyed tonight enormously. You'll get a good notice in the *Express* tomorrow."

And we did. Thank you, David, not only for the notice but also the spark of life you breathed into our party. I went back to the circle bar a new man, all gloom forgotten. And, of course, David led the way. The dailies may have carped here and there, but they all agreed the play got a lot of laughs and would run for years. All except one which said:

"The action of the piece, which concerns dirty work with a horse, takes place in a hotel called the Bull and Cow, and is doubtless intended for an audience of donkeys."

Rather neat, I think. But it could have been written on opening the programme.

What happens the morning after a first night? I can only speak for the way we operate, of course, but the pattern is pretty general. Around mid-morning you assemble with your press representative and advertising agents. Everyone has read the notices and everyone has a good idea of any quotes which can be used – you try not to use good quotes from bad notices – and clearly all forward thinking about the future promotion of the play comes into the discussion. I've only worked with two press representatives over the years. Torrington Douglas was the first and Theo Cowan, who used to be the top publicity man with the Rank Organisation, the second. Theirs is a lousy job.

It's comparatively easy to get publicity for a play in its early days – but a darn sight harder if you are fortunate enough to have a long run. An occasional reminder in the papers is desirable. Not only to let the public know you're still on, but also to let your friends, in remoter parts of the Empire, know you're still alive and kicking. Two other advertising blokes have been with me for all these past years. Reg March, of Phillip Raphael, is responsible for all the posters – on the front of house, in the libraries, on the buses, etc. – and Dougie Read, of Mentor Advertising, is responsible for the newspaper ads, the design of all the advertising and so on. You couldn't wish to meet a more splendid lot and their combined talents have helped many a play along.

One critic complained that "there is no boggling or dismay at the Whitehall. The place is enveloped by a complacency that causes the management to speak already of a two-year run. For all I know, they may be considering a pension scheme for the cast. They are on a good thing."

And, of course, we were. No one actually mentioned a *two*-year run, but we knew from advance bookings and a big library guarantee that we'd get *one* year out of it, at least. Which made it all the easier to await the next big event in our lives – Elspet's and mine, that is – the birth of our next baby.

Louisa arrived on 2nd February 1955, after a good sharp walk round the Serpentine and a hearty lunch at a restaurant just off the Earl's Court Road. Elspet's new gynaecologist, Mr Denny, thought things might be speeded up a bit by these tactics and they were.

"I think," winced Elspet, as we tucked into the *Crème Brulée*, "I think that's the first twinge." It was and a few hours later, in the Princess Beatrice Hospital, our second daughter was born: all 7lbs 12oz of her. What a relief – and how marvellous to know she was all right and not like poor Shelley. Ten days later, we carried her back triumphantly to her newly decorated room, all pinks and blues and bows and ribbons. What a homecoming that was and how different from our empty-handed return three years previously. My sister, Sheila, had produced a son, Nigel, only a few weeks before so there were plenty of proud grandparents buzzing around. All except one – Greggy – who died before he'd seen his "normal" granddaughter. This was our only twinge of sadness, apart from recalling our feelings for Shelley.

So, there I was with a new daughter, a new and successful play and nothing to do except act in eight performances a week. A lot of people might consider that a splendid way of life – but I was restless and determined to find other outlets to fill the daylight hours. My first thought was to start a big band, a long cherished daydream of mine. Tommy Watt and I had remained friends ever since we'd met in the RAF and now he was playing nightly at the Café de Paris with Harry Roy. I suggested that we should form a Basie-type band, using session men: that is, top musicians who hire their services for recordings, special one-night stands and concerts. Tommy would write or arrange the music. We would then rent the musicians and a recording studio to make a specimen disc and I would provide the money. If the BBC or any of the recording companies liked the result we could move on from there.

So the recording was made. "On a Slow Boat to China" on one side and "You Too Can Be A Dreamer" on the other. We went to an agent, Emlyn Griffiths, with the finished result and he was suitably impressed. He, in turn, introduced us to Tom Ronald, of the BBC, and in the fullness of time a series of broadcasts were arranged. The first went out on Friday 14th October – and was an instant success. Tommy's band sounded rather like the latter-day Northern Dance Orchestra and all the musicians and arrangements were superb. Success on the radio meant interest from the recording companies and finally EMI, in the person of George Martin, came along with a contract. (Later, George was to achieve fame as the Beatles' musical arranger.) So there we were: a long series of broadcasts promised, several singles and two LPs to come out on discs. Everything seemed possible. Maybe I was going to achieve my life's ambition and front a big band!

I reckoned without the "regular" big-band operators, though. Naturally they had to pay their musicians week in and week out and they had a tacit agreement with the BBC that they would be given so much air time a year, which helped to pay the "boys" (mostly middle-aged men) and keep their names in front of the listening public. A pick-up band of session men like ours was taking away from their ration. They made their disapproval very plain to the BBC and our contract was not renewed. A great pity and, of course, impossible today when practically all the big bands consist of session men and all the pop groups start life as semi-pros. However our band shot Tommy Watt onwards and upwards and before long he was actually leading the Northern Dance Orchestra. Unhappily his sudden ascent was followed by a sudden descent. His forthright Scots tongue made him many enemies and although he continued as an arranger of some note, as well as writing music for several films, he became bored with inactivity and spends much of his time nowadays as an interior decorator. "Dead dreams of days forsaken . . ."

June saw me negotiating with the BBC for another TV excerpt – this time Act II of *Dry Rot* – and in July the transmission took place. Once more the effect on the box office was electric and this started me thinking yet again about a regular series of full-length farces on television. On this occasion, though, my timing was spot-on for the spectre of ITV was haunting the BBC and they needed some popular old rubbish such as mine to put them on even terms.

On the 23rd August I had lunch at Pastoria's with Alan Chivers, who had produced *Postman's Knock* for the BBC way back in '52 and then, more recently, the *Dry Rot* excerpt. I suggested that I would like to do, say, four or five farces a year. We would arrange everything – cast, director, scenery, wardrobe, etc. – as though it were a theatre production. The BBC would merely pay the bills, put their cameras into the Whitehall, point them in the right direction and that would be that. Alan was very enthusiastic and went back to start the ball rolling. One week later I met Michael Barry, BBC Television Head of Drama, and his assistant, Norman Rutherford, to discuss the project. Their enthusiasm matched Alan's and within a month I was negotiating a four-play two-way contract with Tim Holland-Bennett, then Head of Contracts. One contract was for management, the other for acting. With alterations, these contracts went on without interruption for sixteen years. Only the money changed, really. It did go up, thank God. For my first play I was to be paid the magnificent amounts of forty guineas plus rehearsal payments. Not exactly the sums you hear bandied about these days.

1955 was a prolific year in other respects. Six babies were born to members of the company. Security of tenure doth make fathers of us all. Elspet was super in an Irish play on telly with Liam Redmond – *The Devil Came From Dublin* – and we sold the film rights of *Dry Rot* to John Woolf and Romulus Films. But it was that forty-guinea contract which mattered most, for it started me on that elusive road: the road to stardom. Pardon my euphemism ...

Act X

I cannot claim that I made any startling discovery of a new play or a new playwright for my contractual debut. I relied on a cast-iron, copper-bottomed, dyed-in-the-wool success: *Love in a Mist*. Its author, Kenneth Horne, had written this little play (little in the sense that it was a simple story involving six characters, and one of those never spoke) in 1940 and I personally had appeared in it many times. Once for my mother, twice in the RAF and umpteen times in rep., so I knew audiences loved it and I also knew it should make good television for the viewing public could really get to know the small cast. I'm glad to say I was right, for the day after its transmission Elspet and I woke up to notices like the one Robert Cannell gave us in the *Daily Express*.

WELCOME, Mr and Mrs Rix
"A new husband-and-wife team soared to TV stardom last night in 'Love in a Mist', one of the BBC's finest ever Sunday plays.
"For actor–manager Brian Rix, of London's Whitehall Theatre, and his lovely and talented wife, Elspet Gray, gave a sparkling display as the newly-weds stranded by fog on Exmoor on the first night of their honeymoon.
"At last the BBC has found a clever young comedy team fit to rank with those we see on the imported American films. Now for scripts to match the players."

Well! you can't ask for much more than that can you, except for the scripts. How was it all put together?

It was intended to use Wallace Douglas as director of most of the plays, but he was unavailable for this, the first. So we went to the man who had originally directed it at the St Martin's Theatre in 1940: Richard Bird. Dickie was a dear man and a fine director, but he had trouble with his legs. Fine in the morning session of rehearsals but inclined to put those troublesome pins up in the afternoon and nod off. Occasionally our rehearsals would be punctuated by a loud snore from the stalls, but he always managed to wake up in time to give totally intelligible and intelligent notes. An extraordinary talent.

An equally extraordinary talent was that of our author, Kenneth Horne. Not *the* Kenneth Horne of broadcasting fame, although both men worked next door to each other at the Air Ministry during the war and both held the same rank of Wing Commander. Confusion must have reigned with *their* personal correspondence! Anyway, *our* Kenneth Horne had a marvellous ability to write those small cast plays which were almost bedroom farces (but were really comedies) and which never used a bedroom except in one of his earliest plays, *Jane Steps Out*. The characters explained their situations as they went along – as Robert Cannell put it, "deftly and wittily" – and the audience was able to visualise exactly what was going on or had gone on. We did six on the box – those above plus *Sleeping Partnership*, *Wolf's Clothing*, *Trial and Error*, *A Public Mischief* – and they all went like a bomb. I suppose a similar talent in these days is Alan Ayckbourn.

So that was our author and our director. Then we had our television producer, Alan Chivers. For three weeks he darted about the stalls, watching rehearsals and making notes as to how best he could shoot the finished article. For this particular show he did not prepare a camera script in the traditional studio manner – for he was an Outside Broadcast man to his finger-tips and thought in terms of immediacy – and relied on indicating his thoughts only to his assistant, Mary Evans and to the lighting cameraman, and camera crews. There were three cameras. Two either side of the proscenium arch, resting on platforms, and one which scurried up and down a ramp in the middle of the stalls. It was an amazing sight to see Alan going through the script with

Mary minutes before the off and neither of them being *absolutely* certain he wouldn't change his mind as he was going along. Although it worked perfectly for *Love in a Mist*, Alan gradually abandoned this rather haphazard form of shooting and reverted to the studio technique of camera shots indicated on the script and camera cards issued to his cameramen.

Another hazard, in those days, was the fact we were "live", Any fluffs or dries were in and as we were in front of an audience we couldn't exactly gauge the length of plays, because this altered with the laughter. However, we devised a system, which did us proud for a number of years. On the Friday morning before the Sunday of transmission we would take down the set of the play then at the Whitehall and erect the television set. An invited audience of Old Age Pensioners would come along, at about 11 a.m., and we would dress-rehearse. This was beneficial on two counts. Not only could we check the length of the play, but we could also check the laughs, and any scene which was poor could be rewritten and re-rehearsed before the transmission. Eventually, our Friday dress rehearsals had to go because of cost. Not that the actors received any more loot, but the stage crew took home a fortune. They were paid for an overnight strike (*not* for withholding their labour but for taking down the set!) and an overnight setting on the Thursday night. Then on Friday they worked the dress rehearsal, struck the TV set, put back the play set and sat around in dazed heaps all night from sheer exhaustion. They were in an even worse condition by the time they'd done it all again on Saturday and Sunday, but they woke up sometime on Monday, secure in the fact that they were earning more money than many of the actors! Eventually the BBC jibbed at the price and the Friday dress rehearsals were dropped. Instead we did a rush job on Sunday afternoon. A rush job in so far as it didn't give us much time to put things right.

I'll never forget our first dress rehearsal of *Love in a Mist* on Friday 27th January. Dickie Bird went in front of the tabs and told the audience of OAPs exactly why they were there and also what was expected of them: to join in the fun and feel part of the whole affair. He also mentioned the fact that it was my thirty-second birthday. The audience took his exhortation literally. As I made my first entrance on the stage they joined in the fun to such an extent that they sang "Happy Birthday to You" at the tops of their voices followed by a quick encore of "For he's a jolly good fellow". Alan and Dickie were tearing their hair out. Any attempt to time the play had gone for a Burton. Not only that, I was blubbing and unable to continue anyway.

OAPs can be marvellous audiences but they are a law unto themselves. I've always let them in as cheaply as possible for matinées, and once during *Dry Rot* Hazel Douglas and I watched spellbound as one old dear collected all the teacups after the interval and placed them on the front of the stage. "Excuse me," he'd whisper loudly, at the end of each row, "would you pass your cups along please." There was much shuffling and clinking and along would come the cups. Sir Galahad would then pile them neatly on to his tray, bring them down to the floats and stack them carefully. As there were five rows of OAPs this took some considerable time, for each row had approximately twenty-four cups to be passed along and also our friend was very ancient and his progress from the corner of a row to the corner of the stage was majestically and arthritically slow. Hazel and I just broke up and giggled our way helplessly through our scene. The rest of the cast gathered in the wings, howling with laughter and this only increased our discomfiture. These are times when you wish an old-fashioned stage-trap would open up and swallow you. There was no chance at the Whitehall. The stage floor was solid concrete . . .

Another ghastly occasion when the OAP audience was treated to some gratuitous extemporisation was during the dress rehearsal of *Jane Steps Out*. I was about to kiss Ann Firbank but was supposed to be stopped by Elspet, playing Ann's sister, as she marched furiously in through the french windows. I got nearer and nearer to Ann's face – but still no interruption from the windows behind me. I had no option. I kissed Ann and at the same time whispered (It *is* possible, although highly unsexy),

"Where the hell's Elspet?"

"She not on," osculated Ann in reply. After thirty seconds of kissing the audience were beginning to anticipate the sex act – so I had to stop.

"May I have a cigarette?" I asked Ann.

Her reply came quite naturally: "I thought you didn't smoke."

"I don't," I said, the glazed look of terror entering my eyes, "but it'll give my mouth something to do." That brought forth a good laugh which all helped to pass the time.

"I think you'd be better off kissing me again," said Ann – so I did.

Suddenly we heard running footsteps, and a panting, dishevelled Elspet was on the stage, two minutes twenty seconds late. She gasped out her opening, indignant remark with little conviction and facing dead out front: it didn't take long to discover why. She'd gone upstairs to change, by mistake, into her next scene costume – a nightdress. Suddenly she'd heard her cue, realised her error, grabbed her dress and bundled it on whilst running to the stage. She *had* to face front, for it was completely undone at the back and the scene proceeded with her looking one way and us the other. I don't think our OAPs even noticed!

Anyway, the combined talents of our author, director and TV producer successfully put *Love in a Mist* on the screen. They couldn't have managed without the actors, though, and Joan Sanderson, Basil Lord and Diana Calderwood were splendid. Modesty (and Robert Cannell) prevents me mentioning Elspet and myself, yet again, but modesty does not prevent me mentioning John Slater, who, very nobly, played the non-speaking part of Mr Evans, a duck farmer. Remember, Johnnie was playing the lead in *Dry Rot*, he had recently won the television award for his short-story telling, and he was a big name. There was absolutely no need for him to play Mr Evans, but because he's such a super bloke he let himself be talked into it.

"It'll give the audience somebody they've heard of in the *Radio Times*," I argued. "And this'll give us just the start we need."

"Oh, all right," said John, not too graciously and certainly without displaying his undoubted gift for the English language.

Two days later he was back. "Look, Brian," he said, "I really feel it wouldn't do me any good to play a *non-speaking* part. Do you think Ken Horne could add some words?"

"God almighty, John," was my strident and hysterical reply, "you know the whole joke of this part in this play depends on the old man *not* speaking. I've told the BBC you're playing the part. They're counting on it, I'm counting on it," and all that arm-twisting guff. John was adamant, and then followed our one and only row. At least it was a row as far as I was concerned. John just listened and watched me working myself up into an acute state of high blood pressure.

Finally, and quietly: "If it's worth all that fury, Brian, it must be worth my playing the part." And he did – *and* got a load of laughs.

So, 1956 started with a bang. It also started a pattern of work which went on for many years and which was quite stupid and utterly exhausting. But when you have a burning ambition to succeed and a pathological inability to say no, which is my lot, you are likely to lead a frenetic existence. It was an effort to change our life-style that made Elspet go on and on about building a house in Spain. But that was some seven years later and therefore the telling of *that* story can wait.

No, a factual run-down of the events of 1956 as they affected me personally will paint the picture with little need for embellishment. January, as I have said, was largely taken up with *Love in a Mist* during the days and *Dry Rot* at night. (Put those two titles together and you come up with some very interesting thoughts.) Also, during January, I attended a Sunday cocktail party given by the Spastics Society for the newly formed Stars Organisation for Spastics, and suddenly found myself the Hon. Treasurer. Wilfred Pickles was the Chairman, Vera Lynn the Vice-Chairman. That was another time-consuming job accepted.

In February Romulus Films, headed by John Woolf, started to film *Dry Rot*. Although we were still running happily at the Whitehall, we decided that *Reluctant Heroes* hadn't been affected when the film came out – so why should *Dry Rot* be different?

It wasn't: the film was released at the end of the year and the play continued for another eighteen months. The cinemagoing public is very different from the theatre-going one. The film had some big names. Ronald Shiner played John Slater's part and Sidney James came in for Basil Lord. I clung tenaciously on to Fred Phipps. The rest of the cast too was "improved". Peggy Mount, Joan Sims, Michael Shepley, and Joan Haythorne. Oh, and Heather Sears, in her first film. When she went on to bigger and better things Heather always omitted *Dry Rot* from her biographical details, so just for devilment I thought I would put the record straight here.

Anyway, the result was a funny film, but not, in my view, as funny as the play. I blame this partially on the director, Maurice Elvey, who insisted on having our stage director, Peter Mercier by his side giving him all the stage business. A good idea in theory but we ended up with a filmed version of the stage play, without the theatre audience laughing around to gee it along. Our producer, Jack Clayton, suddenly realised this and persuaded John Chapman to write a chase sequence for the end – this was hurriedly put in and succeeded – for then it looked like a film.

Filming went on until 13th April and rehearsals started on 16th April for our next telly play, *The Perfect Woman*. I had to rewrite the beginning of the play to modernise it, for the author, Wallace Geoffrey, was kindness itself, but felt quite incapable of altering his work. However, he had no objection to my doing some rewriting – so I did – apart from filming at Shepperton during the day and playing at the Whitehall during the evening. Oh yes, and "busking" at the Empress Hall for the SOS Record Star Show on Sunday 18th March, and meeting John Counsell at Windsor about the try-out of our next play for the Whitehall – also by John Chapman – *Simple Spymen*. Not to mention debating with both Johns about the rewrites and also who was to take over from John Slater when he left the Whitehall in June to take *Dry Rot* on tour. John Counsell came up with a suggestion which had me flummoxed: Leo Franklyn. Flummoxed, because I had never seen him work. John suggested he would be dead right for George Chuffer in *Simple Spymen*, which could be done in May at Windsor, and then Leo could go straight into *Dry Rot* at the Whitehall. Although I opened the bowling with Leo's son, Bill, for the Stage Cricket Club I felt this was too tenuous a link to make Leo an obvious choice for the job. John insisted that I go down to Windsor and see Leo work in another play, *Hippo Dancing*. But I couldn't – for theatre, filming and televising took up all my time – so it was arranged that I would be smuggled into the back of the Theatre Royal, Windsor, one Saturday morning to see Leo rehearsing. I did, was duly impressed and Leo joined us in June and never left me for the next seventeen years . . .

On 6th May we televised *The Perfect Woman* – with Wally Douglas directing – and it confirmed our success with *Love in a Mist*. We were on the road to fame and, we hoped, fortune. We knew that fame was coming, though, for on 9th May Elspet and I went on holiday. We took our Jensen (yes, I was in the posh car class by then) to the Costa Brava (oh, not so posh) and everywhere we went we were recognised.

The Costa Brava however was *not* a success, I would like to say we discovered it before anyone else – but we didn't. It was common and *awful*. Not that I'm a snob, my good man, but I've never been one for hordes of people crammed side by side into strips of beach or eating scampi and chips, plus tomato ketchup, in the main restaurant. If you're going to resort to such diabolical dietry, for God's sake do as I do: eat it in the privacy of your own home. On top of all this, it *pissed* down for much of our stay, we felt homesick and wanted to see our lovely Weezla – as Louisa was now called – so we cut short our restful holiday, turned the Jensen's nose north, and went home.

Back to work with a vengeance. *Simple Spymen* at Windsor. Rehearsals for Leo Franklyn to put him into *Dry Rot* and then straight into rehearsals for our next telly piece *Madame Louise*. The author of *Louise* was Vernon Sylvaine and it was a pleasure to meet him for the first time when we were setting up the television version. In my opinion Vernon was the father of modern British farce. Pinero and Ben Travers wittily turned out plays which reflected their times, but sex was apparently bottom-pinching, nothing more. Sylvaine, on the other hand, admitted

148

that one of his characters had balls ... and occasionally used them. Of course, his plays were full of "stock" characters. Of course, transvestism reigned supreme. Of course, his Bunnie Hare character was down-trodden and sex-starved, BUT his Alfred Drayton character (later Arthur Riscoe and Brian Reece) was *rampant*. His *raison d'être* was, frankly, fornicating; and this character, alone, moved British farce forward, and back to its filthy French roots. Of course, this trend has now been exploited *ad nauseam* and if one were to re-present Vernon's plays as part of an historical progression (he had fourteen in the West End) most critics would only notice the obvious characters and writing. One or two might see, through the fog of their own narcissism, Vernon's true worth. Off-hand I can only think of Harold Hobson, Felix Barker, Ronald Bryden and, possibly, B. A. Young and J. C. Trewin who would appreciate him. Others would perhaps give themselves double hernias heaping down expletives on the late Vernon's head. Many critics are actors manqué – some more manqué than others – and it always worries me if a successful author is attacked time and time again, for on those occasions there seems to be a slight whiff of cannibalism about. I have been one for the pot, too, in my time!

My reason for doing *Madame Louise* on television at that time (other than its being a funny play) was blatantly obvious. It gave a wonderful part – the Alfred Drayton one – to Leo Franklyn and it would introduce him as a new leading member of the Whitehall team to a vast audience. It worked and within months Leo's gravel voice and battered face were known to millions.

After *Louise* I was involved in mounting the tour of *Dry Rot*. No real problems. Johnnie Slater was leading the company, two unknown actors were playing my part and Basil Lord's. They were Tony Hilton and Ray Cooney and their coming together was to provide me with my biggest success, *One for the Pot*. Also in the cast was a lovely actor called Andrew Sachs and an unknown actress – still unknown – called Lynda Berrison.

It just goes to show how wrong you can be. We were looking

149

for the female juvenile during auditions and in walked this awkward, snub-nosed girl. She looked terrible. Hair awry, overlong skirt, poor legs but a croaking voice reminiscent of Glynis Johns. It was the voice that did it. We sat up, riveted.

"Where do you come from?" we asked.

"Drama School," was the sultry-voiced answer. "I left today."

Our excitement knew no bounds. We had made a DISCOVERY.

"Go and get your hair done," we said. "Go and borrow some decent clothes. Come back at four o'clock."

Our discovery duly came back. We gave her the job and she was *awful*. But don't waste too much pity. Our ugly duckling turned into a swan all right. Lynda Berrison is now one of Fleet Street's most successful journalists, Lynda Lee-Potter. At least we were right about her going places. We just plumped for the wrong direction . . .

It was about this time, too, that Gilbert Harrison came back into my life. He and I had first met on the film of *What Every Woman Wants*. He was a drama student doing extra work in a pub scene. After that he had worked for me on the tour of *Reluctant Heroes* and had then been my understudy in the early days of *Dry Rot*, but when I went on holiday he was not allowed to go on for me and, not unnaturally, Gilbert handed in his notice. Now he came back to us as the Stage Manager for the tour, and such was his expertise, dedication and sense of humour that I was determined to have him "promoted". Eventually this came about because my old Business Manager, Bill Raynor, was fast asleep on one rather important occasion. My temper knew no bounds and he left. Actually, old Bill was an enormously loyal and devoted manager, but he had snored his way through many an eventful evening, and therefore my rage, although simulated to give me courage, was actually based on reasonable grounds for divorce. So Bill went and Gil came in his place and, many years and several heart-attacks later, is still my General Manager.

After the safe launching of the tour, it was back to telly and *Queen Elizabeth Slept Here* by Talbot Rothwell, based on *George Washington Slept Here* by George S. Kaufman and Moss Hart. You'd think that with those writers the play would still be a world-beater but, although it did jolly well in 1956, today it would be very tame. Extraordinary how quickly styles change. Anyway, Tolly Rothwell has no need to worry. Every time you see a *Carry On* film you are probably witnessing his work, for he has written the great majority of them – much to the joy of countless cinema-goers.

It was during the rehearsals of *Queen Elizabeth Slept Here* that some of us were privileged to witness great courage on the part of two people, Wally Douglas and his wife, actress Anne Craw-ford. Anne had been suffering for many years from a form of cancer, Hodgkin's Disease, and it was only a question of time before the end. At the beginning of October she was around to have lunches with us during the television rehearsals but then she was admitted, for the final time, to hospital. Wally visited her constantly but never once did either ask that he might have some time off from rehearsals. He was there on the dot and when transmission took place on 7th October he said, "Cheerio," and went off to see his beloved Anne. Ten days later she was dead. Not many women would have made so few demands on a husband. Not many husbands would have grieved alone and refused to let their grief intrude, in any shape or form, into their professional lives.

But, for Wally, there was a happy ending. Some time later he met and married one of his stage management during the presentation of *The Lovebirds* at the Adelphi Theatre. Pam and he, plus daughter Louise, are still around today – very much so, for until recently they lived less than a mile from us.

November saw me involved in my second film of the year again with Ronnie Shiner and, in her first film, Catherine Boyle. The title of the film was, I fear, fairly indicative of the audience reaction: *Not Wanted On Voyage*. Michael Pertwee wrote the script which was quite funny, but by 1956 the film fans were beginning to cool when it came to Ronnie and, in fact, I believe this was his last big film part.

Filming began on location in Tangier. It was perhaps typical of the film company that they hadn't bothered to find out that on the day we arrived in North Africa, Tangier was transferred back from International to Arab influence. So we innocents abroad arrived and set up the camera in the main market square. Ronnie and I, wearing genuine Bedouin robes, rode up – Ronnie on a camel, me on a donkey – and were promptly chased by an angry mob of shouting, knife-brandishing Bedouins far more genuine than us. We fled in disorder to the hotel, where someone bothered to find out about the change of rule for the city. We then put two and two together. It wasn't difficult ... Arabs all over the Middle East only had to hear an English voice to go berserk. We'd just committed the enormous folly of Suez ...

So, unlike the Arabs, on this occasion, we packed our tents and stole away to Spanish-controlled Ceuta. There the Spanish authorities only let the Arabs into the centre of the town as they felt fit and they hired them out to us, as it were, for the filming. In spite of Spanish Guards everywhere it was still a hair raising week and we were very glad to get back to England where we finished the film. How did I get a week off from the play, you might well ask? I put the understudy on. In those days no one seemed to mind, but I wouldn't like to risk it today. (Come to think of it, Vanessa Redgrave took nights off from *Design for Living* when she was electioneering in February 1974. Little good it did her. She only got a handful of votes and the play came off soon after – which seems to prove my point.)

It was during the filming of *Not Wanted On Voyage* that I really overstepped the bounds of decency when it came to work. At Elstree from 7.30 a.m. for filming during the day, then a rush back to the Whitehall, as soon as I'd finished, to squeeze in an hour or two's rehearsal for our Christmas television before the *Dry Rot* evening performance. I was only able to do the television in this way because it was *Reluctant Heroes*, but on top of playing my old part I was also *directing* the play *and* rehearsing on Sundays, too, so when Sunday 23rd December was over I was absolutely buggered. No wonder Elspet decided to build a castle in Spain in an effort to slow me down.

In 1956, though, she was adding to the chaos, for not only was she appearing in the television piece with me but by December she was also appearing in *A Touch of Fear* with Jill Bennett and

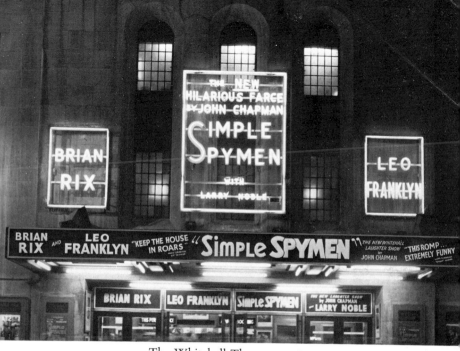

The Whitehall Theatre, 1958

The opening of the repertoire season at the Garrick Theatre, April 1967 (Brian Rix on the balcony)

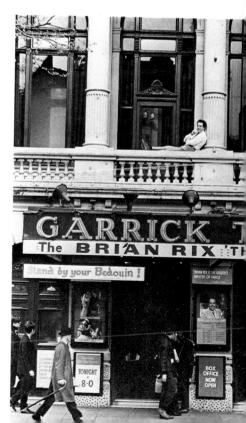

Brian playing father and son in the TV series *Men of Affairs*

With Donna Reading in *A Bit Between the Teeth*

Taking delivery of a new Jaguar
from Mike Harting, 1969

Brian in pensive mood at auditions

Brian and Warren Mitchell in *Men of Affairs*

Brian and Elspet on holiday at Arnside, near Morecambe

Returning from Spain after the car accident, 1965,
left to right Jamie, Brian, Jonty and Louisa

spet Gray and Brian Rix
hearsing *Uproar in the House*:
spet's return to the stage in
67, two years after her car
cident

The Rix family, 1972, *left to right* Louisa,
Elspet, Brian, Jamie and Jonty

Brian with his daughter Louisa, aged 15,
at her first ball, January 1970

At the nets, *left to right* Alf Gover, Jonty, Brian and Jamie

Lord's Taverners, *left to right* Alfred Gover, Ian Carmichael and Brian (in 1970 Brian was President and Ian Carmichael Chairman of the Lord's Taverners, and in 1974 Alfred Gover became President)

Middlesex *v.* Vic Lewis All Stars, 1973, *top left* Brian Rix

---

Middlesex won by 6 wickets

5p LORD'S GROUND 5p

MIDDLESEX v. VIC LEWIS ALL STARS
(F. J. TITMUS'S BENEFIT)

SUNDAY, 10th JUNE 1973

VIC LEWIS ALL STARS	Innings	
1 Gerald Harper	b Latchman	22
2 Michael Parkinson	b Titmus	26
3 Dennis Cox	c Price b Titmus	7
4 David Frost	st Murray b Latchman	35
5 Wes Hall	b Edrich	4
6 Ray Barratt	b Edrich	4
7 Elton John	b Smith	24
8 Vic Lewis	c Edrich b Latchman	19
9 Peter Cook	b Edrich	14
10 Nicholas Parsons	c Price b Crowther	26
11 Ed Stewart	st Murray b Edrich	10
12 Brian Rix	not out	23
13 Malcolm McFee	b Crowther	5
	B 4 , lb , w 1 , n-b	5
	Total	243

FALL OF THE WICKETS
1-46 2-48 3-60 4-88 5-91 6-129 7-163 8-164 9-192 10-202 11-230 12-243

ANALYSIS OF BOWLING

Name	O.	M.	R.	W.	Wd.	N.b.
Price	6	0	19	0		
Jones	6	0	13	0		
Latchman	12	1	42	3	1	
Titmus	8	0	49	2		
Edrich	8	0	56	4		
Crowther	8	0	35	2		
Smith	8	0	20	1		

MIDDLESEX	Innings	
1 M. J. Smith	st Frost b John	52
2 C. T. Radley	st Frost b Parkinson	45
3 P. H. Edrich	b Rix	27
4 J. M. Brearley	c Parkinson b Rix	31
5 N. G. Featherstone	c Rix b Stewart	17
6 Leslie Crowther	c and b Parkinson	8
7 F. J. Titmus	not out	20
8 C. J. R. Black	not out	34
9 J. T. Murray		
10 K. V. Jones		
11 H. C. Latchman		
12 J. S. E. Price		
	B 12 , lb , w , n-b	12
	Total	246

FALL OF THE WICKETS
1-44 2-126 3-141 4-162 5-174 6-212 7-

ANALYSIS OF BOWLING

Name	O.	M.	R.	W.	Wd.	N.b.
Hall	5	0	40	0		
Stewart	4	0	29	1		
Cox	5	0	41	0		
McFee	5	0	16	0		
Parkinson	5	0	38	2		
John	5	0	36	2		
Rix	4	0	26	2		
Lewis	0.5	0	4	0		

Umpires—B. L. Muncer & H. P. Sharp *Scorers—S. Lawrence & N. George

* Wicket-keeper
† Captain

Play begins at 2 p.m. Stumps drawn at 6.30 p.m.
Tea Interval 4.15 p.m. (may be varied according to state of game)

Joanna Lumley with members of the Australian cricket touring team and Brian, Alfred Marks and Leo Franklyn after the show *Don't Just Lie There, Say Something*, 1972

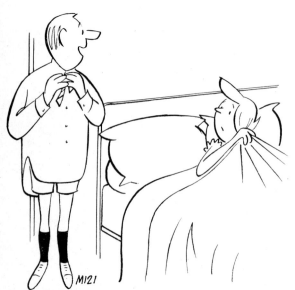

A cartoonist's view of Bri. Rix, *Daily Sketch* 23 M. 1966

"OF COURSE IT'S ME! WHO DID YOU THINK IT WAS—
BRIAN RIX?"

FROM DAILY SKETCH — MAY 23, 1966.

Bryan Forbes at the Aldwych Theatre. I was deeply hurt. She was far too busy to see just how busy I was. To be enjoyed, over-work must be *seen* to be done. That much I *have* learnt over the years. Not much else, though, come to think of it. I still find myself working sixteen hours a day, but at least I've now achieved a sympathetic audience. Thank you for listening. . .

Act XI

My diary for January 1957 has two interesting entries.

"*January 13th. David Jacobs' Party.*" David was at that time the best-known disc-jockey in the country and he and his wife, Pat, lived close to us in Roehampton – around the corner in Priory Lane – and this party was the beginning of a long and close friendship which continues to this day. Unhappily they are now divorced, but they will, however, appear together again in this book.

"*January 23rd. Lunch with Ben Travers.*" So, at last, I was meeting the author of all the best Aldwych farces. And what a charming man he turned out to be. Small, spry and energetic he made me think of a peppery Admiral. Why, I have no idea. He was *not* peppery and he had been a flying instructor during World War I. One of his pupils then was Henry Kendall who also figured very much in my life at the beginning of 1957. Ben and I had met to discuss the television versions of two of his plays to be put on later that year, and he threw himself as heartily into this venture as I'm sure he had thrown himself into the original Aldwych productions of the twenties.

The plays were *Plunder* and *Thark*. Ben tells the story in his own autobiography, *Vale of Laughter*, as to why Tom Walls decided to take off *Plunder* when it was doing so well at the Aldwych. He wanted to put on a smaller cast play so that he could make bigger profits to pay for his losses at the Fortune Theatre. There's an arse-about-face way of doing business for you! Poor Ben was dragged back from watching the Test Matches in

Australia with instructions to write a small cast play with one set. He obliged with *Cup of Kindness*. We did this play on television for our 1959 Christmas production with that lovely actress, Hattie Jacques, in the Mary Brough part. Our production included the line Hattie hates so much:

"Pull up a couple of chairs and sit down."

During our lunch we decided that *Plunder* with its four sets was really impossible to do in the theatre – because we were "live" television and couldn't afford the scene waits – so when it came to the production in August, we were allowed into a studio, the first and only time for many years. In the old Riverside Studios, as a matter of fact, where the film of *Reluctant Heroes* had been made, *Plunder* again repeated its earlier Aldwych success and was enjoyed by a large summer-viewing audience. Actually I've always thought it one of the most immoral farces ever written – or at least an early "black" farce – for the two leading men (Peter Gray and myself, playing the old Walls and Lynn parts) actually commit murder or, at best, manslaughter and get away with it. All Ben had to do with this play was cut it down to size, but I wanted re-writes for *Thark*. I'd always felt the ghost side of the story would be better explained if it was actually *contrived* by the butler "Death". With very little persuading Ben saw the logic of my argument, made the necessary alterations and Johnnie Slater made the most of them when it came to the TV performance. His was a lovely "Death". *Thark*, too, presented set difficulties, for there were three of them and the changes had to go like lightning. My sister-in-law, Rhoda, was very clever and designed three stylised backgrounds in sepia, which blended well with our twenties' costumes but which were really only backcloths with much of the furniture painted on. The cloths shot up and down and the viewing audience never knew the panic and sweat going on backstage. The actors, too, were under pressure. Out of day costumes into full evening dress – all in the space of twenty seconds. One jammed zip or one fumbled fly-button and you'd had it. However, all went well: smoothly directed by Jack Williams, who eventually used the experience he gained with this hybrid form of

155

theatre-cum-television to good effect and went on to bigger and better things with one of the commercial television companies.

February has no diary entries of note. March is more interesting.

"March 1st. Supper with Romany and Richard." Now *that's* a long story. Romany Bain had been at RADA with Elspet and they had renewed their friendship. She was married to Richard Findlater, now an editor of some importance in Fleet Street, but then a struggling biographer and critic and a charming chap. He still is a charming chap, by the way. They had produced one very clever son, Simon, and then went on to bigger and better things: triplets, Roly, Toby and Jenny, and this mass production rather put paid to Romany's acting career. Changing nappies in triplicate plus everything else in triplicate is, to say the least, time-consuming. So Romany turned to journalism and, as journalist, has met considerable success. She also met Tommy Watt at a party in our house and eventually she and Richard divorced and she married Tommy. It's a small old world, isn't it?

"March 2nd. Meeting with Alastair Foot." We were discussing a play which came to nought, but funnily enough, ten years later I did a play of his which he had written with Anthony Marriott called *Uproar in the House* and neither of us could remember what we had met to talk about that decade ago. I wonder if the plot was *No Sex Please – We're British*, which they also wrote? If it was, I ought to kick myself for missing such a money spinner. Thankfully, I.m pretty sure it wasn't. Alastair, unhappily, died before he'd seen the success of *No Sex* so he's not around to consult anymore . . .

"March 3rd. Henry Kendall directs You, Too, Can Have a Body *by F. A. Robinson."* That title is really rather appropriate, I fear, for Henry Kendall and Fred Robinson are both dead, too. Our production was *not* responsible.

Body was Fred's first professionally produced play, originally done by us for television and then presented at the Victoria Palace a year later, by Tom Arnold and myself, with Bill Maynard and Bill Kerr playing the leads. In fact I think *Body* was Fred's *only* professionally produced play, for after its appearance on the ubiquitous telly he was suddenly in demand and went on to write many successful series for the commercial companies, including "The Larkins" with Peggy Mount and David Kossof. Up to March 1957, though, he was a builder's clerk in Hackney who played pub piano and wrote plays for the local Boy Scouts. One of these was *You, Too, Can Have a Body*. His was a marvellous gag-writer's talent, matured by years of near-poverty and wry Cockney humour.

Harry Kendall was overcome by it all.

"'Ere 'Arry, I've gotta 'n idea," said Fred.

"If it's one of those from that *dreadful* Girl Guides' production of yours," replied Harry in his nasal, aristocratic voice, "you can stick it up your woggle."

And so the battle raged. Fred's persistence eventually won the day, for Harry retired to hospital with a heart attack and I had to take over the direction as well as playing the leading part. When the play eventually went on at the Vic. Palace, Harry once more directed, but by then Fred was better known and Harry was a sick man so we missed the edge of his caustic tongue. Except on one occasion.

" 'Ere, 'Arry," came the familiar Fred Cockney, "Brian produced that bit different on the telly."

"It is clear, dear Fred, that in the past you have had two excellent directors – Brown Owl and Brian Rix," replied the elegant, drawling 'Arry. "However, I've seen more cock in my life than those two have had hot dinners. Kindly let me handle it in my own way." Not much you can say to top that.

"*March 18th. Rum Punch at Hornchurch.*" No, *not* a dormitory-belt Jamaican party, but the try-out of a "Pip" Dearsley play. It was, unfortunately, no good but was eventually made into a film with the unlikely title, *And The Same To You*. There was only one part in the play: Horace the punch-drunk heavyweight. There was only one part in the film too: Horace the punch-drunk heavyweight – played by Tommy Cooper. The rest of us, William Hartnell, Vera Day, Sid James, Renee Houston, Dick Bentley, Leo Franklyn and myself, filled in the gaps as best we could between Tommy's appearances. Even after that beating, I *still* think he's one of the funniest men I know.

"*May 15th. Holiday in Fregene.*" Fregene, as you might guess, is in Italy and there Elspet and I enjoyed our first holiday abroad with Louisa. She was sweet and absolutely bowled over by all the attention the Italians paid to her, for at eighteen months she had beautiful eyes under a mass of fair curly hair – and the Italians are pushovers for babies anyway. We had a marvellous time – reflected in her glory – and we had so many volunteer baby-sitters we were able to spend all of five days prowling around Rome itself and each evening, when we returned to the hotel, Louisa hardly noticed our arrival, she'd been spoilt so much. Yes, that was a splendid hol. The only thing that marred it was coming face to faeces, as it were, with the local sewerage whenever we went bathing. Don't make waves . . .

This seems an appropriate place to mention company holidays. In 1957 actors signed for the run of the play – unless they had an early get-out written into their contracts. Nowadays run of the play means twelve months. In 1957 the words meant what they said, and an actor, in theory, could be in a show on the same salary for life.

So, with the long runs we enjoyed and with practically the same members of the cast in each play, it was necessary for people's sanity (though not legally necessary) to give them two weeks' holiday a year. At first I used to let them off one at a time and put the understudy on. This became the most appalling drag. If you had a cast of, say, twelve it meant you had company rehearsals every fortnight and you were without a complete cast for twenty-four weeks, nearly half the year. The audiences didn't like it, the actors didn't like it – in fact only the actor on holiday and the printer churning out the understudy slips seemed to profit – so by 1957 I had devised a far more sophisticated arrangement. I engaged a new actor and actress for the holiday period and they, plus the understudies, used to go on *en masse*. This way I could get rid of a third of the company at a time and the holidays would only last six weeks. Then the stand-by understudies stayed on and the regulars had their holidays. It was all over in ten weeks and the actors were only involved in about three full rehearsals and everyone was happy. I even devised a method of payment which, at that time, was revolutionary, for the adage was still "no play – no pay". I added up the cost of the extra money paid per performance to the understudies and deducted this sum from each artist's salary. Therefore if you were getting £60 per week you would probably receive £40 per week holiday money. If, on the other hand, you were receiving a salary of £40 a week, your holiday money would be, say, £30 per week. I realise this revelation of my munificence (or parsimony, whichever way you care to look at it) is vastly uninteresting, but there might be a handful of you who wonder how we used to cope with hols. Nowadays, the actors generally leave annually and are replaced. Much simpler, I suppose, but you must remember we were a primordial bunch, working out early policies for survival.

"*June 3rd. Lock, Stock and Barrel by Roy Plomley and Arthur Swinson at Richmond.*" I was off again, reading plays, trying out plays and even, once, having a play read by a bunch of actors. I don't know why I bothered really, for my mind was already firmly made up. *Simple Spymen* was going to be the next play at the Whitehall, but one was always hoping the greatest idea ever for a farce *might* emerge. Actually Roy and Arthur *had* an interesting idea. A young, foolish estate agent – very well played by Bill Franklyn – inadvertently let a house he was supposed to sell and sold a house he was supposed to let. You can imagine the complications, and, funnily enough, years later I read about an estate agent who had done just that. Life is *always* stranger than fiction . . .

"*June 20th. Four in Hand at the Theatre Royal, Windsor.*" When we were finishing our holiday in Italy, Elspet had received a cable asking her to start rehearsals immediately on her return for (and I quote) "A Royal Occasion". Actually what it meant was appearing at Windsor for three weeks in the play, along with Peter Gray, Daniel Massey and Genine Graham, but on one night the Queen and all her house-party at Windsor Castle, staying for Ascot, visited the theatre. It was an exciting and memorable performance, though marred somewhat for Elspet. As she took her final curtsy (you don't bow, if you're an actress, when the

Queen is there – you curtsy) she goosed herself sharply on the protruding arm of a chair. Her startled yelp, coupled with the usual jerk, achieved the biggest laugh of the evening.

About this time too, I was voted the Top Television Actor in a poll conducted by the *News Chronicle*. It was really quite a month for both of us, but it's extraordinary how memories fade and it's only old press cuttings or diaries that bring them back . . .

"*June 22nd and 23rd. Le Mans.*" I went to see the race. The most boring, noisy, smelly and uncomfortable experience I have ever had. You rush down there in a queue of cars. At four o'clock the drivers rush across the track to *their* cars and proceed to rush round the course for twenty-four ear-splitting hours. After that, the rushing is over and you start to wander around. The restaurants are full and when you do get a seat the service is poor, the food ghastly and the drinks warm. You may then want to go to the loo. Phew! It's just like being back in the air force again. The smell of urine hits you fifty yards away and, as you get nearer, other smells add to the general beauty of the scene. You try and pretend it's all great fun and go round the side-shows. Bored, bad strippers with sagging tits regale you on one side and the usual fairground rubbish regales you on the other. You then slope back to the grandstand or to the top of the pits or some other vantage point and look with jaundiced eye at the cars still going round, as though on a giant Scalectric track, listen to the indecipherable French commentary and glance at the score-board which is equally indecipherable. After the first hour or two the race is generally decided, anyway, barring accidents. In our case Jaguars took the lead at six o'clock and held it for the next twenty-two hours. It was a procession, not a race.

Finally, in a plethora of boredom, you huddle in your car and try and get some sleep. Four large men do *not* fit too well into one small Saab, so one of us – Nicholas Lykiardopoulos, who had a sleeping-bag – stretched out on the grass of the car park beside our car. It nearly cost him his life. As a freezing cold, misty dawn broke we were awakened from our fitful slumbers by wild shouts from outside. Nicky had just managed to stop a driver, whose rear-window was probably steamed up, from reversing over him. The wheels of the car were actually pinning down the edge of his sleeping-bag. Somewhat shaken by this, and cramped and unshaven anyway, we decided to seek shelter in a local hotel. We had to be joking, of course. The hotels were booked up from one year to the next. However, after a great deal of persuasion, we did manage to get a bath and breakfast in one hotel – which set us up for the heat and horror of the hours ahead. Thankfully, at four o'clock it was all over and we joined the ten-mile traffic jams inching their way out of that hell-hole. You may gather that such shindigs are not for me! Ever since then, I have left motor racing to those funny hearty chaps in deerstalker hats, or those intense aficionados who are as incomprehensible to me as are those who support bull fighting.

My companions, incidentally, were an interesting lot. The plutocrat with the sleeping-bag, Nicky Lykiardopoulos, as his name might suggest, is in shipping. Guy Furneau, a charming chap with glasses, looks like, and is, a boffin. Every time you enjoy, if that's the word, an automatic landing in an aircraft, you can thank him. The organiser of the whole mad social whirl was my, then, brother-in-law, John Georgiades, He was at that time married to Rhoda, Elspet's sister, and I'm not sure what his job was in those days. Something to do with shipping, I suspect; but it could have been computers. He changed his careers with considerable facility and regularity. Some of us even supported him in those ventures. Never mind. All's well that ends well. He now lives in Greece, has a marvellous job – in computers I think – is married again and sends for his children to have splendid holidays in sunny climes. He's been host to his ex-wife, and even I've had an invitation to visit Athens: an invitation I shall certainly accept one day. Time heals all things, even memories of Le Mans . . .

"*July 10th. Mr Stevenson, York House, 10 o'clock.*" Certainly the most important entry in my diary for *that* month, for at 10 o'clock I visited York House and 11 o'clock I paid a deposit on it to buy it – and we're still there to this day. How did all this come about?

Well, Mr Stevenson had an old gardener, Mr Walter, and Mr Walter was, to say the least, underpaid. He got his own back by doing a bit on the side – work, I mean – and we were one of the fortunates for whom he'd do a bit. In our case, it was mowing the lawn and once a week Mr Walter would whip over from York House, attack our lawn with a great deal of ferocity, but a great deal less accuracy (he was very short-sighted), and return, glistening with sweat and wreathed in innocence, from whence he came. Shortly after his retirement, Mr Stevenson mentioned to Mr Walter that York House was too big for him and he was thinking of selling. Fortunately, Mr Walter had heard us saying that we wanted a house looking over Richmond Park so he told Mr Stevenson he thought he had a client. This was 9.30 a.m. As I say, by 11 a.m. the deposit was paid.

Mrs Stevenson was, you might say, a conservationist. York House was built and decorated in 1932. Mrs Stevenson had preserved its style exactly and there were dozens of rolls of wallpaper lovingly stored in the attic to make this preservation possible until well into the twenty-first century. Not wishing to hurt the old lady, we agreed that the interior of the house – all lincrusta and beading and oak – and the exterior of the house – all pealing diarrhoea yellow – was exactly what we wanted. We moved into the house on the 29th November having engaged a progressive architect – now an old friend – Malcolm Radley, to eliminate completely all traces of its middle-class, mid-century ghastliness. We're still at it today – but we're winning, we're winning.

Mr Stevenson was duly grateful to Mr Walter for acting as his house agent and, for twenty-five years, as his gardener. When he left, he awarded Mr Walter the magnificent sum of £25. This did not actually enable Mr Walter to retire in luxury so, fortunately for us, he had to continue working for a number of years more, though he was well over eighty. I think he would be still around if he hadn't received multiple injuries when struck by a car on a zebra crossing. Even then, he recovered and lived on for a year or two. But his spirit lives on, in the shape of his daughter and she and her husband, Mr Brooker, always "house sit" for us when we go away, for Roehampton is a very burglar-prone area. We *never* close!

Next door to York House was an acre of land belonging to the Maharajah of Baroda. It had been bought by the grandfather of the present incumbent for he intended to build a house there and keep his polo ponies at Roehampton Club. This never came to fruition and the land was used quite unofficially by Mr Stevenson and his neighbours, Mr Cunis and Mr Symmons, as a sort of allotment. When I took over from Mr Stevenson, I was determined to buy that land for it was, as it stood, an eyesore. It had its uses, however, for we could have magnificent firework parties there, with a very large bonfire. Mr Walter was very keen on this and built the bonfires and constructed very life-like Guys. One year Dickie Henderson, a guest at the party, came out with the best line. There was the Guy, dressed in Mr Walter's old clothes, perched on top of this monstrous bonfire. There was Mr Walter, darting about and lighting everything in sight. Mr Walter disappeared, the bonfire roared away and the Guy slowly began to topple.

"Thanks, Mr Walter," yelled Dickie, "you can get down now!"

Anyway, the land did eventually become mine by sheer chance. In June 1960 I was playing cricket for the Lord's Taverners at Sunbury and one of the umpires was the old Lancashire and England wicket-keeper, George Duckworth. That year the Indians were the touring cricket side and George was their baggage man and scorer. I knew that the Indian team manager was the Maharajah of Baroda – the grandson of the man who had bought that acre – so in a pause after I had taken a wicket I was chatting to George and asked him what sort of bloke the Maharajah was.

"Oh, HH is a gradely chap," replied George.

"Well if he's all that gradely, George, would you ask him if he'd like to sell me the land at the side of my house?"

"I'll do that," said George. "I'll ask him tomorrow."

And he did. A note arrived at my house advising me to phone HH (His Highness, I suppose that means) at his hotel. I did and a gentleman with a very pronounced Indian accent eventually came on the line.

"I did not even know I had any land in Roehampton. Goodness gracious, my grandfather was a very profligate man."

"Well what the eye never sees, the heart never grieves," was my highly original riposte, "so can we do a deal?"

"I will send my agent round tomorrow and he will advise me." The next morning a blond, heavily moustached Englishman arrived at the door with an ex-Indian Army accent which nearly throttled him. He couldn't have been more helpful, though, and within half an hour we had settled a price at the ludicrously low figure of £6,500 – and that is *very* low for an acre of land in London with building permission for two houses. If you think the *completion* of the sale went as quickly though, you would be wrong. It took a year to go through, for it turned out that the Indian Government now owned the land and there was much to-ing and fro-ing between Delhi and London before the High Commissioner eventually signed the contract. In the meantime I rather stupidly did a deal with my next-door neighbour, Mr Symmons, to let him have half the land for half the price if he did all the legal work, for Mr Symmons was a solicitor. I say "rather stupidly" which is the understatement of the year, for within months that half of land changed hands for the fourth time, with a final sale price of £9,250 more than I had asked. If only Mr Symmons had been in trade ...

Anyway, here I am rambling on about the garden of York House when I haven't actually moved into the house yet. My diary entry is, I think, worth repeating:

"*November 29th. Move house. Elspet pregnant again.*" Now why did I put those two disparate entries down together? I must have known Elspet had another bun in the oven several weeks before, but perhaps some Freudian reaction made me equate a new house with a new life. Anyway, pregnant Elspet was, and we very nearly lost Jamie, our elder son, several times settling into the new house, for our living conditions were far from conducive to peaceful procreation. We virtually camped out in one bedroom for weeks with the roof half down and covered in a tarpaulin which let in

164

both the winter cold and the winter rains. In addition to the move, I was, as usual, up to my eyes in the Christmas television, setting up the first charity ball for the League of Friends of Normansfield to be held at the Hyde Park Hotel in January, and making preparations for the new Whitehall farce *Simple Spymen*, which was to start rehearsals, also in January. I think Ben Travers' telegram, when we did *Thark* at Christmas, just about summed up the situation: "Tharking good luck to all."

January 1958 was, indeed, quite a month. The Normansfield Ball, now an annual event at the Dorchester Hotel, was purely experimental as far as I was concerned, for I had never done such a thing before – on my own bat, that is – and I had to find out the hard way. We charged two guineas, and made £600. Nowadays the price is nearly four times as much, but we make about eight times the profit. You live and learn. The cabaret at the ball has always been its highlight and what names we have had: Vera Lynn, Harry Secombe, Tommy Cooper, Danny La Rue, Ronnie Corbett, David Frost, Millicent Martin, Alma Cogan, Roy Kinnear, Nicholas Parsons, Johnnie Blythe, Cleo Laine, Johnny Dankworth, Leslie Crowther, Christine Holmes, Ann Shelton, Roy Castle, Dora Bryan, Patrick Cargill, Dudley Moore, Alfred Marks, Rolf Harris, Rod Hull, Marian Montgomery, Laurie Holloway, David Jacobs, Frankie Howerd, Janie Marden, Kirri Adams, Jimmy Logan, and if I've missed anyone out, I apologise. Quite a list, and that first year we started off with my old mate Johnnie Slater introducing Jill Day and Dickie Henderson: so that wasn't bad either! Dickie was by then my "blood brother", for towards the end of 1956 Louisa had developed mumps. I had never had that particularly painful disease – particularly painful, that is, for gentlemen over the age of puberty – and was, quite frankly, terrified. I had visions of my one and only becoming my none and lonely, so asked my doctor if there was anything that could be done. He said that if I could find somebody who had had the disease within six weeks, 30 c.c. of that person's blood *could* stir up the necessary antibodies. There was only one person I knew walking around bandy-legged and that was Dickie Henderson, recently returned to the revue at the

Prince of Wales after an unhappy month or two. I rang him up at the theatre and asked if I could borrow his blood. Dickie never hesitated, so after the show, armed with half a dozen bottles of champagne, plus my doctor, I went round to his dressing room. Dickie lay on the couch, his arm bared, and I bent over a chair at the other side of the room with my bottom bared. Our doctor had only packed a 10 c.c. syringe, so three times he had to leave Dickie's arm, march over to my bum and perform the necessary act. All the while a gaggle of giggling chorus girls were peeping round the door which only brought a further blush to my cheeks. And that's how I came to have Dickie's blood in my veins. It served me jolly well, I can tell you, for I *didn't* get mumps, only a sore behind and a terrible hangover, for we finished those six bottles of champagne between us. If you lose blood you've got to replace it somehow ...

So the Ball came and went and was judged a resounding success. The same week saw us rehearsing *Simple Spymen*, and the new cast were rehearsing to take over *Dry Rot* in London prior to going on tour. It was all go, I can tell you; but then I've had your sympathy once about overwork. I can't expect it again.

We opened *Simple Spymen* in my home town of Hull on 17th February and then went to the Theatre Royal, Hanley, and the Prince of Wales, Cardiff. We broke all the house records for those last two dates and still hold them today, for within a year both theatres had ceased to operate – which is all the more sad when you realise they *could* do business if the attraction was right. But in the fifties the touring theatres were really feeling the impact of television, and hardly any successful plays went on the road: so it became a vicious circle, forcing many closures. Still it's good to know that the first professional theatre in which I worked, the POW, Cardiff, will always have my name in the record book – assuming there is one.

Our final touring date was a favourite of mine – and still is to this day – the Alexandra Theatre, Birmingham. It is a favourite for two reasons. The first is that the audience love farce and come along in droves – we hold theatre record after theatre record there – and the second reason is quite simple. The Alex is run by one of the best-loved managers in the business, Derek Salberg. A mad cricket fan, which endears him to me, he has also battled to keep that theatre alive when, frankly, he could have sold it for a vast profit. He chose, instead, to sell it to the local corporation who were committed to keep it open but seem to have done little to make the operation easy. I write only gossip, but if you can afford a million pounds to build your local rep. theatre, surely you can afford a little more than £100,000 to keep your local touring theatre's head above water. It's only a question of distribution ...

It was in the Midland Hotel, Birmingham, that a bizarre incident occurred which led to one of the funniest scenes in the play. Whilst having "coffee in the lounge" – a diabolical habit – I was talking animatedly to Leo Franklyn, as is my wont, and, illustrating a point, slipped out of my chair, clutching my cup of coffee. Leo struggled to help me up, but I stayed on my knees, deep in contemplation, not prayer.

"You know that coffee scene in the third act, Leo. Wouldn't it be funny if I slipped out of my chair and ...?" So a funny coffee scene, as opposed to the funny tea scene in *Dry Rot* was born, and it was in the play that night. It had to be cut when, a year or two later, I suffered excruciating boils in the nether regions and couldn't fall properly, but up to then it was one of the high lights of the play. It's amazing how these highlights are born.

You've read about the tea and coffee scenes but in *Simple Spymen* my childhood memories also proved very useful. John Chapman had written a funny piano scene, with me playing the piano. Well, I *can't* play the piano – anyway, not well enough to get laughs – so I suggested we had a rogue pianola instead. I then remembered a piano stool we had in Hornsea when I was nobbut a lad. The seat opened up, revealing the music underneath. It then looked like a rather square chair and it was possible to sit on the music using the seat, now raised, as a back rest. This went into the play. Someone else had raised the seat (Joan Sanderson, to be precise) and I innocently sat down on the music, promptly going through the seat and getting my bottom jammed. (I hope you notice our childish pre-occupation with bottoms. When we produced *She's Done It Again* in 1970 Irving Wardle in *The Times* commented, "Rix has at last moved from the anal to the genital phase." Oh dear, people noticed!)

Leo then raced round to help me up and my arm was caught in his sleeve. We then went into a glorious bit of jacket business which we had actually started to do during the last ten days of *Dry Rot* but had saved to put in the new play. Everything happened to that jacket – inside out, upside down – and finally Leo, who was impersonating a vicar at the time, intoned, "Thou art indeed a bloody fool, my friend." Collapse of stout audience, but even greater hilarity was at hand, for Leo then noticed that my false moustache (we were disguised!) had disappeared. Much frantic searching with me finally finding it firmly affixed to Leo's bottom (Mr Wardle was *right!*). This wasn't the end (no pun intended), however, for I then had to accompany Joan Sanderson as she sang "Pale Hands I Love". Unfortunately, the pianola roll dictated that I played "Yip I Addy I Ay" and the result was chaos and a very funny curtain. Sometimes *not* being able to play a piano helps ...

Simple Spymen opened at the Whitehall on 19th March 1958 to our usual curate's egg press, but I think *Plays and Players* sums it up well:

"People know that at the Whitehall they'll get plenty to laugh at. And *Simple Spymen* doesn't let them down. It is a lot of fun. The team work magnificently and in the seasoned Leo Franklyn, Brian Rix has a foil who will help him to make the rafters echo with mirth for several years to come."

That critic was right. With the aid of a television excerpt on 10th April, we roared away for another three years. The audience loved the slap-stick, for it was probably the most knock-about farce I have ever done, and old Leo gave his funniest performance ever. But all the others in the cast contributed a great deal (so did the director, Wally Douglas) and I would like to mention them here. Apart from Joan Sanderson there was Ray Cooney, Toby Perkins, Charles Cameron, Gerald Anderson, Larry Noble,

Merylin Roberts, Peter Allenby, Peter Mercier and Andrew Sachs. Eventually my sister, Sheila, took over from Joan and was very good, too. One final point about the cast: only a handful are now active actors. The rest have retired or died – and you can't give up the profession more certainly than that . . .

Act XII

James MacGregor Rix was born on Sunday 27th April 1958: the first son in our family. He's always been a reasonable boy, even choosing the day of his arrival with care for, by making it a Sunday he enabled me to be around when he popped up for air. His reasonableness continued and as a baby he only cried when he was hungry and the rest of the time was all sunny smiles or sleep. He's now bigger than I am and will probably tick me off for even *mentioning* this, but it has always amazed me how our kids' personalities developed along fairly predictable lines from their earliest days. I suppose all families are the same, but I can only speak for mine.

Anyway – there was Jamie, safe and sound, and Elspet, Mr Denny and the Princess Beatrice Hospital – plus the indefatigable Sister Kelly – had done their job splendidly for the second time. Three months later Jamie was christened, and his godparents make up an interesting cast: John Slater, a Jew; Michael Walsh, a Catholic; Romany Bain, a Methodist; Rhoda Georgiades, a Presbyterian. We only needed a Moslem, a Hindu and a Rosicrucian to cover the field.

So, after two successful launchings – Jamie and *Simple Spymen* – there followed five rather abortive ones. First *You, Too, Can Have a Body*, at the Victoria Palace, which had a run but was never really successful. Next a meeting with Willis Hall in June to discuss a television play. The BBC commissioned it, but failed to set a date for delivery. They are still waiting!

Then there was the television production of *On Monday*

Next ..., the Philip King farce about a struggling provincial repertory company presenting a ghastly new play. Elspet and I had seen it, as Philip's guests, on our honeymoon in 1949 at the Comedy Theatre and, as we were from a struggling provincial repertory company, we thought it was very funny. So did the audience, but it had a rather specialised appeal. We found this out when we did the telly version, for the vast viewing millions understood not at all the basis of the play and cared even less. A pity, for it was funny and so were we. I played the old Henry Kendall part of the frustrated director, and Harry himself directed the play proper.

Just before the transmission he remembered a gag he'd put in the Comedy Theatre production. The juvenile, Ray Cooney, had a line which went something like, "He's never been able to look Milady in the face ever since he caught her hiding the Ace of Spades in her fan."

Harry Kendall, "In her what?"

Bemused Juvenile, "In her fan."

Harry Kendall, "Well, I suppose it's all right if the Lord Chamberlain passed it."

I put the line in and there was one dirty-minded bloke in front who got it. He guffawed loudly and the rest of the house followed suit. The then Controller of BBC Television was watching the play with his family at home and, according to the letter he wrote me, they all reacted violently against this line, and he regretted that it had been perpetrated on a family audience, especially as it had been a Sunday. That was the only ticking-off I ever received from the BBC (except one from Michael Barry justly criticising our production of a panto *Boobs in the Wood* which did *not* enhance the festivities on Christmas television, 1960) but it really seemed rather pathetic, especially when you consider the lines that come out of the screen these days.

Fourthly, there was lunch at Les Ambassadeurs with Sydney Box who declared he was going to launch me into film stardom and offered me a three-picture contract – which I accepted with indecent haste. I didn't realise that Sydney had done a deal with

Rank to provide pictures for their so-called National Circuit, which, in reality, was all the old beat-up cinemas grouped together in one last desperate bid to keep Bingo at bay. Our little offering *The Night We Dropped a Clanger* actually *did* make money but I think it was the only one that did. Anyway, just after we'd finished it, Sydney Box suffered a stroke, so my contract lapsed and my dreams of sitting on the right hand of Cecil B. de Mille rather fell by the wayside.

The fifth abortion was, perhaps, the most disappointing. I'd always fancied myself as a tycoon running, with absolute precision and complete success, a television station. Now it was known that soon the Independent Television Authority would be offering up another batch of minor stations to the Lords and Ladies, the local newspapers and the monied merchants in the smaller centres of population. It so happened that I was at some dreary Variety Club luncheon at the Savoy and when it was over I went along for a pee. Standing next to me in the stalls was Henry Hall – this *is* Henry Hall peeing – and after the usual exchange of pleasantries Henry suddenly enquired if I was interested in forming a consortium to make a bid for the Devon and Cornwall ITV station. Was I interested? Stopping only to rinse the hands – that obligatory gesture to hygiene all men perform when two or more are gathered together – we raced back to Henry's office and by five o'clock in the afternoon the nucleus of our company was formed. David, the Earl of Westmorland, to give us our aristocratic support; Henry and I, showbusiness; John and Roy Boulting, the film side of the entertainment world – who brought in the big guns of British Lion – helped by David Kingsley, plus Shepperton Studios. Not a bad start for a quick slash and a late afternoon's phoning round. Eventually Kenneth Horne (the comedian this time, not the writer) came on the board plus a number of West Country tycoons, and our application was drafted by no less a luminary than Lord Goodman – then, plain Arnold. We were pretty confident, but knew our main rival was a group headed by Peter Cadbury who had been doing all his ground-work long before us. Every Lord Lieutenant in the West Country was on his board, plus all the local papers, so they had a very strong chance. In the end they were granted the franchise ' as Westward and we were the unlucky runners-up. Our application was frowned upon, for British Lion was then supported by a government subsidy and, if we'd been given the licence, it would probably have seemed like nepotism. Still, it was a near thing; but that's no compensation. The winner's rostrum is the one to be on, not those others, a step down. But I did meet and enjoy greatly the company of the two Davids, the Boulting twins, Ken Horne and dear old Henry "Here's to the next time . . ."

As opposed to my foray into Independent Television, my association with the BBC provided some fruitful opportunities at the end of '58. I did two televisions which included Dora Bryan – always very popular with us – one being *Nothing But The Truth* and, unlike my first night at Ilkley ten years before, the curtain *did* stay up and all went well. The second play was written by an interesting character, Raymond Dyer. At least he *was* Raymond Dyer when he toured in *Dry Rot* and when we did his farcical chiller, *Wanted, One Body*, but he then went on to higher things – *Rattle of a Simple Man* and *Staircase* included – and changed his name to Charles Dyer. (It's rather like that old joke about two North Countrymen who went on holiday, a Mr Sidebottom and Mr Ball. They stayed in separate hotels and when Mr Ball went round to pick up his mate he was told at reception that there was only a Mr Sidi Botam from Arabia staying there. "In that case," said Mr Ball, "would you tell him his old chum Mr Testiclees from Greece has arrived.")

Then came the incident which led, eventually, to an increase in police pay. On the morning of Wednesday 17th December, M'Lud, at 09.00 hours precisely, I was proceeding in an orderly fashion, driving my red Jensen, from York House to the Whitehall Theatre, where I was rehearsing the forthcoming television production *A Cuckoo in the Nest* by Ben Travers, for the British Broadcasting Corporation. As I was approaching Putney Hospital in the Lower Richmond Road I had occasion to halt my car for I was being waved down by a motor cycle policeman, known in the vernacular as a "speed cop". The policeman, whose name I subsequently discovered to be Eastmond – otherwise known as "Buster" – alleged that I had contravened the Road Traffic Act by exceeding the 30 m.p.h. speed limit in a built-up area, and that information would be laid against me and that proceedings could follow. I recommenced my journey but one hundred yards ahead, I was again waved down, this time by a civilian, whose name I subsequently discovered to be Mr Gerald Garratt, a senior Civil Servant and a Deputy Keeper at the Science Museum. Mr Garratt offered to act as a witness on my behalf, for he had been following me from Roehampton Lane, a distance of two miles, and at no time had I exceeded 32 m.p.h. and that discrepancy could be accounted for by a fault in either his speedometer or mine. I accepted, with gratitude, Mr Garratt's offer to speak on my behalf and we had just finished exchanging names and addresses when PC Eastmond walked over and demanded to know, in what can only be described as a bellicose manner, why we were talking. Mr Garratt replied that he would no doubt find out in court, whereupon a scuffle broke out and Mr Garratt was dumped through a hedge bordering the side of the road and within sight of a queue waiting for the Number 37 bus.

Feeling that I was witnessing the intimidation of a witness I appealed for the co-operation of any member of the queue willing to come forward and act as a further witness. No help was forthcoming. Indeed the queue turned as one man (or woman) and looked the other way. I then telephoned the local police station in Putney and eventually a police car arrived and Mr Garratt was bundled in, under arrest, and taken to the station. I followed in my own car. After three hours of questioning, – we were in separate rooms – Mr Garratt was released with no charge laid against him and, with profuse apologies from the police, I was allowed to proceed to the Whitehall Theatre where all the company had dispersed for lunch, feeling, no doubt, there was indeed a cuckoo in the nest, but this time at Putney Police Station.

This incident might have remained of a private nature but for two factors. Firstly, a member of the bus queue reported the

174

incident to one of the daily newspapers and secondly, I in turn reported the incident to the late Mr George Jeger, then the Managing Director of the Whitehall Theatre, a Justice of the Peace and a Member of Parliament for the constituency of Goole. Mr Jeger was suitably outraged and, if I might express a personal opinion, M'Lud, I feel Mr Jeger, being a member of the Labour Party, saw this as an opportunity to make political capital out of the incident to the discomfiture of the Conservative Home Secretary, Mr R. A. Butler.

In the event, all the newspapers carried the story as front page news on the morning of Thursday 18th December and Mr Garratt subsequently received "substantial damages" for assault and false imprisonment, in addition to being indemnified as to his costs. I, in turn, received a letter from the Commissioner of Police saying that no further action would be taken over the allegation of exceeding the speed limit. I hung the letter among my Christmas cards.

George Jeger, in the meantime, had a field day and nearly a year later, on the 18th November 1959, Mr Patrick Gordon Walker (Smethwick Labour) moved:

> "That this house regrets the failure of the Home Secretary adequately to explain the payment of £300 out of public money in the case of Garratt *v* Eastmond in which the alleged misconduct of a Metropolitan Police officer was involved."

The result of this motion was super. The Home Secretary' "Rab" Butler, promised an enquiry into the police generally' This enquiry decided, amongst other things, that police pay was inadequate and was a major stumbling block when it came to attracting the right calibre of man into the force. This was remedied forthwith and police pay went up considerably.

One final point. As a result of this case I have often been approached with diffidence by the police when asked to do "good works" – police balls and the like – for apparently I am known as a man who dislikes them. Nothing could be further from the truth. After all, it's *almost* due to me that they were able to pay the HP on their black and white tellies. If they want to move into the colour bracket I am quite willing, for a small consideration, to drive up and down the Lower Richmond Road with a retired Civil Servant in tow. I'm sure we can help again . . .

After this front page incident, after nine successful years at the Whitehall, after three years of wildly successful television productions, after people coming up to me in the streets to shake my hand, you might excuse my presumption in thinking I was pretty well known. The doorman at Wandsworth Town Hall disabused me of this belief. Rotary had asked me to present the raffle prizes after the show and the man who did the asking was our vet, then treating Bastien for a particularly lovely condition known as wet eczema. Anyway, he assured me that we would be met at the door and all would be well. Unfortunately he omitted to tell the doorman about these arrangements and also omitted to have anyone awaiting our arrival. The doorman did *not* recognise us.

"Where's your tickets?"

"We have no tickets. We are guests, here to present the raffle prizes."

"We get bleeding try-ons like that, mate, every night of the week. No ticket, no entrance."

"Look, I'm Brian Rix and this is my wife Elspet Gray. You must have seen us on the box."

"How can I watch the bleeding box when I'm 'ere every bleeding night?"

We were about to leave when a flustered Rotarian ran up and whisked us past the glowering doorman and, with profuse apologies, ushered two tight-lipped Rixes into the hall and to a table peopled by our local MP Sir Hugh Linstead, Evelyn Laye and her husband Frank Lawton. To cover our confusion Elspet turned to talk to Sir Hugh. Unfortunately *her* confusion was such that she mistook our MP for our vet.

"Bastien is so much better since you gave him those pills," she trilled. "All that nasty weeping has stopped but he still looks a trifle poxy." Sir Hugh was, to say the least, nonplussed. Under the table I kicked Elspet, who suddenly realised her *faux pas* and you could see the blush spreading upwards from her toes. By the time it reached the roots of her red hair I had grabbed her and was treading the light fantastic. Sir Hugh stayed, open-mouthed, at the table wondering, no doubt, if all actresses were as scatty. After that Elspet always voted for Sir Hugh, even though she is, at heart, a Liberal. What you might call a poxy vote.

It's extraordinary, though, how often actors are asked to help out, for nothing of course, and how often they are treated in an offhand manner when they turn up, late and tired, after a show. One of our own "dos" for Normansfield provided a classic example of this. A member of our committee had arranged a dance at the Ealing Town Hall (how glamorous can you get?) and asked me to bring along some of the company and "Would Terry Scott do the cabaret?". I prevailed on Terry to help out, and Helen Jessop, Basil Lord, Elspet and I went along in support. We had asked for a table. No table. We had asked for a few sandwiches. No sandwiches. We had asked for a drink. No drink. In desperation I carted everyone off to the bar and bought a round. As I was doing this Elspet and Helen overheard a couple discussing us.

"I think they've been treated rather badly, don't you?" said one.

"What's so special about them?" came the reply. "It's their job!"

At the end of January 1959 Elspet began to rehearse a new comedy by Kenneth Horne (you're right, the author, not the comedian) called *Wolf's Clothing*. In the cast with her were Muriel Pavlow, Derek Farr, Patrick Cargill, Angela Browne, Ronald Adam and Viola Lyel. It was a charming little comedy, but was lost in the vastness of the Strand Theatre when it eventually opened there. But for Elspet the happy rehearsal period became a nightmare, for on 9th February her mother died: an Elspet too, but known as Elsie. She was a highly intelligent woman (she had achieved Honours in Languages many years before, when women found it difficult to do such things) who had stagnated for thirty years in India, where her abilities atrophied. As a widow she was lonely and her great happiness was to stay with us and help look after Louisa and Jamie. As Elspet was about to go on tour with the new play, Elsie moved in, *in loco parentis*. On the last Monday of rehearsals it was a freezing cold day and she had walked up Clarence Lane to meet Louisa from school. We sat down to lunch. Elsie, looking very cold, made a strange little noise and pitched forward – dead. She was buried at Farnham, alongside Greggy: two victims of the British Raj. Too little to do, too much to eat and drink and smoke. How many Greggys and Elsies are there left in the world? Quite a few, I think, and most of them seem to be living out pretty boring lives in the South of Spain where the pattern is repeated. Those left must be very tough, though, for they last longer than Mr and Mrs MacGregor-Gray. RIP.

I've already mentioned Sydney Box and *The Night We Dropped a Clanger*. Well we began to make the film at the end of May. Cecil Parker, Leslie Phillips, William Hartnell, Hattie Jacques and Leo Franklyn, plus me – twice!

Twice because I played my own double. This was a particularly popular type of film at the time, sparked off, I suspect, by *I Was Monty's Double*, and in fact ours was a sort of skit on that subject, well written by John Chapman. It *was* a funny film, it *did* make money on the disastrous national circuit and, for once, I felt I gave a reasonably good performance as the pompously brave Wing Commander and his stupidly simple lavatory attendant double. The film was directed by Darcy Conyers and was produced by the two of us for £65,000, which is ridiculous when you consider the cast we put together and the amount we had to pay for a process called "travelling-matt" which enabled me to play with myself. In case of doubt, I will rephrase that statement. I was able to talk to myself and walk round myself far more effectively than in the old "split screen days", and really the whole thing looked pretty good. We also had Cecil Parker being very funny and it was a delight to appear with such a consummate comedy actor.

People seeing the film never knew the circumstances under

which I played the part. For the first and only time in my life (touch wood) I was suffering from boils. This dreadfully painful condition always rouses unfeeling laughter whenever it's mentioned, but wait till you have 'em – *everywhere* – like I had for eighteen months. Every time I sat down in the film you could see me gingerly lowering myself on to a chair where I squatted on an air ring, thoughtfully provided by the prop. department. After the day's filming I returned to the Whitehall in a hire car, painfully perched on the same air ring, and performed as best I could in *Simple Spymen*, cutting all the falls, particularly those in the coffee scene.

To heap Pelion upon Ossa, it was at that time I took delivery of a beautiful canary-yellow drophead Aston Martin. The damn thing had been ordered months before and you can imagine the excitement when Mike Harting drove this gleaming piece of sexual imagery through our gates. (Incidentally, I mention Mike specifically, not only because he is an old friend but particularly because he and George Abecassis – who runs HW Motors – always take me out to a splendid lunch on Motor Show Press day and I would hate any omission on my part to preclude future lunches.) Anyway, there was my latest toy and there was I, with at least three boils on my bum, trying to get into the driving seat in what can only be described as the cockpit. Agony! So the omnipresent air ring was again pressed into service, but unhappily it raised me to such a height that my thighs were jammed firmly under the steering wheel and manoeuvring the car, except in a dead straight line, was quite out of the question. My lovely yellow bird stayed silently in the garage for two months until the boils moved to another part of my Job-like body.

Those boils provided me with a further embarrassment. I was being treated by a very well-known skin specialist, Dr Muende, and all was well when I went to his rooms in Welbeck Street. Unfortunately, from time to time I had to visit the St James's Hospital in Lyle Street so that some dreadful torturer could stab one of my fevered furuncles in order to grow a culture. The pain at the end of the journey was pretty grim, but so was the trip up Lyle Street. Many of London's scruffiest whores used to hang out there – literally, sometimes – and seeing all the pilgrims with suppurating sores wending their weary way up to the hospital provided them with much ribaldry. It brought new meaning to that old rugger song:

We've the pox and the clap
And we don't give a rap
For our ambition is to spread
disease . . .

By now Ray Cooney and Tony Hilton had completed the first draft of the play which eventually became *One For The Pot*. At that time, though, it was called *Dickory Dock* (the leading character's name was Hickory and the pun is theirs, not mine) and was tried out with considerable success at the Richmond Theatre, then run by a dear chap, Freddie Piffard. Although there was much wrong with the play, it had that indefinable quality which made it a success from the word go. The fact that one actor played four parts was such a good theatrical trick, that the audience never seemed to query, as they do in so many farces, whether or not the jokes and the actual story-line were a bit thin. Incidentally, the two leading parts were well played at Richmond by Ray Cooney himself (I'd given him a week off from *Simple Spymen*) and Raymond Dyer. Ray Cooney was then Raymond Cooney and shortened his name later. Raymond Dyer was not yet Charles.

That reminds me of the other name-dropping story. A young man went to a solicitor to find out how to change his name.

"What is your present one?" queried the solicitor.

"Fred Smelley," came the reply.

"And what name have you chosen as your new one?"

"Bert Smelley," was the answer. There's nowt so queer as folk . . .

So 1959 drifted to a close. Not particularly peacefully because of my boily behind, but successfully, anyway. *Simple Spymen* was still doing well. So was the film of *Clanger*. *Dickory Dock* was clearly the answer as far as the next play was concerned and I was about to make my second film with Darcy Conyers. After

Sydney Box's illness my contract had lapsed, but thanks to my television association with British Lion I was able to move the subjects over to them and we were to make *The Night We Got The Bird* at Shepperton Studios starting on Leap Year's 29th February. A week earlier I attended the insurance doctor's surgery (all leading artists are insured when making a film), was asked to leave the customary sample and was handed a small milk jug. Once inside the loo I was regaled with an interesting sight. There, on the window sill, was a motley collection of vessels, vases and vials, each one full and each one labelled with the name of the donor. Courtesy forbids that I specify those billed in such a unique fashion but in the film were Dora Bryan, Ronnie Shiner, Irene Handl, Leo Franklyn, Johnnie Slater, John le Mesurier, Robertson Hare, Liz Fraser and Kynaston Reeves. We all want our names in lights – but this was ridiculous.

The film was written by Ray Cooney and Tony Hilton and was an adaptation from a play by Basil Thomas called *The Lovebirds* which had enjoyed a reasonable run at the Adelphi Theatre, starring Ronnie Shiner and Dora Bryan. The result of our efforts was a very funny, albeit simple, film which is still shown constantly on both BBC and Commercial Television. Unfortunately, the critics loathed it – I think the fantasy element about a man reincarnated as a parrot got on their collective wicks – and we didn't get a particularly good release date. A pity, for it should have made a lot of money. Years later, when it first appeared on BBC telly, something like eighteen million people watched it. If that lot had paid money at the cinema box offices, I'd have retired years ago!

Later in the year we made another John Chapman film *The Night We Sprang A Leak* but because *Bird* hadn't done particularly well on its release they changed the name to *Nothing Barred*. This, like *Bird*, only did moderate business, but it was well served by Naunton Wayne, Charles Heslop, Ann Firbank and Leo Franklyn, with a superb vignette from Wilfred Lawson, playing an old drunk who turned on the tap in the bathroom and instead of being greeted by water heard a choir singing a hymn. His reaction and conversion were miraculous to behold. In fact he *had* heard a choir: all escaped convicts making their way through London's sewers and singing so I could find their direction and let them out. A bit of a stinker for me – literally – for I had my head down a Tedworth Square sewer for one full day's shooting. The resultant scene got many laughs but at the expense of one set of outraged olfactory nerves – mine – for they recreated those odorous moments for days afterwards. Honestly, if I was a sewer rat I'd give myself up.

When the film of *Bird* was due for release all the usual tub-thumping went on – which included my appearance on "What's My Line?" as the guest celebrity. The panel were blindfolded and the guest was supposed to disguise his or her voice and then the panel had to guess in twenty questions who it was. All very childish and a terrible insult if you were not spotted early. In my case I'm glad to say I was recognised by Gilbert Harding at his first attempt, which is not surprising for I was using the voice of a parrot and the parrot had had a lot of publicity when we were making the film. In addition I had the parrot with me, and he decided to take over the programme for at least ten minutes. The audience roared with laughter as he hopped on to Eamonn Andrews' shoulder, grabbed his pencil, split it in two and then proceeded to besmirch his dinner jacket with valuable guano. In fact, the blasted parrot got so many laughs that the last four contestants had to be sent home and asked to come back the following week. Eamonn will never forget the night *he* got the bird. Nor, I'm sure, will the Duke of Bedford. He was in the film too – sewing mailbags. What a way to publicise Woburn.

Other television appearances in 1960 followed the usual pattern. *Is Your Honeymoon Really Necessary?* received a singular accolade by being included in the BBC's ponderously titled 20th Century Theatre series, as did the Ted Willis play version of Richard Gordon's *Doctor in the House*. With me in that cast was Dickie Henderson and at thirty-six and thirty-eight years of age respectively, we must have been the oldest medical students in the business! Playing one of the nurses was Sheila Hancock, already climbing steadily upwards in her career. The Lord's Taverners did a well-received show called *Upgreen – And At 'Em* or *A*

Maiden Nearly Over. All the best-known Taverners were in the cast and we performed for nothing and the BBC fee went to the charity. They seemed to have stopped those sort of handouts these days.

The big disappointment in 1960, from a television point of view, was our pantomime *Boobs in the Wood*. Conceived early in April by BBC's Norman Rutherford, authors Ray Cooney and Tony Hilton, plus myself, we thought we had come up with the perfect answer for a Christmas farce and pantomime rolled into one. All the usual Whitehall favourites were to be in the cast, Wally Douglas was directing, the music was to be specially composed by Tommy Watt and we only needed to import our Principal Boy. We first went for Maggie Smith but she, perhaps wisely, was unavailable, so our choice fell on a very clever girl, Carole Shelley, who eventually went to America and made a big success as one of the English girls in both the Broadway and film productions of *The Odd Couple*. Rehearsals started in October, four weeks before the recording date, and many of us had to spend the first week learning to sing and dance (poor Dougie Squires had a hell of a time with my two left feet) and all proceeded well until the dress rehearsal on Friday 25th November. That was an unforgettable day. Elspet (who was pregnant again) went into labour and Wally and I practically had babies too when we witnessed the shambles around us at the theatre. In the first place, they were still hanging the cloths and putting up the set and lighting, on the tiny Whitehall stage, when the audience was in and it was time for the curtain to go up. When, one hour later, it did rise the cacophony of noise from our sixteen-piece orchestra was so great that not a single word of any song could be heard and in such a small theatre the audience were blasted out of their seats and completely deafened. This loss of hearing also resulted in a complete loss of laughter, so we went through the entire rehearsal in a state of total bedlam and total silence. Oh, it was *awful*. A despairing group of us connected with the production met afterwards and various suggestions were made. In the first place it was decided to move the band from the pit to the back of the auditorium. Then the comedy scenes came under close scrutiny and many alterations were made which meant rehearsing every spare minute before the actual show on the Sunday. Only one scene was untouched – a bell-ringing sequence – and Tony Hilton had a fixation about it. He bored the pants off everyone by going on for hours about Dan Leno and how funny it had been in *his* day. Eventually, in desperation – for we had millions of other problems to solve – we left it in and it proved to be exactly as we had expected: a load of old bells. Arguments, discussions, suggestions went on all afternoon and evening in my dressing room, only stopping, as far as I was concerned, when I went on in *Simple Spymen*. After the show, we were off again but at midnight, tired and dispirited, we wended our weary way home. All except me. I went round to the Princess Beatrice to see how Elspet was progressing and found, to my amazement, that I was the proud father of a second bouncing boy and Jonathan Robert MacGregor, who arrived at 12.15 a.m. on Saturday 26th November, has continued to bounce ever since.

Of course, I felt awful about missing the event and this just added to the general air of gloom sparked off by the panto. Elspet was unhappy that *I* was unhappy and that pack of cards built up till they all collapsed in a heap when it came to the performance and recording time on the Sunday. Everyone was exhausted by their efforts to re-rehearse and relearn whole tracts of script and I personally was out on my feet as I hadn't slept for three nights – the combination of Jonathan's arrival and worry about the show saw to that.

Boobs in the Wood really *was* a boob. I should have listened to Wally Douglas who said at the outset we ought to hire a big theatre. But no, I wanted the publicity to come to the Whitehall. I got the publicity all right, but entirely the wrong kind, for in September I had signed, with much ado, a new three-year BBC contract and *Boobs* was my first effort under this latest agreement. Hardly an auspicious beginning and Michael Barry was quite entitled to write that rude letter. He was very sweet, though, when I did my next TV farce and sent me a telegram saying, "You've got your colours back!"

Other unhappy events in 1960? A try-out of a ghastly play at

Wolverhampton by Michael Pertwee called *Thin on Top*. It nearly closed down the rep. company who performed it and nearly discouraged Michael from ever again writing a stage farce. Thank God it didn't, for his next one – ten years later – was greeted by paeans of praise from everyone, including the press.

I was also involved in a libel action against the *Daily Mail* and their then theatre critic, Robert Muller. Mr Muller reviewed, adversely, a play by John Chapman called *Brides of March* – which was nothing to do with any of us at the Whitehall – but in so doing he implied that we only put on smut at that theatre. As we prided ourselves on "good, clean, family fun" we were naturally incensed, and sued. The *Daily Mail* huffed and puffed a bit at the outset, but as soon as they knew we had retained Gerald Gardiner, now Lord Gardiner, they hurriedly settled out of court and we received £1,500 damages and costs. Still, not really my favourite pastime – litigation.

Other *happy* events in 1960? My Mum and Dad's Golden Wedding Anniversary on Sunday 12th June. A super occasion celebrated by all the family and many friends on a glorious summer's day in the garden at The Mount in Hornsea. The Thousandth Performance Party at the Whitehall on 11th August for *Simple Spymen* and the Tenth Anniversary of our stay at the Whitehall on 12th September were two other splendid shindigs.

Oh, and yes . . . I made sixty-five not out in a benefit cricket match against Middlesex.

Act XIII

Jonathan's godparents were a little less mixed, ecumenically, than his brother's, when it came to his christening on Saturday 18th March 1961. Admittedly Dickie Henderson was a Catholic – but Tim Manderson and Auntie Billie (Elspet's widowed aunt Isobel Wilson, a lovely lady, who has acted as a grandmother to our kids since Elsie died) did follow a more conventional pattern. What makes Jonathan unique, though, as far as our family is concerned, is that he was actually given a Bible by one of his godparents – Dickie – so that *must* equal Jamie's denominational diversity. Actually, Jamie attended his brother's christening with a huge plaster on his forehead, for a week before he had been hit by a metal swing on which Louisa was playing in our garden. We heard her horrified shriek and saw Jamie staggering towards the house streaming blood, and it really looked as though his eyes had gone. Luckily, we happened to be having lunch with two doctors – so first aid was promptly at hand.

The reason for two doctors to lunch? We had decided to try cellular injections for Shelley, to see if it could help her retardation in any way, and the foremost exponent of that therapy at that time was a Dr Henri from Paris, and our then family doctor, Dr Fermont, was in attendance. Unhappily, it didn't seem to help Shelley much, if at all, but it did give her a fear of injections which has lasted to this day. Poor love – but we were still at the stage when we believed you could help organically. Now we are sure you can't: not with a mongol, anyway.

Life seemed to be party after party in those days, for a month after the christening came the "do" at Pastoria's Restaurant to celebrate our passing the Aldwych Theatre record of ten years seven months and four days for one farce team, in one theatre, in consecutive plays. We invited all the old Aldwych crowd who were still around and along came Ralph Lynn, Bunny Hare, Winifred Shotter and, of course, Ben Travers himself. On our side we had everyone who had ever been in one of our farces, plus a few friendly columnists such as Bill Boorne. It *was* a do, I can tell you (the hilariously imaginative invitation and menu reflected the atmosphere), with Ralph Lynn topping the evening with a superbly funny speech – a speech he may have made hundreds of times, in one form or another, but a lesson in timing for all that.

But one man missed the gaiety of this party, and he, along with my father, had really made it all possible. He was, of course, my Uncle Bert who had quietly supported me over the years – who had, funnily enough, stayed at Pastoria's whenever he came up to London for my first nights – and who had died at the end of January. In so doing he missed not only the Aldwych record-breaking occasion but also the most obviously successful first night I have ever had, *One For The Pot*.

We opened on 2nd August to an ecstatic press from the newspaper Lords Spiritual and Temporal: *The Times, Daily Telegraph, Guardian, Sunday Times* and *Observer*. The hewers of wood and drawers of water were, as is their wont, less enthusiastic but nothing could take away from the fact we had a hit: a palpable hit, in fact. Immediately we were playing to capacity and this astounding business continued throughout the rest of the year, the whole of 1962 and was only affected by the dreadful winter of 1963. Everyone who was anyone came to see it and one of my happiest memories is seeing the late Princess Royal, in the front row, falling about and laughing as loudly as any fishwife. President Ayub Khan watched from a box, surrounded by members of the Special Branch, all watching him and ignoring the antics on the stage. The Churchills came; Prince Charles and Princess Anne were photographed sneaking out the back way with all the overflowing dustbins in the foreground; and one performance was interrupted towards the end by a car thief being chased by the police. He rushed in past our stage doorkeeper, Bert Trickett, and ran on to the stage pursued by two large custodians of the law. Hurdling over the footlights, he ran to the back of the stalls, up the stairs into the foyer, out through the front doors, hailed a passing taxi and escaped, leaving behind two perspiring, puffed-out policemen and a totally bewildered audience, who were wondering if it was all part of the play. I saw all this happening, vaguely, from the wings, for I had just rushed round to make another entrance, as yet another brother, from a cupboard. That entrance was normally greeted with an enormous laugh, but on this occasion there was total silence. I was as bewildered as the audience until it was explained to me what had happened, so in my curtain speech I, in turn, had to explain it to them. This, too, made every front page.

Some people, however, *can* keep news to themselves. I know women are supposed to tattle about everything but I can honestly say that Elspet was like a clam for nearly a year when it came to the preparation of my "This Is Your Life" on BBC Television. They had wanted to do the programme in 1960, but Elspet was expecting Jonty so felt it would be safer if they could postpone. They could, and Elspet (plus my father and mother and a great many friends) kept absolutely shtum for all that time and I had absolutely no inkling at all that it was going to happen. In fact, they caught me at a party and we were at least a couple of hours late arriving.

Let me explain what happened. On Sunday 17th September I had two dates. One was a cricket match for my brother-in-law, Peter Mercier, at Ewell. After that I was supposed to go home, change, pick up Elspet and drive off to the depths of Surrey for a house-warming party given by Johnnie Koon, who runs a number of splendid Chinese restaurants in town. As I was packing my cricket bag I noticed that Elspet kept on at me to be back early from the cricket, but I got a bit stroppy about this for Johnnie's invitation said the party would last till dawn.

"So why should I hurry back if I'm enjoying myself after the match?" I queried.

"Because it will look very rude if we're not there on time," said Elspet rather lamely.

"Bollocks," quoth I, and went off happily to play cricket, confident I had won that round of repartee.

Well, it so happened that I *did* enjoy myself at the match and didn't get home till 8.30, wanting a leisurely bath first before dressing for the party. Elspet was frantic, but I still didn't twig that anything was up and about 9.15 we drove off to Surrey and met the first of the autumn fogs. Two hours later we finally found our way to the Koon household, in a state of great tension to say the least, and were met by a distraught Eamonn Andrews and a number of his equally panicky production acolytes. *Still* I didn't guess and wandered off with Eamonn to have a drink. That was it. A hidden film camera appeared, the book was thrust into my hands and we were off, with me giggling weakly the while and wishing I hadn't been so beastly to Elspet – for you're supposed to love your wife in "This Is Your Life". Anyway, the programme wasn't ruined, in spite of our late arrival, for it was recorded and shown several weeks later. I had a terrible lump in my throat for most of the time. My father came on and dried.

"What do you think of your son's achievements?" prompted Eamonn.

"Not bad," was the laconic reply, and there my father stuck and no amount of help from Eamonn could get him going on his rehearsed story. Donald Wolfit was the very opposite. Eamonn couldn't stop him and by the time Donald finished he'd ascribed to me many parts I had never played. Colin Cowdrey made me very proud when he said I could certainly have made a county cricketer – but Colin is notoriously kind. A BBC studio manager was produced, who claimed he was with me in the RAF, but I honestly couldn't remember him at all. Two old age pensioners and an ardent fan enlivened the proceedings. Hattie Jacques dealt with charity. George Radford was flown from Canada, and the rest of the Whitehall was represented by Wally Patch, George Jeger, John Chapman and all the children (plus their parents) who had been born to members of the company over the past decade. By now I was blubbing quite openly and kneading Elspet's hand as though it were dough. The knock-out punch came when our own kids arrived and Leo Franklyn, dressed as a nanny, wheeled on Jonathan in his pram, followed by an over-excited, barking Bastien. I *know* it's mawkish – but my quick was *really* touched that night . . .

It was even more affected by Brian Reece. Brian and I were always being confused, because of the similarity in our names – not our looks. People would congratulate me on "PC 49" and congratulate him on the Whitehall, so we decided to appear together in a telly and let people sort it out for themselves. We chose to do *Wolf's Clothing* – which Elspet had done at the Strand – but there was a general post in casting. I played Derek Farr's part, Elspet took over Muriel Pavlow's, Brian played Pat Cargill's and Jan Holden came into Elspet's role. Bunny Hare and Fabia Drake were there instead of Ronald Adam and Viola Lyel, whilst a striking blonde, Jacqueline Jones, was the *au pair* girl, instead of Angela Browne.

Rehearsals were somewhat confused. Elspet was ill and confined to her bed for a week and Brian had to keep going to Westminster Hospital for some pretty grim-sounding injections. They not only sounded grim, they were grim, for poor Brian had bone cancer and within a year he was dead. He was a super bloke and just before he went into hospital for the last time he took our two families up the river in his boat and gave no indication of the fear in his heart. Not long afterwards the problem as to who was "PC 49" and who was at the Whitehall was finally and irrevocably solved. I would it had been some other way.

1961 also saw my first and only appearance with a very funny lady, Thora Hird. I did two comedy shows with Dickie Henderson and played cricket with Ray Lindwall. And so to 1962 . . .

That was a pretty dull year because we were so *successful*! Ridiculous, isn't it? Every night I pointed the car in the general direction of the Mall and every night when the curtain went up there would be yet another full house with maybe twenty or thirty standing. The cast – Basil Lord, Leo Franklyn, Terry Scott,

Peter Mercier, Larry Noble, Sheila Mercier, Helen Jessop and Hazel Douglas, plus my doubles, Stuart Sherwin, Pearson Dodd, Gerry Dawson, and understudies Christine Russell and Jean Cook – grew as complacent as I did so that practical jokes to "corpse" your fellow actors – always a fatal sign – became the order of the day. I remember one elaborate joke I perpetrated night after night on Terry. In the play I had just taken some peculiar drug and went off barking like a dog and Terry, as a furious father, would yell, "Look at him – just look at him. 'Alf way up that lamppost." This would be greeted by the necessary audience laughter, and all the cast left on stage would turn round to follow Terry's gaze – so it was a suitable time to get them all going. The antics I got up to were unforgivable and unrepeatable in retrospect. All except the one on Terry's last night. As he yelled his line about the lamppost, and as they all looked off left through the windows, there *was* a lamppost, there *was* a dog and it *was* lifting its leg. I had dressed my understudy Gerry Dawson, in a dog-skin, had a lamppost built and a phallic tube and soda siphon completed the necessary effect. The whole joke cost me about £5, but it cost a lot more in actual fact for the cast were quite incapable of another word and it was some time before we won the audience back. Oh dear – I blush with shame when I think about it.

The director of *One For The Pot* was Henry Kendall and, frankly, he was too ill to really care what happened. My usual director, Wally Douglas, had been appointed Programme Controller of Westward Television (our rivals in the race for Devon and Cornwall) so Henry had seemed a natural successor, for he was an inventive actor and had been a good director. By our time, though, his heart was a permanent worry and he was a very tired man who was delighted to do very little. In the event, it didn't make much difference because *One For The Pot* was practically actor-proof and director-proof. In the theatre, that is. On the screen, whether television or film, it meant not a thing: all the elaborate theatrical effects, which were marvellous before your very eyes, paled into insignificance and obvious trickery when put in front of the camera. I know, because our television excerpt was not as effective as usual and when I made the film in South Africa in 1968 it was practically unwatchable. Still, one shouldn't speak ill of the dead: thank God, it never achieved any film circuit, so author Ray Cooney and I, who saw the finished article together in a small viewing room near London airport, can hug our secret horror together and never need to admit we were in any way responsible!

But to get back to Henry Kendall. In August 1962 we did the television of Philip King's wonderfully funny farce *See How They Run* and Harry played the Bishop. A little short of breath but certainly not short of laughs. He then went off to Le Rayol, in the South of France, to holiday with Countess Hollender and her two daughters. At the same time Elspet and I went on holiday to Cavallière - a few miles away - and one night, or rather one morning at about three o'clock, we were woken by that awful shrill, frightening clanging which only the phone can make when you are fast asleep. It was the Hollenders in great distress. Henry had collapsed and was clearly dying. We rushed over as he breathed his last. There then followed the most bizarre operation, for Harry had to be cremated and his ashes taken back to England. Try doing this in France. The nearest crematorium was in Marseilles and it took five days to arrange for the necessary coffins - you need three - and for the necessary permission to come through. I spent those five days in the company of Pat Hollender and a number of French undertakers - all looking like small French character actors - in various French funeral parlours, surrounded by various French plaster saints and various French exaltations to the life hereafter. Poor Harry. That particular holiday did him no good at all.

There was a service of praise and remembrance for him at St Martin-in-the-Fields on the 11th July. I read the lesson and Alan Melville gave the address. I wish I'd had the courage to tell my favourite Harry Kendall story. We were driving to Birmingham to see the last try-out of *One For The Pot* at the Alex and in those days there was no speed limit on the M1 so I was showing off my Facel Vega's paces. As we approached 145 m.p.h. Harry, looking slightly ashen, said, "You know, dear boy, I have never been as fast as this before, even when doing a vertical dive in a Sopwith Pup." And there let us leave Henry Kendall AFC, sometime pilot, actor and wit.

1962 saw the start of a new type of programme for me on television. It was called "Dial Rix" and the idea was that I would ring up a relative of mine, also played by me, and the story would spring from the opening conversation. The programmes were to be fifty minutes in length and they were to lampoon some aspect of our society. For example, there was *What a Drag*, which had a go at cigarette advertising; *No Plums in the Pudding* which tilted at Christmas office parties and so on. It was a good idea, nearly ruined by extraordinary programming on the part of the BBC, who seemed to put the shows on with absolutely no set pattern, and also by our first director, Darcy Conyers. Straight out of the film studio, Darcy thought in wider terms and bigger budgets than television, with the result that we had spent practically all the money for six programmes by the time we had made the first three. Luckily, Wally Douglas resigned from Westward and came back to mount a rescue operation. Several authors wrote the scripts – John Chapman, Ray Cooney, Tony Hilton and Christopher Bond. It was Christopher Bond's *Come Prancing* which had the greatest impact and achieved my biggest-ever audience of some eighteen million viewers. It is sad to record that the opposition programme that night was the once great Tony Hancock.

John Chapman's *Between the Balance Sheets* did well too: it formed the basis of his farce *Diplomatic Baggage* which Donald Albery and I subsequently presented at Wyndham's Theatre in 1964. But eventually, after nine programmes, "Dial Rix" ground to a halt for want of new ideas. Authors realised that one fifty-minute programme could contain the basis for a film or a play, and no one wants to give away those chances or that sort of money, so that was that. A pity, but I was finding false ears and noses and wigs were beginning to look a bit odd in my desperate search to change into yet another relative!

1963 started badly – and sadly. The winter was the worst in living memory and our lovely capacity business melted away, unlike the snow, which stayed around for nearly three months. I was very depressed and needing a break, so Elspet and I joined forces with David and Pat Jacobs and flew off to Jamaica to have a marvellous holiday in the Plantation Inn at Ocho Rios.

In those days BOAC didn't fly direct, so we were put up for one night at the Plaza Hotel, scene of Neil Simon's very funny *Plaza Suite*. It was all very posh, but I found the television programmes piped to our rooms rather depressing and the static electricity positively alarming. However, it was lovely to wander round New York, free of charge, as it were, and we really did a crash tourist course in about four hours. My over-riding impression of the city was a load of rusty fire escapes and overflowing dustbins: not a pretty sight. *We* all looked very pretty, though, when we went to lunch in the Plaza Grill, particularly David, who had just been voted "Britain's Best Dressed Man of the Year" and was wearing a snazzy Italian red jersey cardigan – all his more formal attire being packed ready for the flight to Kingston. The head waiter took one look at David, literally saw red, and held up a restraining hand. Voice quivering with indignation, he enquired from "Britain's Best Dressed Man" if he honestly thought he could sit down in the Plaza Grill dressed like that? "Britain's Best Dressed Man" replied that he thought he could. The head waiter was puce (he and David's red cardigan made a fetching twinset) and adamant. Suddenly Pat Jacobs had an idea. David had left his very smart velvet-collared overcoat in the cloakroom and it was black. Would that be all right? The head waiter, replied that it would. So that is how "Britain's Best Dressed Man" came to be sitting in the Plaza Grill, eating his Chicken Maryland, with his overcoat flapping around his ankles.

The Plantation Inn had the richest bunch of people I've ever met under one roof. Oil millionaires, gambling millionaires, property millionaires – practically all American and Canadian. You would never have known we were the poor relations, though, for the manager of the hotel, Sydney Attwood, was a lovely man who had once been Head of Artists' Bookings for the

BBC and recognised quality when he saw it! Really, he was very kind and although our stay cost a bomb, it could, I suppose, have cost twice as much. We were also able to take advantage of David's women's programme "Wednesday Magazine", which was then appearing on BBC television. We filmed each other gambolling in the waves, snorkeling, eating vast buffet lunches surrounded by tiny yellow birds: all of which was intended to regale David's lady viewers. There was only one snag – the camera had a wobble and all but three minutes of film was useless – so the dear ladies were saved from what would surely have been chronic boredom.

It was in Jamaica that I was described so breezily by the local journalist as London's best known fart actor. David, too, came in for his share of Mr Malaprop's perception. He was written up as "London's best-known dicks jockey". I accept my accolade. I wonder if David accepts his?

We left Heathrow in a blizzard and returned in a blizzard. Unhappily there was another blowing in my business world, for when I rang up my mum and dad to say we were safely returned, I sensed a note of strain in my father's voice. After a little shilly-shallying he came to the point and it wasn't easy for him. He was a man who had never admitted failure, and to have to admit it to me, one of his own children, was almost more than he could bear.

Briefly, the bank had foreclosed and all the money I had patiently built up over twelve years at the Whitehall, some £90,000 had gone. You see, my old man was a stubborn devil who believed not at all in limited companies. The business had to be his and his brother's. The rest of us, their children, could take our place all in good time: when they were dead. So all their companies – shipowning, shipbroking, garage, radio, petrol and theatrical – were lumped under one partnership: all for one and one for all. Several fell on hard times, the bank wouldn't extend any more credit – though, God knows, they had enough collateral – and that, very simply, was that. For years I had argued and pleaded with him, pointing out the inherent dangers of his business methods, but I was his youngest and there was never a hope of budging him. But now he had to admit I'd been right. It was a pretty grim telephone call, I can tell you.

So, on the morning of 23rd February Rix Theatrical Productions ceased to exist and Brian Rix Enterprises Limited took over our main asset, the ailing *One For The Pot*. My father went into a decline and, less than three years later, he was dead. He would probably have died anyway, but it seemed that his own stubbornness, aided by his bank manager, proved a fatal combination. I think his accountant, who also died about the same time, can be counted as part of the aggregation; but then accountants are only there to advise, not to lead.

By a strange coincidence, the only play of merit I tried out in 1963 was *Who's Your Father?* by Ray Cooney. I knew who *my* father was, all too well in that year, but as time has gone by I have come to understand him more and sometimes wish he was around so I could tell him. Anyway Ray's play went on at Richmond and it was not a success. It had six very funny business scenes, but the plot – about an escaped convict who has been in prison so long that his own son doesn't know him – came across as old-fashioned and definitely 1920s. What to do with those six scenes? Ray is nothing if not resourceful. The plot was altered to a Russian ballet dancer who defects to the West (based on you-know-who), the six scenes slotted in nicely, thank you very much, and there was another eventual smash hit, *Chase Me, Comrade!*

One interesting programme I did in 1963 was television's "Talking Sport" on BBC2. In this I pontificated on my ideas for revitalising cricket and argued the points with such experts as Colin Cowdrey and Freddie Trueman, whilst Peter West held the ring and Ian Carmichael acted as devil's advocate. My thesis, if you can call it that, was eventually beatified by being published in the *Listener*, and on rereading the article I'm amazed how many of the points have been taken up, especially in relation to one-day cricket. Common sense, I suppose ...

1964 was really the beginning of the end for me at the Whitehall. On 11th May George Jeger was given notice to quit by his new boss, Felice Cooper, and, as he went after nineteen years, he predicted that I would follow him within two years. He was right, almost to the day, but of course at the time I scoffed at the idea.

When old Louis Cooper died, way back in 1961, he left the theatre to his two daughters and his son. His widow, Alice kept a watching brief, but George Jeger was really left in sole charge. Over the years one daughter, Felice, bought out the rest of the family, as and when they wished to sell, and suddenly there she was at the top of the pile – and the first person to go was George, who had always been at loggerheads with her. After his departure, it was easy to see why. She was, at times, unpredictable and no amount of patience on my part could cope with the situation as I now found it.

But I am being precipitate. 1964 did not see *my* exit from the Whitehall scene. Rather, it saw the arrival on 15th July of *Chase Me, Comrade!* Harold Hobson in the *Sunday Times* was, as usual, kind – "Brian Rix gives the public what it wants – his joy is communicated" – and this really sums up most of the press reactions. However, it was left to Ronald Bryden, then of the *New Statesman*, later of the *Observer*, to make the most sweeping statements of all:

"There they are: the most robust survivors of a great tradition, the most successful British theatrical enterprises of our time. Curious that no one can be found to speak up wholeheartedly for them – no one, that is, outside enthusiastic millions who have packed every British theatre where they have played.

"It's particularly curious considering the current intellectual agitation for a theatre of the masses, a true working-class drama. Everything, apparently, for which Joan Littlewood has struggled – the boisterous, extrovert playing, the integrated teamwork, the Cockney irreverence of any unself-conscious, unacademic audience bent purely on pleasure – exists, patently and profitably, at the Whitehall. Yet how many devout pilgrims to Stratford East have hazarded the shorter journey to Trafalgar Square to worship at the effortless shrine of the thing itself? How many Arts Council grants have sustained Mr Rix's company? How many *Evening Standard* awards went to *Dry Rot*? How many theses have been written on the art of Colin Morris, John Chapman or Ray Cooney? The time has come, surely, to fill the gap."

Two of the pilgrims to help fill the gap were Margot Fonteyn followed closely by the excuse for the whole play himself, Rudolf Nureyev. Both were overwhelming in their obvious enjoyment and in their personalities. Dame Margot was so delightful and charming, it was difficult to realise the pinnacle she held in the world of ballet. Nureyev provided an excuse for an extempore party and if he felt any resentment about the play he never showed it and was, shall we say, extremely gracious.

Others to be delighted by the success of *Comrade* were my newly found backers. For the first time in fourteen years at the Whitehall I had to seek outside support. Now that production costs were creeping up and all that hard-earned capital had disappeared a year earlier I felt I should, as it were, go to the normal market and seek out my "angels". There was no lack of support treading around to fill the gap ...

Close on the opening of *Comrade* came my co-productions with Donald Albery. A musical *Instant Marriage* at the Piccadilly with Joan Sims, Stephanie Voss, Paul Whitsun-Jones, Wallas Eaton, Rex Garner and Bob Grant who also wrote the book; Laurie Holloway composed the music. But it was really too broad for public taste and staggered along for a year, losing most of its money. At the beginning, some lady threatened to sue us for pinching her idea, but as Bob Grant had already pinched it from a French farce nearly a hundred years old, there was little she could do about proving her point and nothing more was heard of it.

Diplomatic Baggage with Elspet, Charles Heslop and John Chapman opened at Wyndham's. Derek Royle stole most of the notices with a marvellously acrobatic performance as a silent French waiter, but the leads, too, were well received. Unfortunately, away from its natural home at the Whitehall, *Baggage* was not the riot everyone expected and this production, too, lost most of its money. Ah me! The vicissitudes of production. *Sic transit gloria mundi* ...

Apart from being involved in all these late-summer productions, Elspet and I were also involved in building our castle in Spain. Walter Gotell had stumbled across eleven acres of land between Algeciras and Tarifa, on the southern tip of Spain, when he was filming in *Fifty-five Days in Peking* near Madrid. He promptly sold us two and a half acres and we started to build. Not without many misgivings on my part, but Elspet was determined that this would be the beginning of a new life. Away from the theatre, away from incessant phone calls, away from the office. Away from the tensions of London and so on and so on. Of course, she was right. Instead, we had the tensions of Spain, incessant cables from the office, incessant blocked-up drains and so on, and so on. Ironically, when we sold the place ten years later, it was Elspet who wanted to sell and I who wanted to stay ...

But in the beginning all went smoothly. We agreed our plans, obtained our Bank of England permission, appointed our builder, rushed over one October Sunday to clear up any outstanding problems, returned to our respective theatres, learnt our Spanish and hoped for the best. We needn't have worried. Six months later, to the day, the house was built, exactly as planned – which says a great deal for the builder, José Maria Perez Lorenzo. There were only three important omissions, as we subsequently discovered. The foundations of one wing were not bound to the main part of the house and as they were on clay soil, that wing slowly and majestically slid down the hill. José Maria put that right. Then they had forgotten to put in any drainaways from our cesspit, so a horrified Elspet one day saw a large, damp, odoriferous patch spreading like a slimy bog in front of the windows. As there were fourteen people staying in the house, it was not surprising that its progress was rather rapid. José Maria put that right. Finally, there was no water. At least there was, but we had a header tank on the roof, which was too high up to be filled by the local pressure, with the result that after one bath the house was like a parched desert for several hours. José

Maria put that right. The header tank was removed and the water just gushed straight through. Perfectly satisfactory, but unfortunately our two hot-water tanks did not have expansion chambers: as the hot water expanded, so did they, and burst. They happened to be placed above two wardrobes, so a pile of clothes had an unexpected washday. José Maria did *not* put that right, for by then the poor man had gone out of business. We were one among too many.

Evening Standard, London, 12th March 1965

BRIAN RIX GOES TO THE PALACE

"Brian Rix, the actor from *Chase Me Comrade!* at the Whitehall Theatre went to lunch with the Queen at Buckingham Palace today.

"Also there were Princess Margaret and the Earl of Snowdon, Air Commandant Dame Jean Conan Doyle, Director of the WRAF, Mr Justice Widgery, a Judge of the High Court, Sir Peter Runge, President of the Federation of British Industries, Mr Charles Forte, Chairman of Forte & Co., Mr Clifford Kenyon, Labour MP for Chorley, Dr David Stafford-Clark, Physician in Charge, Department of Psychological Medicine, and Director of the York Clinic, Dr George Thalban-Ball, organist of the Temple Church and professor and examiner of the Royal College of Music."

I love the words "also there" don't you? Some of those "also there" have done quite well, really. One's a Lord Chief Justice. At least two have been knighted; whereas the headliner is still dropping his trousers to get a laugh. Actually, Princess Margaret and I reached that topic fairly quickly and I had the temerity to mention my jock strap – but in what context I cannot say.

But seriously, though, folks, it *was* an exciting occasion and I would be less than honest if I did not admit to feeling very honoured when I received the invitation. Actually our group had been asked earlier, but the Queen had developed chicken pox, I think it was, and we were postponed. Relief came when the alternative date was suggested and I doubt if any of us had engagements we couldn't break!

I prepared for the occasion by having only one small cup of tea at breakfast (imagine the embarrassment if you had to be excused in the middle of lunch) and primped and prepared myself in my Whitehall dressing room before driving the few hundred yards up the Mall to the Palace gates. I felt very important as I was waved through to the inner courtyard, where I parked by the covered entrance and was greeted by a courteous equerry who *had* seen a lot of my plays, which helped to break the ice. Up the stairs to an ante room, where the lunchees nervously toyed with glasses of sherry or small gins and tonics. Suddenly the barking and scuffling of dogs: a vast number of corgis (at least it seemed vast) flooded into the room and there was the Queen looking, I may say, twice as attractive as in any portrait or photo. We lined up, were presented, and luncheon was served. The Queen sat on one side of the oval table. Princess Margaret sat opposite her, with me on her left. Conversation flowed fairly easily, with each side of the table rather keeping to themselves. However, when we went back into the ante room for coffee there was a general musical chairs, with the Queen moving over to us and Princess Margaret to the other lot.

We left exactly two hours after we arrived. A fascinating two hours, I can tell you. I can't even remember what we had to eat, but I do remember that when I got home, Elspet was in her oldest jeans getting on with the spring-cleaning. How are the mighty fallen . . .

Act XIV

I began my 1965 summer holiday at 5.30 a.m. on Sunday 17th July when the BEA plane took off for Gibraltar and, unfortunately, I began it alone. Our house in Spain was finished. Elspet had been over to see to all the basic furnishings and fittings, and the two of us were to go ahead as the advance guard before the hordes descended on us. We reckoned without Jonathan. When he went to bed on Saturday night he was accompanied by a high temperature. Elspet, being a good mum, decided to stay, until the doctor had seen him, and catch a later flight: so at midnight we were ringing up Heathrow making all the necessary alterations. Hardly an auspicious beginning to our change of life-style. For me the change was pretty temporary, anyway, as I only had a month off before returning to the dreaded treadmill. I was lucky to get a month but Stanley Baxter came in for one – prior to playing *Chase Me, Comrade!* in Australia – so it all slotted in very neatly.

I arrived at La Farandula – the name of our Spanish hideaway which means "the ambience of the theatre" – by 8.30 a.m. and could hardly believe it was all ours. The sun was shining hotly. Two young maids were sweeping and dusting. A crate of our belongings, sent from England, lay outside ready for unpacking, and the Gotells wandered over and asked me to breakfast. Idyllic – or so it seemed – but the problem with me is that I always want everything to be right *now*, and that can cause an awful lot of aggro to anyone involved, myself included.

When I returned after breakfast to open the crate I began to look round. No garden. No terraces. No swimming pool. No driveway. If I could have installed them then and there I would have done, for the adrenalin was up and it was all systems go. Later that night Elspet arrived – Jonathan was on the necessary antibiotic – to find me with a full head of steam and a list as long as your arm of things to be done in the morning. Change of life-style? We were about to add compound interest.

For a week we charged everywhere. Buying, organising, arguing, cajoling. We even suffered the unheard of in Spain: a burglary. On our fourth night we went to bed with a howling gale blowing – the Levante is very insistent in high summer – and about four o'clock I woke up with the curtains almost horizontal. "That's one hell of a wind which can blow them up like that," I thought and returned to snoresville.

In the morning I went to put on my jeans and couldn't find them. Elspet was making breakfast so I yelled through the door to ask if she'd moved them. Having been assured she hadn't and having been reminded that I was always mislaying things, I went on with the hunt. Eventually I found my jeans lying outside on the balcony. Now, no wind I know can actually lift a pair of trousers through a window, deposit them outside and remove 4,000 pesetas from the hip pocket. We'd been burgled and I was going to report it. Elspet got in a flap.

"Look, we're foreigners. We've just moved in. Do you think . . .?" etc. etc. . . .

Yes, I definitely *did* think and I went to get my briefcase which had been by my trousers. You're ahead of me. No briefcase. Now panic *did* set in. All our traveller's cheques – gone. All our documents – passports, driving licences, bail bond – gone, too. We were up the creek, and no mistake. What made it worse was that I had actually woken up and seen the bloody burglar, for he was the one pushing the curtains horizontal – not the wind.

> It wasn't the Almighty
> Who lifted her nightie
> It was Roger, the Lodger, the sod.

We raced out of the house into our hired Seat 600 and started the arduous climb up our unmade drive. Suddenly Elspet yelled and there was my briefcase nestling between two rocks. The lock was smashed, but everything, except money, was there. What a relief! Off we went to the local police in Tarifa who were very polite, kept the briefcase (they still have it) and plainly disbelieved us. They *never* have burglaries in Spain, or so they would have you think. They had to change their minds later in the day when three more burglaries were reported: our wind in the willows had had a field day. The police said it couldn't be a Spaniard, only a passing Moroccan. They don't have burglars in Spain, you see.

Anyway, that wasted a morning, so the pressure was even greater on us in our efforts to be prepared for the family and guests. Well the guests were hardly guests; they were really family too – the Mandersons. On the Sunday they arrived. Three Rix children, one nannie and two Mandersons, Tim and Anne. We were rather short of breath and rather short of temper but ready to receive them in fair shape. However, there was no towel-rail in the guest bathroom, no soap dishes and no loo-paper holder, so next day down came our indefatigable builder's foreman, armed with a small sledge hammer and chisel plus the necessary toilet accessories. We heard this awful banging, raced along the corridor, and there was a gaping hole in the bathroom wall showing the entire contents of our guests' wardrobe. Tim and Anne were graciousness itself as they dusted down their plaster-covered clothes, but worse was to come. Florentino – such was the foreman's name – proceeded to mend the hole and install the equipment with the same cement mix. Inadvertently, he also installed the Mandersons' luggage which we discovered, some two hours later, firmly cemented to the wall. Tim and Anne's graciousness slipped only minutely, for they, like us, were beginning to cotton on to the fact that the Spanish operate in a different way from the English. Once you settle for that you can sit back and relax. At least the Mandersons could, but Elspet and I couldn't. Oh no. We were preparing for the next invasion – the Georgiades – and two weeks later they duly arrived, all five of them. We must have been out of our tiny minds. It was like running Butlin's with none of the facilities, and four weeks after the start of my changed life-style, I returned exhausted and practically penniless to the hard labour of one performance a night at the Whitehall and our lovely housekeeper, Mac – Mrs MacDonald – to minister to my every need.

Meanwhile, back at the hacienda, Elspet soldiered on and I was determined to see she did. Each Sunday morning I caught that 5.30 a.m. plane and arrived at La Farandula in time for breakfast. Then Sunday could be spent in the sun, checking up on all that had happened in the preceding week and all that was to happen in the coming one, before returning on Monday morning to the peace and quiet of London.

I did this once too often. It was now late summer. The schedules changed and I had to fly back on Sunday night. Driving along the road to Gibraltar, which was very rough and dark, I suddenly saw a mule. I swerved to avoid it and hit it with the passenger side of the car. The passenger was Elspet and she took the brunt of the whole ghastly business. The mule was killed, the car was destroyed and Elspet lay unconscious, with blood everywhere. I thought she was dead. The horror of that moment will never leave me.

By a miracle, a car was coming towards us. This, on a deserted country road. By an even greater miracle it turned out to be a taxi and the driver plied his hire a few yards from the hospital in Algeciras. I lifted Elspet into his car and we were off like the wind and within twenty minutes life-giving plasma was being pumped into her, for her face was cut in two and she'd lost a great deal of blood.

The greatest miracle of all was yet to come. The best local surgeon for that kind of work, a Dr Ramos Arguelles, had returned that night from holiday and from 1 a.m. till 6 a.m. he laboured, stitching Elspet up. How successful he was can be judged by the fact that after one further plastic surgery operation in London, carried out by Gerry Moore of East Grinstead fame, Elspet was appearing in *To Dorothy, a Son* on BBC Television by Easter Monday the following year.

The hospital in Algeciras was a lesson to us all. The nuns merely saw to the running of the place, the *practicantes* – rather superior male nurses – administered the drugs, and members of the family did the nursing. Our family was rather young to provide that service, but again luck was with us, for staying at the big local hotel, the Reina Cristina, was a senior nursing sister, Rosemary Eyres, who volunteered to stay with Elspet until she was better. Rosemary was sweet, kind, utterly practical and very essential. Our new neighbours and friends, too, were splendid. John and Pat Donnithorne, from the Reina, sent along soft pillows; Walter and Yvonne Gotell; Nancy and Tarleton Winchester (Nancy had been an Assistant Stage Manager with Ronnie Shiner when the Whitehall first opened); Purple and Cecilia Blatch (he got that name in Ceylon when a local newspaper carried a headline describing his rugby exploits – "Cecil Blatch's Purple Patches"); Cristi Lieb and her brother Alan; Roland St Oswald: all, and many more, provided us with grapes and sympathy. I'll never forget one occasion in Elspet's room when Dr Arguelles brought in two fellow doctors to survey his handiwork. Also there were the Spanish Donald Peers, Pedro Terol, and a blind Canadian author called Sidney Bigman with his girlfriend Stephanie. Rosemary was around, of course, plus Elspet's sister Rhoda with her youngest daughter, Zoë, and her nannie, Ruth. The local fire chief, Señor Palmer, was booming away (he was a raw-boned, red-headed Spaniard whose Scottish family had landed over a hundred years before in Southern Spain, but he still looked as Scots as Elspet's father with his red hair and his bristling moustache), our builder José Maria Perez Lorenzo was lending valuable support, as were the local handyman, Manolin, and his two children. A total of fifteen people crammed into a room twelve feet by ten feet, not forgetting Elspet in bed and me passing round the sherry and *tapas* like a maniac. Into the middle of this bedlam strolled one of the *practicantes* to give us our injections. Actually, I think the 20 c.c. syringes contained ox-tail soup – such was the admixture and the amount – but whatever it was it was supposed to be good for us. Without further ado he went over to Elspet – who obediently rolled on to her tum – whipped up her nightie and whipped in the needle. The medical men present kept on looking, everyone else decorously averted their gaze, but kept on talking. Our *practicante* friend then came over to me, indicated I should drop my trousers, repeated the performance and strolled out again. The only concession he made to professional ethics was knocking the ash off his fag before he actually started the injections . . .

I flew back to England, with a lump of plaster on my right temple and Louisa, Jamie and Jonty lumped around me in the aircraft. I went on that night at the Whitehall and as the *Sun* reported the next day:

"He was cheered when he appeared. The cast had to abandon their opening lines because of the storm of applause."

I had to abandon my opening lines because I was blubbing so much. Elspet returned nine days later and was greeted with a *Daily Express* headline which outdid mine in mawkishness: "When a woman's looks could vanish in a flash." The story, though, by Ann Leslie was perfectly readable and did sum up how lucky Elspet really was to be alive and in one piece. The postscript to that story, though, would have taken a further five years to tell. The mule belonged to the Dowager Marchioness of Bute. In Spain you have to fence, hobble or tether animals so they can't do what this mule did – wander on to the road. We sued, of course, for damages and five years later we settled. I'm glad we were young enough to wait that long . . .

Anyway I was back in the West End for my fifteenth anniversary at the Whitehall. I little realised it would be my last. It was the end, too, for Larry Noble who really felt after all those years that he'd had enough. Possibly that was an omen, but, in the event, he went and in his place came Derek Royle, who had done so well in *Diplomatic Baggage*. We soldiered on, with me desperately trying to buy the lease of the theatre. Twice, we were grouped round the conference table – accountants, solicitors and bankers – and twice Felice Cooper stopped negotiations. She had remarried and thought her husband, who was near retirement from the United States Air Force, might want to take over the running of the Whitehall. In the event he didn't, but by then I had left and Paul Raymond stepped smartly into the breach. If only I had been more patient – but life is full of "if onlys".

I think the catalyst which made me leave the Whitehall was the death of my father. Whilst he was around I felt I should carry on in the old way, but once he was gone there was none of that feeling; just one of frustration at being in the same sort of plays, in the same theatre for so long with nothing tangible to show at the end of it all. Really my success had made the Whitehall a very valuable property and I was unable to share in this. Coupled with the growing tension between Felice and myself it was more than I could bear, so when Leslie Grade offered me a summer season at an astronomical salary to take *Chase Me, Comrade!* to Morecambe, I accepted. My father had died, after a series of strokes, on January 10th 1966. I accepted Leslie's offer two weeks later. You don't have to be a psychiatrist to see the connection.

On the 2nd March it was announced I was leaving the Whitehall on the 21st May and then Danny La Rue and Barbara Windsor would come in with *Come Spy With Me*. What was *not* announced was that I had the option to go back to the Whitehall after Christmas; but when that time came *Come Spy With Me* had still a long way to go to get its money back. I owned a quarter of the Danny La Rue show and was as anxious as anybody to see its success, so I packed my belongings, which had been stored at the Whitehall and crossed Trafalgar Square to the Garrick Theatre. This was all done with Felice's agreement. The week I opened there, she threw us out of our offices . . . Ah, me. Poor old Gilbert Harrison was practically dictating in the street.

What had happened after my exit to make way for Danny? Well we had a lovely holiday in Spain – the garden was growing, the terraces were laid – and returned to the grind of twice nightly at the Winter Gardens, Morecambe. It was bloody diabolical! The houses were dreadful and the sweat and effort really weren't worth the huge pay cheque at the end of the week. Frankly *Chase Me, Comrade!* was too sophisticated for the Morecambe audience, most of whom were day-trippers anyway and had left the town before our first house started. I began to wonder if I meant anything away from the West End and the Whitehall.

I needn't have worried, for when we took the play on tour after Morecambe, every theatre was packed to capacity. Ours is an extraordinary business and this was further proved conclusively when at the beginning of the *Comrade* tour I took my first tentative steps towards experimenting with a repertoire. Briefly, Dickie Henderson in *Bang, Bang Beirut* by Ray Cooney and Tony Hilton (subsequently retitled *Stand By Your Bedouin*), and myself in *Comrade* split the week. You'd have thought a new play with Dickie would have done better than our old one. Not a bit of it. The public expected to see Dickie in cabaret or variety or television situation comedy, not in a play. They stayed away in droves and flocked to see the established legitimate theatre lot – us. If we'd gone into the variety theatres the business would have been reversed and yet Dickie was hysterically funny in his play, as we had been in ours at Morecambe. Odd, isn't it?

So, back to London for Christmas, the television of *One For The Pot*, the decision to leave well alone at the Whitehall and my arrangements with John Hallett, the Managing Director of the Garrick, to try out my repertoire idea there. I was going to start off in March 1967 with one play *Stand By Your Bedouin* and then, five weeks later, add a second, *Uproar in the House* by Anthony Marriott and Alastair Foot. Those two plays would be presented on alternative weeks and then we would add a third play *Let Sleeping Wives Lie* by Harold Brooke and Kay Bannerman. I was able to arrange excerpts from all these plays to be televised by the BBC and was confident all would be clear to the vast British public.

How wrong can you get? The British public was totally unclear. The British public thought I was doing three one-act plays. The British public thought the plays were flopping and coming off after one week. The British public frankly didn't care a damn and merely wanted to know there was *one* funny play on in *one* theatre. And that quite simply was that. All my airy fairy plans to take one play out of the repertoire and put it on the road came to nought and after six months I had lost so much money I had to face reality and revert to one play, *Let Sleeping Wives Lie*. I was able to arrange the transfer of *Uproar in the House* back to the Whitehall – but with another management who paid us a royalty – and poor old *Stand By Your Bedouin* bit the desert dust. To run a repertoire successfully you have to have fairly unlimited funds – like the National Theatre or the Royal Shakespeare – for frankly it is not a strictly commercial proposition. I had approached the Arts Council on a number of occasions for this altruistic backing, but there was little hope of it ever being forthcoming – hence my attempt to go it alone. I had presented quite a good case. My London productions would *have* to tour. I would be able to attract a number of artists who were only interested in short runs or a particular play. I would be able to switch from low comedy, to farce, to high comedy with consummate ease and so on. In the end, lack of funds forced me to present three plays which were identical in concept – with casts who were playing similar parts – for financially I was unable to ring the changes. This, coupled with the reasons already given, made the whole idea a nonsense. Still, it was a fantastic effort really. We rehearsed three new farces and opened them "cold". We received, in the main, very good notices. We had a team of splendid hard-working actors headed by Leslie Crowther, Derek Farr, Leo Franklyn, Elspet and myself. Marvellous support came from Dennis Ramsden, Helen Jessop, Andrew Sachs, Bill Treacher, Anna Dawson, Alan Tilvern, Sheila Mercier and Wendy Padbury. The plays were directed by Wally Douglas, with settings by my sister-in-law, Rhoda Gray. The entire office work was done by Gilbert Harrison, plus one secretary, Jennifer Wilson, and eventually an assistant, David Wilson. Nor was television ignored. Apart from our three excerpts, we also presented in 1967 *Look After Lulu*, *Is Your Honeymoon Really Necessary*, for the second time, *Money for Jam* – a new play by a sixty-three-year-old ex-tobacconist and contributor to *Punch*, T. M. Learoyd – and the television version of *Chase Me, Comrade!* Not bad for a tiny company, run from a tiny office with a tiny office staff. I'd like to see *any* of the subsidised companies *anywhere* do the same, with the same staff and resources. No wonder poor old Gil Harrison retired to hospital with a heart attack. Not, thank God, with fatal results and not, thank God, before he'd done all the necessary work.

Incidentally, Elspet received a jolly pleasant pat on the back for one of her performances:

DAILY EXPRESS STAR AWARD
"To actress Elspet Gray in *Look After Lulu* for a wide eyed and winning study in naughtiness in the face of a cliché-ridden translation by Noël Coward of a classic Feydeau farce."

Not bad for someone playing the female lead in two plays in the repertoire, plus two telly pieces at the same time, plus seeing the kids off to school every morning. Oh it's a glamorous life, ours is ...

On the other hand the *Daily Express* was singularly untruthful when *Uproar in the House* was transferred to the Whitehall. What made it worse was that the notice was written by Jamie's god-father, Michael Walsh, and he had been in my dressing room a few days before the transfer and *knew* why we had to do it. He also knew we had arranged quite favourable terms and yet this is what appeared on the 20th October.

It Looks As Though The Joke Is On Mr Rix
"Mr Rix brought the play to London as a vehicle for his own company, but dropped it. And he has nothing to do with this venture which could restore the Whitehall as the house of farce." Etc. etc.

Ooh, I was hopping mad, I can tell you. It was some time before I could bring myself to speak to Michael, but time heals all things and he's a very kind bloke, really, if you forget he's a journalist.

Then, after the collapse of the repertoire came the collapse of my brother-in-law's computer firm and if I may again quote the *Express*:

"Brian Rix, Britain's King of Farce, has lost thousands of pounds in a computer firm which has gone into liquidation."

This time it was the whole truth that was published and I was hopping mad for quite a different reason.

· · · · ·

After the hurly burly of 1967, the hue and cry, the hullabaloo, the huffiness, the humour and the humiliation, 1968 seemed humdrum in comparison.

Elspet left *Let Sleeping Wives Lie* and Rona Anderson took over. *One For The Pot* was filmed, disastrously, in Pretoria. Almost as disastrous was the try out of Michael Pertwee's *Birth of a Nation* at Richmond. Luckily he persevered with the rewrites. Elspet and I appeared in a successful Kenneth Horne comedy, *A Public Mischief*, with that delightful and indefatigable Dame Cicely Courtneidge. The Whitehall Theatre, which had been losing money since I left – tee hee hee – was put up for sale but was too expensive for me to buy. We had a sneak thief at the Garrick who came in through the pass door and took Elspet's handbag. The following week Rona came in, and so did the thief again: to have a go at *her* possessions. I presented the transfer from the Newcastle Playhouse *Close the Coalhouse Door* at the Fortune Theatre. It never really took off, but it was a marvellous show. Everyone who saw it loved it and I'm always proud of being associated with it. The only reason it ran as long as it did was because critic David Nathan drummed up a lot of left-wing support and his column provided me with a splendid platform to keep the coalhouse door from closing too quickly.

However, *Coalhouse* came off early in 1969 and *Wives* followed soon afterwards. We took the production on tour and then opened the splendid little theatre at Weston-super-Mare. I played my part for four weeks, whilst Simon Merrick played Leslie Crowther's. Then Leslie Crowther came in for six weeks and Simon Merrick took over from me. I went on holiday. All very civilised, but I was preparing for our next Garrick production and for my lengthy and very happy association with Michael Pertwee which still continues to this day.

The play was *Birth of a Nation*, now rewritten and retitled *She's Done It Again*. It opened at the Garrick on the 15th October to the best notices I have ever had from *all* the papers. It turned out to be the shortest run I had ever had, too. There must be a moral in that somewhere ...

Act XV

"I have no doubt at all about what has been the principal theatrical event of the week. The Master is back again, and London can once more be gay. Michael Pertwee's farce, *She's Done It Again*, is the funniest in which the great Brian Rix has ever appeared. There are difficulties in the way of communicating a proper sense of its delicious and delirious qualities. But what looks feeble and hackneyed on the page glows with glorious life in the Garrick Theatre."

Harold Hobson *Sunday Times*

"It is easily the funniest show I have seen this year."

Irving Wardle *The Times*

"Almost continual laughter at the Garrick Theatre last night."

John Barber *Daily Telegraph*

"A furiously funny frolic." Weston Taylor *News of the World*

"The lark's on the wing, Brian Rix in his element and all's right with the world ..." Felix Barker *Evening News*

– and so on, and so on. Hardly a dissenting voice anywhere. You'd think with raves like that we'd have run almost indefinitely. We opened on 5th October 1969 and closed on 23rd May 1970 – the shortest run I have ever had. What went wrong? Difficult to say really. Possibly the play showed its slightly old-fashioned background: it was based on an earlier play *Nap Hand* by Guy Bolton and Vernon Sylvaine. Possibly the women in the audience didn't like to see pregnant women in a farce or men impersonating pregnant women. All I know is that we had a super cast: Simon Merrick, Anthony Sharp, Leo Franklyn, Derek Royle, Robert Dorning, Michael Kilgarriff, Margaret Nolan, Hazel Douglas, Anna Dawson and Elaine Baillie. All I know is that the audience *did* laugh almost continuously and that we had recouped our capital by Christmas. All I know is that we had lost it all again by May. In other words – I *don't* know!

My pride was hurt, of course, particularly as I had never failed to make money with any play in which I had appeared and I was determined to redress the position on this one. I did: by taking the play on tour for fourteen weeks, which is a long time to be away from home. I drove back every weekend, including one mammoth Sunday dash from Loch Lomond to Hornsea – driving my mother to her house – and straight on from there to Roehampton, a distance of six hundred miles, all done well before tea time. Towards the end of the tour I noticed my right hand was becoming claw-like and useless and I had to go on an extensive course of injections to restore full power and mobility. The tension of driving thousands of miles to get home caused me to grip the steering wheel too tightly and as a result I nearly lost the use of my right hand – a great help to an actor! However, my grip was still strong enough to hold a pen and, much to my pride and relief, I was able to sign the cheques returning all the original capital subscribed by my backers, plus a small amount of profit. It all goes to show that there is still a lot of activity in the provinces – if you provide the right attractions. I don't mean comedy and farce only. The provincial audience is very catholic in its taste and I firmly believe the future strength of the theatre lies more and more in the regions and farther and farther away from the West End. Convenience and price are two major factors; but civic pride enters into it, too.

Why, then, should the West End audience be indifferent to *She's Done It Again* and yet the provincial audience receive it with rapture and capacity houses? I'm not really certain, any more that I am *certain* about the constituents of a good farce. I've a pretty good idea, but there'll always be some clever devil to prove I'm wrong. Just before *She's Done It Again* opened, the *Sunday Times* published an article by Robert Lacey under the heading "Beauty Of The Well Timed Gag" which put forward some of my theories – and I still think they stand up. I was quoted as saying:

"My plays are total escapism and and are meant to be. But in order to escape, the farce has to be founded on some aspect of everyday life. The secret is to take something fairly recognisable to everyone – life in the army, tax problems, American methods in British business – establish it firmly as a context people will believe in, and then push the situation to its extreme."

Well *She's Done It Again* reacted positively to that bit of litmus paper. When first written as *Nap Hand* in 1939 it was conceived as a result of the birth of the Dionne Quintuplets. Our regeneration was sparked off (in thought only) by recent multiple births caused by the so-called fertility pill. Except no one in our play had really had quins. We merely assembled a bunch of babies together and said they had been produced by one mother. This deception was further complicated when it turned out that one of our five borrowed babies was black. I think you could say that was pushing the situation to its extreme.

I went on:

"Civil Servants are 1969 figures of fun. And policemen don't get laughs as they did before 'Z Cars'."

How then did we get at bureaucracy in *She's Done It Again?* Well, author Michael Pertwee had the brilliant idea of a tax inspector who was staying at the hotel – in which the play was set – fully aware that the proprietor was fiddling his tax but totally unable to use his knowledge for he was perpetually on the brink of disaster himself, as he'd brought a voluptuous dumb blonde with him for a dirty weekend and was terrified of being found out.

I qualified this further in my interview:

"I think there's a strong vein of cruelty in all humour. People laugh at other people's discomfiture, because they're damn glad not to be in that predicament themselves. That is why the adulterer, or the man (or woman) who wishes he were – and don't most people wish that at some time or another? – will fall about when he sees an adulterer getting caught on the stage. British audiences will laugh at homosexuality and deafness, even though neither is comic at all. But they won't laugh at blindness, though it could be argued that being deaf, being cut off from communication with other people, is the more tragic situation. It is a terribly difficult line to draw, but if a particular character rings true to the plot, and if you aren't just exploiting his weakness for cheap laughs, then he is a legitimate figure of fun."

She's Done It Again once more reinforced my theories. One of the great successes of the play was Derek Royle's brilliantly funny performance as Professor Hogg: old, absent-minded, deaf and dotty. The audiences found him the funniest part of the evening and the critics acclaimed him, without exception. Yet senility, in truth, is sad almost beyond endurance.

I continued:

"The whole point of good farce is that it teeters on the edge of tragedy. It always threatens ultimate catastrophe, and this is what sustains the dramatic tension. But by a slight twist it makes people roll about with laughter. It is tragedy with its trousers down."

The libidinous, nervous tax inspector; the Reverend Hubert Porter, terrified of being discovered in his contribution to the great quintuplet deception; the crooked hotel proprietor, nervous, too, because all his machinations could go wrong; the dotty old Professor Hogg delivering babies by grace and by God. All these characters, and more, in *She's Done It Again* were threatened by ultimate catastrophe.

I went on to praise the actors:

"All my company are actors first and comedians second. If an actor is to play a farce role well he must convince the audience completely. But he must also have a meticulous sense of timing."

I have already paid tribute to the cast of *She's Done It Again* but when we went on tour a new luminary on the farce scene came in for Simon Merrick. His name, Peter Bland. He had played the Indian servant in *Conduct Unbecoming* for a year and wanted to broaden his range, so he auditioned for our tour. As he walked on the stage I felt he had the necessary qualities. He only had to speak a couple of lines and I was sure. The complete farceur was there. Tall, smallish head, large nose, pop eyes and an inner turmoil, plus a ridiculous sense of the ridiculous. I have used Peter on every possible occasion since then and his notices bear out my immediate reaction to his first audition. That's how it goes. Right with Peter Bland. Wrong with Lynda Lee-Potter. But back to that vital question of timing:

"I really do savour the pleasure of timing a line perfectly. It's rather like changing gear properly or playing a good stroke at cricket, and of course there's the sexual element. It's like making love really well, it's a deeply physical feeling. But then laughter itself is deeply physical – it involves an extraordinary explosion of energy that can hit you like a sledgehammer in the theatre. A responsive audience whips you on so it hurts, like a horse under a jockey. And it's so physical, you know, that on a humid day you actually get fewer laughs – the closeness makes laughing physically more difficult."

I then went on to refer to Ronald Bryden's article in the *New Statesman*:

"A critic once said that my plays are vulgar in the truest sense of the word – of the people, and that is something of which I am very proud. I am proud that my audiences contain so many coach parties, and I resent the implication that coach parties are some sort of sub-human species. Thank God for them, because without them much of the West End theatre just could not keep going."

Well they came in droves to *She's Done It Again* when it first started and again when it went on tour. They just went missing in the vital months of February, March and April 1970, with dire results. But for all that the play *did* fulfil my next claim:

"If you can get an audience to roll about with laughter, and it's an open honest laughter, then you've achieved some sort of very precious liberation, a release from tension and violence. I think our farces achieve a rare suspension of time, people forget their everyday troubles and worries. And I think the effect of this release on people's everyday behaviour is healthy and positive."

Did *She's Done It Again* fulfil my claims? According to Harold Hobson, most emphatically, *yes*:

"Rarely have old bottles contained such joyous new wine as is to be found in *She's Done It Again*. Several times during the evening I was on the point of rising from my seat and demanding, 'Where's your Georgie Feydeau now?'."

I wish he had done. Michael Pertwee would have been very pleased. You don't hear many shouts of "Author, author" these days ...

But then Michael is an exceptional man. Most authors are pleasant chaps and Michael is one of the more pleasant. He is also one of the more efficient, for if a scene proves difficult in rehearsal or if an actor or director is unhappy, Michael has no delusions of grandeur and will retire forthwith to the nearest loo or cupboard or corner and produce a phenomenal number of rewritten pages in a phenomenally short time. If those are unacceptable, he will try again, and so on, until he runs out of loos, cupboards, or corners and all his powers of imagination, or straightforward cribbing, have been exhausted. To add to all these graces, he is married to a beautiful Indian lady, Maya, and anyone who doubts Michael's abilities as a writer could hardly fault his ability to pick a knock-out as a wife. You will gather I admire his co-efficiency in more ways than one.

During the tour of *She's Done It Again* I came up with an idea for a television series which stretched Michael considerably. As he'd made such a splendid conversion of one Vernon Sylvaine farce, why couldn't he do more? I put up the idea to Vernon's widow, Marie, who readily agreed. I put up the idea to the then Head of Television Outside Broadcast Events, Bryan Cowgill, who readily agreed. I put up the idea to Michael Pertwee himself, who readily agreed. What was this brilliant idea which brought forth such ready agreement? Quite simply, it was to take six Vernon Sylvaine farces, cut them down to fifty minutes each, tour them in pairs in the provinces as a double bill and then record them for television, making up a series of six programmes for eventual transmission.

The advantages were numerous. Costs would be kept down, for the BBC were to give me a fixed sum which could not be exceeded and the tour was to make up the rest of the money. The plays would tour for two weeks before being televised and thus they were run in and ready to go. We were actually able to record a hundred minutes of screen time in one evening – an incredible amount in drama terms. (One must pay tribute here to our director, Wally Douglas, and the Manchester Outside Broadcast crews, who came under the enthusiastic leadership of the Northern Head of Network Production, Derek Burrell-Davis, and who really worked themselves into the ground on those recording Sundays.) The actors gained enormously, both in confidence and cash, for they were really able to work on the plays by playing them in front of the public and they were also paid a lot more money: a fee for each television programme, and, of course, their normal theatrical salaries for the touring side. They had to work hard, but so did everyone else. Michael Pertwee did a splendid job, cutting down the numbers in the cast (Vernon wrote in the days when actors were cheap), cutting down the number of sets and modernising one or two plays which were beginning to show their age. Rhoda Gray designed a very clever aluminium frame into which slotted various double-clad sections of the sets (one side would be, say, a bookcase, the other side of the section might be a cocktail cabinet) and the whole lot was built cheaply and well by Stanley Moore. Gilbert Harrison organised the entire affair splendidly from the office point of view – with the close co-operation of the BBC Artists' Contract Manager, John Moore, and I've already mentioned our director/producer, Wally Douglas, who worked like a beaver. No – the advantages were, as I have said, numerous.

There was only one snag. The first day of the transmission of the series "Six of Rix" coincided with the first day of the 1972 power cuts. Half the country was blacked out during our weekly run – with the exception of the last programme – so a great many people were unable to see *A Spot of Bother*, *Aren't Men Beasts!*, *Madame Louise*, *One Wild Oat*, *Will Any Gentleman?* and *What The Dr Ordered* in their truncated, modernised form, even assuming they'd wanted to – and the whole idea rather fizzled out in a welter of empty grates, cold suppers, freezing rooms and heated arguments. Rather sad, because it *was* a good idea, it *was* comparatively inexpensive and four of the six plays *were* funny. Ah, the slings and arrows of outrageous fortune . . .

I suffered those slings and arrows in profusion on one incredible night during the "Six of Rix" tour. We finished at Bradford on the Saturday night and opened on the following Monday in Southsea. However, it was Whitsun, so my family had gone down to the small cottage we own in Brixham, Devon, and I drove down to join them for the Sunday. It was too far to drive in one night so I stopped off at the Raven Hotel, Droitwich, to break the journey. I arrived about 1.30 in the morning, and there, waiting for me in my room, in this rambling old hotel, was a cold supper and half a bottle of plonk. By 2 a.m. I had supped, bathed and was fast asleep. By 4 a.m. I was awake and bursting. I fumbled my way in the dark to my private bathroom, closed the door and opened my eyes. There I was, stark bollock naked in the well-lit corridor of the hotel and no key to let myself back into my room. In front of me was the trolley containing the remains of my supper. I hastily smoothed out the crumpled red paper napkin to cover the parts, hid the cheeks of my bum with a plate and walked down the lengthy corridor of the hotel feeling acute embarrassment and rather like a couple of eggs in aspic. To make matters worse I was two floors up and had to proceed, with due caution and stealth, down a vast staircase in search of the night porter. I eventually found him, vacuum-cleaning away, and such was his mirth, he nearly fell over the bloody machine, when he saw me. However, in due course he recovered and escorted me – still bursting and still caparisoned in plate and napkin – back to my room, where he let me in with his pass key. How I avoided being seen by anyone else I shall never know, for the hotel was full, but when I went to pay my bill in the morning it was clear that the night porter had carried the good news from Ghent. I was greeted at the reception desk by many a muffled snigger and many a smirk was hidden behind a cupped hand.

Funnily enough, a version of this scene was in my next West End play *Don't Just Lie There, Say Something!*, again by Michael Pertwee. Old Leo Franklyn was supposed to lock himself out of a room, looking for the loo, in much the same way as I had done. I've said it before and I'll say it again: farce has to be founded on some aspect of everyday life.

Incidentally, many of the titles of the plays I present come from me and *Don't Just Lie There, Say Something!* was no exception. We had been discussing titles, all one morning when we were on holiday in Spain, and this was the sum total of a great deal of artistic endeavour! My younger son, Jonathan (then aged eleven) came up with a beauty – *Not On the Table, Darling, You'll Take the Polish Off* – but we couldn't make it fit, somehow. But it's worth remembering for another time . . .

Don't Just Lie There tells the story of an unfaithful Minister of State for Home Affairs and his innocent Parliamentary Under-Secretary who is unwittingly dragged in to all the imbroglios caused by his senior's sexual shenanigans. (And if you knew the difficulty I had to find out the correct spelling of *that* word, you wouldn't believe it. It's not in my *Oxford English Dictionary*, the *Encyclopaedia Britannica* or Roget's *Thesaurus*. Even *The Times* didn't know, but eventually an old friend of ours – Tony

Lawrence, who happened to be staying with us – phoned the local library. They found the recalcitrant word in the American *Webster's Dictionary* – shades of Frank Sinatra's "Songs for Swingin' Lovers" and "Too Marvellous For Words".)

The cast was good and the girls were beautiful. Alfred Marks, Leo Franklyn, Peter Bland, Joanna Lumley, Deborah Grant, Nina Thomas, Donna Reading, Michael Cronin and I made up the happy throng. We were received, thank God, by almost total press silence, for the papers were on strike. I say thank God, as this was probably an apostolic blessing in disguise. The two or three notices we did receive were ghastly and only Jack Lambert in the *Sunday Times* was kind. However, the bad notices and/or the silence seemed to have no effect and we ploughed on to excellent business in spite of everything, including power cuts. We were lucky that we only had to use our generator on six occasions and the cuts came either before the first act or during the interval prior to the second act, so the audience could see us well illuminated for at least half the evening and roamin' in the gloamin' for the rest. It really worked rather neatly and the audiences on those six occasions were marvellous – reacting as they did during the war – all for one and one for all. It was quite inspiring, really. Brought tears to the old eyes.

Don't Just Lie There, Say Something! was just one of those plays. The very opposite of *She's Done It Again!* One, with its marvellous notices, faltered; the other, with everything against it, prospered.* When Alfred Marks left and was succeeded by Moray Watson business actually went *up*, and we were a year old! We had many cast changes amongst the girls too. Debbie Grant contracted glandular fever and Claire Neilson stepped in at short notice to help us out. Debbie returned. Then Joanna Lumley fell ill and left. Once again Claire stepped into the breach. Eventually all the girls left, except for Donna Reading, and in their places came Myra Frances, Heather Barbour and Alexandra Bastedo. Still no ill-effects. (Mind you, the girls were still beautiful.) And I forgot to mention that on the third night of the pre-

---

*On reflection, I wonder if Jilly Cooper's article in the *Sunday Times* about the play worked the miracle? Cherchez la femme!

London tour, Leo Franklyn was involved in a car crash, Michael Cronin took over at ten minutes' notice and the Brighton audience gave him a great reception at the end. Actually, Leo's accident might be one of the reasons we had such a poor first night. All our rehearsals to improve the play were curtailed by his absence and we had to open in London with the unedited version since there wasn't time to rehearse Leo in the new scenes and you can't put an apology in the programme. *After* the first night we started work and by the third week in London the play was trimmed, improved and going like a bomb. Ah yes, that's another hazard added to the West End these days, but in 1972 we were still only suffering black-outs *without* the bombs.

So, *Don't Just Lie There, Say Something!* was on and doing well at the Garrick. At home we were living under siege conditions. Apart from the rota electricity cuts, we were without heat or cooking facilities for other reasons: our kitchen was being rebuilt by the indefatigable Jim Stratford. This face-lift took nearly six months, and it added considerably to the cold and misery of that winter for if we *did* achieve any heat in the house it rapidly rushed out of the nearest hole in the wall. But I became a dab hand at "do it yourself" in a minor way: successfully changing the colour of all the kitchen furniture. I was so carried away by my own prowess that when Elspet had a slight spat with the gateposts I attempted my "do it yourself" methods on her car. The result was an object lesson in "*don't* do it yourself" and the subsequent bill from the coach-builders was well over a hundred pounds. I had turned a minor scratch into a major respray. My daughter, Louisa, did even better with that gatepost a few weeks later, when she was a learner driver. I had taken her round the block in Elspet's car and she was doing splendidly. Splendidly, that is, until she attempted to get into our drive. As she approached the gate her foot slipped off the brake on to the accelerator and with no effort at all, there was the entire brick and concrete gatepost lying on the crumpled bonnet of the Renault. That bill came to one hundred pounds for the gatepost and two hundred pounds for the car. Even my little spray-gun couldn't inflict that amount of damage. I should add that, undaunted and undeterred, Louisa passed her driving test three weeks after the accident – with no trouble at all. I'm glad the examiner couldn't see the rubble round our drive.

Apart from rushing about with a spray-gun, playing at the Garrick Theatre every night and failing as a driving instructor, I was trying to promote the idea of the two leading characters in *Don't Just Lie There* becoming the basis of a television series. Michael Pertwee eventually agreed to write the series and we found a customer in Patrick Dromgoole of HTV. The end product came out (again during power cuts!) as *Men of Affairs* with Warren Mitchell as the Minister. It was a funny series, but we made the simple error of showing the critics a private viewing of two of the simplest episodes so the press was *not* kind. Added to that was the complication of HTV being a small boy taking on the big 'uns, with a networked series at peak viewing time. The closing down of television at half past ten in the evening gave many of the stations a chance to reschedule and *Men of Affairs* lost its prime spot. However, on HTV it soldiered on at 8.30 and was never out of the "Top Ten".

As I say, it was a funny series but, looking back, I would think it had one main fault. Practically every story had the Minister chasing the girls. I know this was the basis of the whole idea – but I'm afraid it gave the series a predictability which seems to be the bane of most Sit. Coms. on television. As Ministers we were able to move around the world into all manner of situations – but our feet remained firmly rooted in our original territory, in spite of some magnificent sets. Mind you, we must all take some blame for this, if there *is* any blame, that is! It certainly can't be laid at Michael Pertwee's door, for he provided a selection of story lines from which, almost invariably, we seemed to choose the ones involving the Minister's sexual capers. By we, I mean our television director, Derek Clark – a lovely man – our producer, Wally Douglas, Warren and myself.

A final problem came towards the end of the series. Some minor dispute at the studios meant a recording had to be postponed. On this occasion Warren earned his colours and no mistake. The audience were already seated and in need of entertainment. Warren obliged. He rushed off into Make-up and emerged some short time later as Alf Garnett and proceeded to regale the audience with his cabaret act for nearly an hour. Ay, there's the rub. *Till Death* still appears on television; *Men of Affairs* does not. But where our series did have a consistent run – the West Country, Wales and Australia – it *was* a smash.

Don't Just Lie There, Say Something! came off, really, in error. After eighteen months, business had dropped a little and, as I was expecting to make the film of the play, continue the television series and had been offered my first pantomime lead, it seemed I could take a break from nightly performances at the theatre and have myself a sabbatical. The play came off when it was really still full of life and we went on a short tour which never played to less than capacity and which nearly had me in an early grave. The girls were part of the trouble. I had taken them out on tour using a clause in the old West End contract which allowed you to extend the London run up to eight weeks in the provinces. Unhappily, because it did ensure you *could* have a bumper tour if you wished, this clause has now disappeared. *I* wished, but the girls didn't, and if girls want to be difficult – oh, bloody hell!

Apart from their keening, I was having problems with the film. In October 1972 a note had appeared at the Garrick, on Pinewood Studios notepaper, written by a veteran film producer, Edward Dryhurst, expressing his interest in making the film of the play. Were we interested? Of course we – Michael and I – were. It seemed to be cut and dried. Eddie seemed to have Rank backing for the picture, which was to be made at Pinewood. It was all an illusion, really. Eddie only hoped to have Rank backing and when it came to the crunch we found we had taken the shadow for the substance. Michael had written the film script and had received no payment. We had "sold" the film rights, without any contract. I had taken the play off and was out on tour without any job to follow. HTV had invested money for the script, but that had largely gone on other pre-production expenses. We were, to put it mildly, up the creek without a paddle.

I took the law into my own hands. Michael and I were still the owners of the film rights and Michael was the owner of his film script. We found a film producer ready to help us out – Andrew Mitchell – and he and our director, Bob Kellett, worked miracles in the shortest possible time. Frank Poole, and the Rank Board agreed to finance the film for £150,000 which, in these days, is peanuts but this meant Pinewood Studios were out and the film would have to be made on location. Bob Kellett's offices and basement in Breams Buildings, off Chancery Lane, were pressed into service and ninety per cent of the film was shot in temperatures approaching a hundred degrees Fahrenheit. The cast shared a communal dressing room which was also the production office. It was chaos, but by cool management on the part of Andrew Mitchell and even cooler direction by Bob Kellett, a very passable film was made for £138,000. Whether it will ever be seen or not is another matter. A lot of inexpensive films never see the light of day (or the dark of the cinema) nowadays, but it was a big success in South Africa – where it could only be viewed by white audiences, presumably because it showed white politicians in bed together with a girl (white) between them – and perhaps it may still be a big success elsewhere. Anyway, I'm keeping my fingers crossed. Incidentally, the film had Leslie Phillips as the Minister, and as Terry-Thomas played the part in Australia, Michael Pertwee could claim a splendid quintet of actors in that part: Alfred Marks, Moray Watson, Warren Mitchell, Leslie Phillips, and T.T. What you might call a Nap Hand ... *or* a Running Flush ...

Act XVI

1973 was a *very* good year – for much of the time. After the little female problems of the *Don't Just Lie There* tour (all right, I *know* I sound like a male chauvinistic pig), the difficulties under which we made the film seemed but naught in contrast and it was marvellous to be actually paid by someone else for doing a job, and also to let that someone else worry about the day-to-day management of the production. This euphoria went on for several months. Immediately after the film I went into seven more episodes of *Men of Affairs*, then had five weeks' holiday in Spain (when the first five chapters of this book were written) ending with a forest fire which nearly consumed our house – aircraft had to bomb the flames to put them out – plus a glorious sightseeing trip around Granada, the Sierra Nevada and Ronda before our return to England, or rather, Scotland, for we raced up to Ardnamurchan to see that most lovely part of north-west Britain. Then came six more televisions, and all this as a *paid actor* away from the theatre. Such a thing had never happened to me before. It enabled me to have a few days' holiday with Louisa when she left Art College before going on to the Yvonne Arnaud Theatre at Guildford as an Assistant Stage Manager. It enabled me to see Jamie progress from the Colts XI to the 1st XI in cricket at St Paul's. It enabled me to see Jonty skippering his prep school XI at Tower House in his last season before going on to St Paul's. Oh, it was *lovely*.

It was lovely, too, to have my evenings at home and enjoy the social life which I had missed during the whole of my marriage.

I don't know how Elspet stood this deprivation! Even the occasional spats over the constant rewriting of the television series faded into insignificance with the first gin and tonic before dinner and I could happily have continued in that vein for many months longer. However, television series *do* come to an end. Films *are* in short supply. So it was back to the theatre again in December with my first leading role in a pantomime. Before that, though, there was one final fling with a four-day trip to Moscow. Marvellous value for money, Thomson mini-holidays: Michael and Maya Pertwee, plus Elspet and me, had a ball. We were allowed to see over the Bolshoi Theatre, because I had a letter from the Russian Embassy explaining, in Russian, that I was an actor of "some repute" (at least, I think that's what it said!) and this opened all the necessary doors and gave us a chance to see that lovely theatre when quite empty. We also saw the Bolshoi Ballet operating in the Hall of Congress, which is a vast building inside the Kremlin walls and which houses six thousand people in one audience. My overall impression was of a poorish *corps de ballet* (I think we saw the 3rd XI) operating inside a three-storied aircraft hangar, with a huge NAAFI on the top floor (approached by escalator) shovelling all manner of food and drink into the audience during the inordinately long intervals.

We were amazed to find in Moscow that the pound actually meant something. If you wanted to visit a restaurant, Intourist would only accept pounds, not roubles. This, I suppose, is because there is no official exchange and the Russians are trying to build up their stock of convertible currency. Fascinating, though, to find your Diner's Club card operating just as effectively in a Moscow restaurant as in one in the Fulham Road.

Then it was farewell to Borsch, Blinis with Caviar, Vodka and Russian champagne, and hail to the Earl Haig rehearsal room at Parson's Green. Martin Williams, the efficient, pleasant and youthful General Manager of the New Theatre, Cardiff had decided upon Robinson Crusoe for my pantomime debut. The decision was actually made for him because he has a hiring agreement with Derek Salberg at the Alexandra, Birmingham, and as the pantomime costumes and sets become available – so they go to Cardiff. Robinson Crusoe suited me fine though. As you may remember it starts off in the land of Green Ginger in Hull. This *is* the name of a street and, as my father had his first office there, you could say I was the most perfectly cast actor *never* to play Robinson Crusoe. I played his stupid brother, Billy.

Before signing my agreement it was decided that a brand-new book would be written by Michael Pertwee. The idea was to present the pantomime in broad farce form. We were all confident it would work splendidly and rehearsals, amiably conducted by Alexander Doré, reinforced this conviction. Everyone chuckled away and Peter Bland and I had visions of our cross-talk act going down in panto legend. We were brought down to earth with a bang on that first never-to-be-forgotten matinée on the Saturday before Christmas. The noise was indescribable. Hundreds of shrill Welsh voices raised, not in song, but in childish chatter. Hundreds of shrill Welsh voices were mobile too. They thundered round the auditorium, demanding to be taken to the toilet, demanding ice creams, sweets and chocolates. Demanding everything, in fact, except words. When that first never-to-be-forgotten matinée was over, so was our enthusiasm for dialogue. It was cut, cut, cut and get to the funny business. What funny business? In truth, not a great deal. We had neglected the one fundamental fact about pantomime: children want their comics to be seen, not heard. So it was back to the drawing board with a vengeance and rehearsals were the order of the day until we finally achieved some sort of fun out of the chaos. Dickie Henderson came to see us one matinée (he was being hugely entertaining at the Double Diamond Club in Caerphilly) and afterwards pronounced judgment.

"Next time you do a pantomime, Brian," he said, "let some other silly sod speak the plot. You get yourself four cast-iron knockabout scenes and make sure you come on right at the end, before the walk down, in the best scene of all, otherwise you'll hand the panto to the speciality acts who are just doing their everyday thing."

How right he was and if ever I do a panto again I shall immediately demand a radio mike and a list of tried and tested funny scenes which have worked for the last hundred years.

The Cardiff season was, in truth, rather like being in a well-paid prison. Not the fault of the management or the audiences; just the weary repetition of the day-to-day routine. I stayed at the Angel Hotel where I had a very pleasant suite and was able to get on, in the mornings, with this book. Then it was a quick lunch and into the theatre for the matinée. A short tea-break in between and then off again for the evening show. Fine whilst the houses were full but not so good when the miners' strike, the three-day week, the power cuts and the forty per cent reduction in lighting and heating hit us. I froze in my hotel room, then repaired to a freezing steak-bar warmed only by the personality of Dot, its manageress. Then on to my cell-like dressing room, which was also freezing, before facing a freezing audience who had all come from freezing homes. The only light relief (if I may coin a phrase) was provided on Election night when Peter Bland and Michael Cronin (he was a super Davy Jones) joined me in a riotous piss-up watching the results come in on the newly liberated telly (up to the election period it went off, by law, at 10.30 p.m. all to save a few lumps of coal or to prove that self-flagellation can *still* be fun . . .).

Anyway, on 2nd March 1974 it was all over. By 4th March Elspet and I were winging our way to the Coral Reef Hotel in Barbados in the company of Leslie and Jean Crowther. "Lucky devils" you may think, but we were going out with a solemn duty in mind: to support our ailing Test team in the Third Test at Bridgetown. It was marvellous. Leslie swears it's the best holiday ever and I think he's right. Every day during the five days of the Test, small groups of enthusiasts, the four of us amongst them, left our hotels and proceeded by bumpy bus to the ground, there to cheer on the English team. We had a job on the Saturday: with twenty thousand people crammed into a ground holding fourteen thousand – a handful of English, even with loud voices like Leslie's and mine – found it difficult to be heard above the din. If I thought that first never-to-be-forgotten Cardiff panto-mime matinée was noisy I was now being disabused.

We had another noisy reception of a more pleasant kind when Leslie and I did a cabaret at our hotel for the team and their supporters. Several hundred squeezed into a space normally holding less than one hundred, but they were a marvellous audi-ence and we both found difficulty in coming off! Next day we marched up and down the beach, proudly receiving plaudits from all and sundry and as our team went on to achieve a noble draw we felt we must have raised morale somehow. Our morale was considerably lifted too, for our guide and mentor round Barbados was the splendid Wesley Hall, once the terror of the English batsmen, now a respected Senator and the nicest fast bowler I have ever met. Going round the island with him was royal progress, indeed. We basked in his reflected glory. We basked in the sun, too.

Then – it was back to work and the inevitable rehearsal room at Parson's Green. This time, it was more familiar ground – for we were preparing Michael Pertwee's new farce – *A Bit Between the Teeth* – based on an idea by Brian Rix. How did I get into the act? Well, for years I had been an editor for, collaborator with, and intermediary between a playwright and his scripts. This time, I was a little more positive, by striking the first spark which kindled the flame. Years before, a friend of mine was involved in an incident which must haunt the dreams of all car-driving adulterers. He came out of his girlfriend's flat to find his car had been stolen. The police *had* to be called. My friend had no trouble explaining his predicament to them for, after all (nudge, nudge – wink wink), we are all men of the world – but he had hell's own delight explaining to his suspicious missus exactly why he'd been parked in North London when he was supposed to be on business in Birmingham. This struck me as being a good basis for yet another twist of the farcical adulterer's tale, and Michael Pertwee and I discussed it at length. We came up with a load of soggy tape-recorded notes – and little else. Then at Christmas 1973 I was smitten by flu, which meant nursing my temperature in bed by day and playing, albeit groggily, at the Garrick Theatre by night. During this enforced period of rest, I listened to our taped discussion about the new play. Worried, I rang up Michael and we both agreed that we were way off the mark. "How would it be if . . .?" was the gist of our conversation and Michael idly remembered a scene from his play *In the Bag*. This sparked off further thoughts, feeding a feverish but fruitful dream, which was my lot after this phone call. I rang Michael back. He was now all systems go, and on Monday 1st January 1973 we met at my house and discussed all the various permutations. Michael went away, satisfied that he had enough, at least, to start a synopsis. He put typewriter to paper on the 2nd January and by teatime on Sunday 7th January the play was written. It has remained substantially the same to this day. The only problem was the title. At the beginning of the play my character, Fogg, a jeweller, was burnishing stones and cutting them with a dentist-type brace and bit. I suggested the title *A Bit Between the Teeth*. The rather boring opening scene has disappeared. The title has remained – much to many people's bewilderment . . . Now you know.

For a long time I had been wanting to start a play off at Guildford and this, too, had been the wish of my old friend Laurie Lister, then Director of the Yvonne Arnaud Theatre. Now this wish became reality and *A Bit Between the Teeth* was successfully launched at this delightful theatre on 10th April 1974. We were immediately offered seven London theatres for the play's West End home but, such is my suspicion of a London summer, I had already made arrangements to take the play to South Africa, and would not contemplate bringing it into London until September. Actually, I had set my heart on 12th September which was the beginning of my twenty-fifth year presenting and acting in farce in the West End. To say in April that you want to open a play in London in September is not easy – for the theatre scene is constantly changing – but one manager, Larry Parnes, who ran the Cambridge Theatre, was prepared to settle on that future date and take a gamble. It would be pleasant to record his unqualified success, but at this present time it is not possible so to do. I'll explain why in a minute.

So there we were. A big success at Guildford. A big success on a short four-week provincial tour and then a big success in South Africa. How did I come to be taking a play there, against all my natural instincts? Quite simply, I was too late to get a summer season booked in England; touring is useless in mid-summer; Australia was out – for their Equity will only accept the "stars" of a show – so when South African impresario, Pieter Toerien, suggested a tour of his country, it seemed the logical thing.

Pieter is naturally persuasive, a super bloke to work for and with, as well as being a member of the Progressive Party. We only agreed to go to South Africa if we could play to "mixed" audiences. This was impossible, but Pieter arranged the next best thing: that we would play to various racial groups in their own theatres. You *think* this is the next best thing until you get there. We discovered, in Cape Town, that many whites will not visit the Nico Malan, because it is "Whites Only" – but was built with rate-payers' money paid by both whites and coloureds – and therefore these dissenters, quite rightly, feel this segregation is neither fair nor just. You go across Cape Town to play at the Joseph Stone Auditorium in Athlone. This is a theatre for the non-white population, but many non-whites keep away because they feel, quite rightly too, that they should be able to go to the Nico Malan as they've helped pay for it. It's a ridiculous situation that would be Gilbertian were it not so sad. The only compensation for us was that we played to capacity houses and had the satisfaction of seeing a number of charities benefit from our appearances at the Joseph Stone. The cast played for out-of-pocket expenses only, Pieter Toerien put on the play for nothing, Michael Pertwee and our director, Wally Douglas, accepted no royalties and the various causes did well. The main cause, though, of non-segregated audiences benefited not at all . . .*

However, we pressed on and did what we could to present a "liberal" viewpoint to any who were prepared to listen. Actually practically everyone we met *was* prepared to listen and it would be presumptuous to claim that we really influenced them in any way. Many in South Africa are already sailing before the

* It has now. The Nico Malan went multi-racial in March 1975.

winds of change and we can claim no credit for those enlight-
ened voyagers. They were already embarked when we got there.

By "we" I mean Elspet, who was with me as a "camp follow-
er", and the super little cast, Jimmy Logan, Peter Bland, Donna
Reading and Vivienne Johnson. I was received with great courtesy
by many people, including the Minister for Sport, Dr Piet Koornhof, and I am happy to report that, before we left Africa, Pieter
Toerien was able to announce the formation of a "non racial"
club at the Intimate Theatre, Johannesburg, which he runs with
his ebullient partner, Shirley Firth. This club is open to all races
and enables club members to see any Intimate Theatre production
at reduced prices as members of *one* audience on club nights.
May it prosper and be the harbinger of good things to come.

South Africa itself – apartheid apart? That's a bit like the old
gag – "but apart from that, Mrs Lincoln, did you enjoy the play?".
Well it's a beautiful country. We saw Cape Town and Table
Mountain in all its glory; drove across the Garden Route to Port
Elizabeth and East London. Flew to Johannesburg for our season
at the Civic Theatre which is run by the amiable Michal Grob-
belaar, another manager aware of the need for non-segregated
audiences.* Jo'burg was rather like being in the middle of Shaftes-
bury Avenue. Muriel Pavlow was there. Robert Flemyng, Robert
Beatty too. Then there was Andrew Cruickshank, Slim and
Christine Ramsden, not to mention hosts of lesser-known actors
and actresses. You could have gone from one party to the next,
but I sat on the balcony writing my book and Elspet coped with
Jonty who had flown out to join us for the holidays. As we left
Johannesburg Jamie flew out, too, and we all went for a fortnight's
working holiday (working for me, that is) at the Oyster Box
Hotel, just outside Durban.

There, Elspet and I celebrated our Silver Wedding Anniversary
on 14th August 1974. It was quite a party. The day dawned
bright and sunny and we received an early phone call from Louisa,
who had opted to stay working at Guildford until she went to
drama school. She needed the money. Then we helped prepare

* This too has nearly come to pass. The Civic Theatre now allows in audiences
of different races – as yet on different nights.

a barbecue in a cottage by the sea and eventually all the cast, plus sundry guests, including Peter Bland's family, arrived. We were presented with splendid gifts organised, I suspect, by Jimmy Logan, and a roistering time was had by all. How we made the show that night I'll never know, particularly as we started with those most lethal concoctions, champagne cocktails. Make it we did, but I imagine we looked distinctly sleepy.

So our eleven-week tour of South Africa finished. We had played to record business and had, in a minor way, made friends and influenced people. Not as much as the British Lions, though, who were amongst our audience in East London and whose victories, I'm sure, have influenced South African political thinking almost as much as Mozambique. Only one thing was left to do and that was a four-day trip to the Kruger Park. Now that is *fantastic*. To bed by candlelight (in the Northern part anyway) by 8 p.m. Up at first light and then slowly cruising along the roads to see all those magnificent animals. We saw our first elephant within two hours and we were chased by one of those ten ton monsters as we startled him turning a corner. My foot went hard on the floor and the boys managed some magnificent photos out of the rear window. I have never been so frightened in all my life!

Yes, South Africa is a beautiful country if you can close your eyes to Soweto or those signs "Whites Only". I can't . . .

So, it was back to England and one week in Brighton before opening at the Cambridge Theatre. Our first night went very well, really, but our press was as usual mixed, with the best notices being reserved for the Sundays. John Barber of the *Daily Telegraph* was probably the kindest of the dailies, for he found it all highly diverting:

First Night   *Telegraph* 13 September 1974
SUPERB COMEDIANS IN
RIOT OF CONFUSION
By John Barber

"In *A Bit Between the Teeth* at the Cambridge, Michael Pertwee has reduced bedroom farce to its barest essentials – a cast of

235

five, a mountain of misunderstanding, and a London flat with nine exits and entrances. But come in a bit closer.

Of the five characters, two are superbly resourceful comedians – Brian Rix, the bespectacled knight of the woeful countenance himself, and Jimmy Logan, who can wag his jaw like an irate rolling-pin.

Add two shapely undressed girls, and the obligatory copper, and you have the indispensable basics for updated bed-to-bedlam Feydeau.

"But if the ingredients are few, they have been stirred with alarming ingenuity, and the result is very funny indeed. The show is a riot of comic confusion, with never a dirty joke or leering innuendo. And the director, Wallace Douglas, whips it along at a stunning pace.

The secret of its success is that the plot is built on panic. Mr Rix, a prim-and-proper jeweller with a stammer, discovers to his horror that his married philandering partner has used his car, and his name, on a date with a girl. But the vehicle disappears, with girl with it.

"So the police descend on Mr Rix – who just happens to be hiding his partner's pretty but rain-soaked wife, who just happens to have taken off her clothes to dry.

I cannot explain how husband and wife are kept apart, nor the girl in the pantry, the cat in the fridge, the tin of exploding beans, nor lines like: "What was the Countess de Le Touquet doing with Diane's handbag in the back of the stolen car?" But I promise you, they made a kind of insane sense, granted Mr Rix's one fatal lie to the law.

"As never before he is struck scarlet with shock, paralytic with fright, rigid with moral disapproval. Mr Logan bullies him superbly, a man to bluff you matily into digging your own grave.

Donna Reading and Vivienne Johnson are delectable, and Peter Bland's policeman is a triumph of cunning bewilderment. I admit the fun slackens, especially towards the end. But I laughed and laughed."

I said earlier it would be pleasant to record Larry Parnes' unqualified success in waiting for us at the Cambridge. Our business started off splendidly and in no time at all we had nearly half our money back. We expected a small recession just before Christmas but the West End generally was totally unprepared for the bottom falling out of the business in such a startling way as it did the week ending 14th December 1974. What caused this dramatic slide? Well, in the first instance the news media had been grinding away for months about the desperate financial situation facing the country. People were beginning to count their pennies – especially with Christmas coming up – and venturing into West End theatres was an expensive business, particularly if you had the added expense of parking and restaurants. These problems might have been overcome if the IRA had decided not to put the boot in, and the bombs around our Stage Doors did not exactly make welcoming sounds. Indeed there are prophets of doom who predict at least twenty "dark" London theatres for much of next year. Meanwhile we all sit around and wonder if those bloody bombs *will* start again, and if we *are* all going broke.

So what does the future hold for me? Well, Elspet and I are still together and *that's* a blessing. Louisa is at the London Academy of Music and Dramatic Art, already a full member of Equity and determined to be an actress. Foolish, headstrong girl! Jamie is about to take his "A" Levels and wants to go on to University and read English and Drama. That sounds like another good man gone wrong. The only sensible one, at the moment, is young Jonty who, at fourteen, is more interested in his incipient moustache and golf than the theatre. But, alas, there is time yet for a change of heart. What about me personally? Eventually, I suppose, I shall tour *A Bit Between the Teeth* and I am talking to Louis Michaels of Triumph Productions about a summer season with the play at Bournemouth.* I am talking to Duncan Weldon and Paul Elliott (also of Triumph) about taking the

* I am now touring *Bit* with great success *and* going to Bournemouth!

237

play to Canada and Australia. Then again, I am mixed up with them regarding the presentation of a new Terry Scott farce and the Haymarket production of *The Case in Question* with Sir John Clements. Conversations have just started with Michael Grade regarding a television series for London Weekend and with Patrick Dromgoole of HTV. Pieter Toerien wants me to go back to South Africa. I have taken an option (with Pieter) on a super play, *Harold and Maude*, which *might* be produced by the Royal Shakespeare Company.* Again it might not. An actor's life is all ifs and buts. You can settle for a few months' ahead – sometimes a couple of years – but there's always that area of uncertainty which surrounds every facet of our profession. Why do we do it? I shall never know. At best it offers riches beyond the dreams of avarice. At worst, it offers grinding poverty beyond the nightmares of beggars.

Maybe we are performers because of a white-hot burning desire to create works of art. Maybe we are children at heart, who like dressing up. Maybe we just like the money and the work when it's there and the enforced idleness when it's not. Maybe we're all egocentrics who want to see our names in lights.

Perhaps the only permanent memorial I shall leave is that, as a result of my importunity, four theatres – the Whitehall, the Garrick, the Cambridge and the Winter Gardens, Morecambe – now boast shower baths. How else could I present good *clean* fun?

Before you put down this book, turn off the bedside lamp and go to sleep let me tell you, appropriately enough, a fairy tale:

Once upon a time there was a famous theatrical couple who, when our story begins, were making their respective ways up the ladder of success and were idyllically married. One day the wife rushed into her husband's dressing room just as he was preparing for the evening performance.

---

* Recently I rang up the Aldwych Theatre and asked for the Manager.
"Oh," said the switchboard operator, "you've just missed him. He left five minutes ago for Stratford. But," she added, "you'll get him there, I should think, in half an hour."
"Do you know, love, where Stratford-on-Avon is?"
"No, haven't an idea."
So I gave her a geography lesson.

"Oh, darling," she said, "I have just come from the press show of your new film. Darling, it was fantastic! The critics actually stood at the end and *cheered*! No one has ever seen anything like it *before*. Imagine, darling – the critics *cheering*! Oh, it was magnificent, darling. The most exciting moment of my life. Oh, how I wished you'd been there, for it was *your* performance they were cheering, my darling. *Your* performance. The film itself was good, too, but you were *miraculous*! The artistic merit and truth behind the author's words were there for all to see, of course. The costumes were magnificent. The direction – faultless. The lighting and make-up sans pareil. There was one tiny moment when you appeared to have no lips – but that was nothing. Oh, my darling, you are going to be a great star, probably the greatest star in all the theatrical firmament and if my being with you should in any way impede your meteoric rise, then I must leave you, my darling, for it would be wrong of me to stand in the way of one who is destined to straddle the world like a Colossus, hear the thunder of applause from countless international audiences, be showered with blandishments from all the critics and receive the just financial rewards for one who is truly great. So choose, my darling, and if it be your wish that you make your way like some mythical deity – lonely but unencumbered – then you have only to say the word and I will go through that door never to impose myself on your dear life again."

Came the reply, "Yes, yes, yes. What do you mean, no lips?"

And that, I think, says it all . . .

Except for one nagging question. Have I convinced you that I *do* know my farce from my elbow?

Mr Charles Lewsen of *The Times* thinks not:

"It is time to say that, for all his twenty-five years at the trade, Mr Rix does not understand farce."

I'm glad to say that Mr J. C. Trewin, perhaps a more experienced critic, flew to my defence:

"Now in his twenty-fifth year as a farceur Brian Rix would have been surprised at a recent accusation that he has never understood farce, a subject in which he could take a doctorate with ease."

So there we have two disparate views. I can only leave the members of the audience, or the reader of this book, to judge who is right.

CURTAIN DOWN

ndex

becassis, George, 179
ccolade, 97
ce of Clubs, 97
dam, Ronald, 177, 190
delphi Theatre, 122, 151, 181
lbery, Donald, 193, 198
ldwych Theatre, 153, 154, 187
lexandra Theatre, Birmingham, 166-7, 228
llenby, Peter, 169
llie (author's nannie), 2, 5, 6
mpleforth College, 15
nd The Same To You, 157
nderson, Gene, 102, 103
nderson, Gerald, 168
nderson, Rona, 212
ndrews, Eamonn, 182, 189
nne, Princess, 187
nthony and Anna, 40
ny Other Business, 55
quila Airways, 112-14
ren't Men Beasts!, 220
rguelles, Dr Ramos, 205, 206
rnold, Tom, 156
"Around the Shows", 100
rts Council, 210
rts Theatre, Cambridge, 25
skern Main Colliery, 45-7
tkinson, Alex, 122
ttenborough, Richard, 124
ttwood, Sydney, 194
uer, Mischa, 102
ustralia, 127, 202, 225, 226
yckbourn, Alan, 142

Ayrton, Randle, 17
Ayub Khan, President, 187

Babes In The Wood, 72
Baillie, Elaine, 214
Bain, Romany, 156, 170
Baird, Anthony, 103, 127
Baker's Daughter, The, 86-7
Bang, Bang, Beirut, 209
Bannerman, Kay, 209
Banzie, Brenda de, 124
Barbdaos, 230-1
Barber, John, 213, 235
Barbour, Heather, 222
Barker, Felix, 149, 213
Barker, Vere, 77, 78
Barlow, H. J., 80, 81
Baroda, Maharajah of, 163-4
Barrington, Jonah, 117-18
Barry, Michael, 139, 171, 184
Bastedo, Alexandra, 222
Bastien (author's labrador), 73, 83, 84-5, 96, 103, 107, 176, 190
Baxter, Beverley, 92
Baxter, Stanley, 202
BBC, 97, 100-1, 116-18, 123, 138, 139, 141-6, 170, 171, 173, 181, 182, 183, 193, 196, 205, 219-20
Beatty, Robert, 234
Bedford, Duke of, 182
Bennett, Jill, 152
Bentley, Charlie, 69
Bentley, Dick, 157

Berrison, Lynda, see Lee Potter, Lynda
Between the Balance Sheets, 193
Bickmore, Dr G. H., 7-8
Bickmore, Gwen, 7
Big Bad Mouse, 35
Bigman, Sidney, 206
Bird, Richard (Dickie), 142, 143-4
Birmingham, 80, 166-7
Birth of a Nation, see She's Done It Again
Bit Between The Teeth, A, 57, 231, 232, 235-7
Bitter Rice, 85, 86
Blanche, Marie, 34, 35, 36, 39
Bland, Peter, 217, 222, 229, 230, 234, 236
Blatch, Purple and Cecilia, 206
Blind Goddess, The, 72
Bloom, Leslie, 76, 77
Blythe, Michael, 25
Bolton, Guy 214
Bond, Christopher, 193
Boobs in the Wood, 171, 183, 184
Boorne, Bill, 92, 187
Boorne, Peg, 92
Bootham School, 11-12, 13-14
Boulting Brothers, 172, 173
Box, Sydney, 56, 171-2, 178, 181
Boyle, Catherine, 151
Brian Rix Enterprises Ltd, 196
Brides of March, 185

Bridlington, 64–6 67, 86
Bridlington Chronicle, 72
Brighton, 235
British Lion, 172, 173, 181
Bromly, Alan, 119, 120
Brooke, Harold, 209
Brooker, Mr and Mrs, 162–3
Brown, Ivor, 93–4
Browne, Angela, 177, 190
Brownlow, Alexander, 26
Bryan, Dora, 165, 173, 181
Bryden, Ronald, 149, 197, 217
Buckingham Palace, 200–1
Burrell-Davis, Derek, 219
Bute, Dowager Marchioness of, 207
Butler, Janet, 74
Butler, R. A., 175
By Candle Light, 73
Byron Productions, 97

Cadbury, Peter, 172
Calderwood, Diana, 129, 145
Cambridge Theatre, 25, 232, 235, 238
Cameron, Charles, 129, 168
Cameron, Earl, 67
Campion, Gerald, 55–6, 126
Cannell, Robert, 141, 145
Cannon, Dennis, 67
Captain Carvallo, 67, 97
Cardiff, 23–4, 166, 228–30
Cargill, Patrick, 165, 177, 190
Carl Barriteau Band, 42
Carmichael, Arthur, 19
Carmichael, Ian, 19, 196
Carmichael, R.P., 19
Carousel, 97
Carstairs, John Paddy, 126
Carry On films, 151
Cary, Falkland, 35, 114
Casey, Emily, 103
Cavalliere, 192
Chapman, Mrs Constance, 77
Chapman, John, 81, 98, 103, 121, 125, 128, 129, 130, 131, 147, 167, 178, 181, 185, 189, 193, 198
Charles, Prince, 187
Chase Me, Comrade!, 196, 197–8, 202, 208–9, 210
Chivers, Alan, 119, 120, 139, 142–3

Christie, Agatha, 124
Chu Chin Chow, 27
Civic Theatre, Johannesburg, 234
Clark, Derek, 224
Clark, Wynne, 129
Clayton, Jack 147
Cleaver, John, 74
Close the Coalhouse Door (by Alan Plater, based on stories by Sid Chaplin), 46, 212
Cocktail Party, The, 96
Coliseum Theatre, Harrow, 25, 127
College of Dramatic Art, Stratford, 17
Collins, Colin, 32, 59, 60–1
Come Prancing, 193
Come Spy With Me, 208
Comedy Theatre, 80, 81, 91, 171
Conduct Unbecoming, 217
Connies, 77
Conyers, Darcy, 121, 178, 180, 193
Cook, Jean, 191
Cooney, Ray, 149, 168, 171, 180 181, 183, 192, 193, 196, 209
Cooper, Alice, 117, 197
Cooper, Felice, 197, 208
Cooper, Jilly, 222
Cooper, Louis, 81, 197
Cooper, Tommy, 157, 165
Cosford, 49–50
Costa Brava, 148
Cottingham, 3–4
Counsell, John, 124, 125, 147–8
Courtneidge, Dame Cicely, 212
Cowan, Theo, 136
Cowdrey, Colin, 189, 196
Cowgill, Bryan, 219
Crawford, Anne, 151
Cronin, Michael, 222, 230
Cross, Cecil (Hugh), 26, 27
Crowther, Jean, 230–1
Crowther, Leslie, 108, 165, 210, 212, 230–1
Croydon, 28, 50
Cruickshank, Andrew, 234
Cruttwell, Hugh, 123

Cookoo in the Nest, A, 173
Cup of Kindness, 155

Danum Hotel, 47
Daily Express, 136, 141, 20[...] 211
Daily Graphic, 90, 118
Daily Herald, 90
Daily Mail, 87, 90, 185
Daily Sketch, 118
Daily Telegraph, 91, 187, 21[...] 235
Daily Worker, 92, 93
Dangerous Corner, 37
"Daphne's", 56
David Garrick, 18, 28
Davis, "Taffy", 27
Davis, Robert, *see* Hartford Davis, Robert
Dawson, Anna, 210, 214
Dawson, Gerry, 191
Day, Kenneth, 76
Day, Vera, 157
Dear Miss Phoebe, 97
Dearsley, "Pip", 157
Deep Are The Roots, 67
Defoe, Daniel, 19
Denham, Reginald, 37
Denny, Mr, 137, 170
Dermody, Frank, 74, 88, 8[...] 95, 103
Desert Rats, 70, 122
Design for Living, 152
Devil Came From Dublin, The 140
"Dial Rix", 193
Dick Barton, Special Agent, 3[...]
Dickory Dock, 180–1
Difference of Opinion, 55
Diplomatic Baggage, 198–[...] 207
Dish Ran Away . . ., The, 80 81
Doctor in the House, 182
Dodd, Pearson, 191
Donnithorne, John and Pat 206
Don't Just Lie There, Say Something!, 221–5, 227
Doré, Alexander, 229
Dorning, Robert, 214
Double Diamond Club, Caerphilly, 229

242

Douglas, Hazel, 144, 191, 214
Douglas, Louise, 151
Douglas, Pam, 151
Douglas, Torrington, 116, 136
Douglas, Wallace, 125, 129, 130, 142, 148, 151, 168, 183, 184, 191, 193, 210, 219, 220, 224, 233, 236
Drake, Fabia, 190
Drake's Drum, 40
Dresdel, Sonia, 35
Dromgoole, Patrick, 224
Drummond, John, 93
Drury Lane, 97
Dryhurst, Edward, 225
Dry-Pool Group, The, 19
Dry Rot, 103, 121, 124, 125, 127, 128–37, 139, 140, 144, 145, 146–7, 148, 150, 152, 166, 167, 168, 173, 198
Duckworth, George, 163
Duke of York's Theatre, 55
Dyer, Raymond (Charles), 173, 180

Eagle Has Two Heads, The, 62
Eastchurch, 44
Eaton, Wallas, 198
Edinburgh, 26–7
Edward, My Son, 65
Elizabeth, Queen, 200, 201
Elliott, Paul, 237
Ellison, John, 101
Elstree, 152
Elvey, Maurice, 147
EMI, 138
Empire Theatre: Chiswick, 127; Hackney, 127; Nottingham, 27; Wood Green, 127
Empress Hall, 147
ENSA, 28–9, 37
Equity, 116–17
Ervine, St John, 40
Evans, Mary, 142
Evening News, 92, 213
Evening Standard, 91, 92, 102, 123, 198
Everett, Wally, 52, 56, 58
Exercise Bowler, 55
Eyres, Rosemary, 206

Farr, Derek, 98, 177, 190, 210
Fermont, Dr, 186
Festival of Britain, 101
Fifty-five Days in Peking, 199
Finch, 9, 10
Findlater, Richard, 156
Firbank, Ann, 144–5, 181
Firth, Shirley, 234
Flea in her Ear, A, 38
Flemyng, Robert, 234
Florrie (Rix family maid), 5
Folkestone, 121, 124, 135
Fonteyn, Margot, 198
Foot, Alastair, 156, 209
Forbes, Bryan, 126, 153
Formby, George, 97–8
Forrest, Joan, 120
Fortune Theatre, 154, 212
Foster, Mrs Helen, 117
Four in Hand, 159
Fowler, Harry, 126
Fox, Douglas, 7
Fox, Mrs, 8
Frances, Myra, 222
Frank, Elizabeth, 91
Franklyn, John, 65, 66
Franklyn, Leo, 61, 62, 67, 147–8, 149, 157, 167, 168, 178, 181, 190, 210, 214, 221, 222–3
Franklyn, William, 67, 126, 148, 159
Fraser, Dennis, 28
Fraser, Liz, 181
Fregene, 158
French, David, 7
French for Love, 38
Furneau, Guy, 161

Gainsborough Films, 56
Galloping Major, The, 77
Gardiner, Lord (Gerald), 185
Garner, Rex, 198
Garratt, Gerald, 174
Garrick Theatre, 2, 5, 30, 103, 208, 209, 212, 213, 223, 224, 231, 238
Geoffrey, Wallace, 147
George Washington Slept Here, 150
Georgiades, John, 161
Georgiades, Rhoda (*née* Gray), 66, 68, 71, 122, 135, 155, 161, 170, 204–5, 206, 210, 219–20
Georgiades, Zoë, 206
Germaine, Marie, 74
Germany, 127–8
Gielgud, John, 21
Gilbert, Sister, 104
Glasgow, 26
"Golden Shot, The", 118
Goodman, Lord, 172
Gordon, Richard, 182
Gordon Walker, Patrick, 175
Gotell, Walter and Yvonne, 199, 202, 206
Grade, Leslie, 208
Grade, Michael 238
Graham, Genine, 159
Grand Pavilion, Bridlington, 64–5
Grand Theatre: Halifax, 122; Leeds, 26; Swansea, 82
Grant, Bob, 198
Grant, Deborah, 222
Gray, Elsie (author's mother-in-law), 177–8
Gray, Elspet (author's wife), 14, 57, 66, 67–8, 71–3, 74, 75, 83, 84–6, 88, 91, 95, 96, 98–9, 100, 102,–3, 104–6, 119–20, 121, 122, 123, 126, 127, 129, 130, 134, 135, 137, 140, 141, 144, 145, 148, 152–3, 159, 164, 176–7, 183, 184, 188, 190, 198, 199, 202, 203, 205, 206–7, 210, 211, 223, 228
Gray, James MacGregor (author's father-in-law), 87–8, 134–5
Gray, Peter, 155, 159
Gray, Rhoda, *see* Georgiades, Rhoda
Greene, Richard, 122
Griffiths, Emlyn, 138
Grobelaar, Michael, 234
Guardian, 187
Guildford, 227, 232, 233
Guilty Party, 55

Haggett, James, 69–70
Halfpenny Breeze, 121
Hall, Henry, 135, 172, 173
Hall, Wesley, 231

243

Hall, Willis, 170
Hallett, John, 209
Halsted, Henry, 99
Halton, 13, 48, 51, 54
Hamlet, 22
Hammond, Peter, 121
Hancock, Sheila, 182
Hancock, Tony, 193
Handl, Irene, 181
Hanley, 166
Hanson, Harry, 64
Happy Family, The, 100, 101
Harding, Gilbert, 182
Hare, Robertson ("Bunny"), 97, 181, 187, 190
Harper, Gerald, 123
Harrison, Gilbert, 150, 208, 210–11, 220
Harrogate, 29, 32–8, 40
Harrogate Herald, 36
Hart, Moss, 150
Hartford-Davis, Robert, 125–6
Harting, Mike, 179
Hartnell, William, 157, 178
Hastings, 74, 76
Hasty Heart, The, 66, 71
Hay Fever, 14
Hayes, Walter, 90
Haythorne, Joan, 147
He Found Adventure, 11
Helliwell, Arthur, 101
Henderson, Dickie, 108, 163, 165–6, 182, 186, 190, 209, 229
Henderson, Michael, 117
Henri, Dr, 186
"Henry Hall's Guest Night", 135
Heslop, Charles, 181, 198
Hilton, Tony, 149, 180, 181, 183, 184, 193, 209
Hippo Dancing, 148
Hippodrome Theatre: Aldershot, 127; Golders Green, 127; Margate, 67
Hird, Thora, 101, 190
His Excellency, 97
H. M. Tennent Ltd, 56
Hobbs, Jack, 27
Hobson, Harold, 1, 93, 149, 197, 213, 218
Hoiles, George, 79

Holden, Jan, 190
Holland-Bennett, Tim, 139
Hollender, Countess, 192
Hollis, Gerry, 72
Hollis, Walter 72
Holloway, Laurie, 198
Holly and the Ivy, The, 97
Home and Beauty, 97
Home at Seven, 97
Horne, Kenneth (writer), 141, 142, 146, 177, 212
Horne, Kenneth (comedian), 172, 173
Hornsea, 4–6, 8–9, 17, 18, 23, 28
Houston, Renee, 157
Howard, Trevor, 35
HTV, 224, 225
Hull, 3, 8–9, 15, 18–19, 25, 79
Hull Daily Mail, 79
Hundred Years Old, A, 62
Huntley-Gordon, Tony, 124
HW Motors, 179

I Was Monty's Double, 178
Iden, Rosalind, 23
Ilkley Gazette, 59, 61, 62
Ilkley Repertory Company, 59–63
Impey, Betty, 103
In the Bag, 122, 232
Indoor Fireworks, 37
Inspector Calls, An, 67
Instant Marriage, 198
Interval Club, 65
Intimate Theatre, Johannesburg, 234
Irene Vanbrugh Memorial Fund, 97
Is Your Honeymoon Really Necessary?, 182, 210
ITA, 172
Ivory, Jim, 52–3

Jacobs, David, 108, 154, 165, 194, 195
Jacobs, Pat, 154, 194, 195
Jacques, Hattie, 126, 155, 178, 189
Jamaica, 194–5
James, Sidney, 147, 157
Jane Steps Out, 142, 144

Jeger, George, 81, 109, 117, 175, 189, 196–7
Jessop, Helen, 99, 103, 177, 191, 210
Johnny's On The Spot, 123
Johns, Glynis, 150
Johnson, Bryan, 25
Johnson, Noel, 35
Johnson, Vivienne, 236
Johnston, Brian, 101, 117
Jones, Jacqueline, 190
Joseph Stone Auditorium Cape Town, 233
Jubb, Betty, 6

Kaufman, George S., 150
Kellett, Bob, 225, 226
Kendall, Henry, 101, 154, 156, 157, 171, 191, 192–3
Kelly, Sister, 170
Kerr, Bill, 156
Khama, Seretse, 86
Kilgarriff, Michael, 214
King Lear, 21, 22, 24, 25, 28
King, Philip, 17, 35, 114, 119, 171, 192
King's Hall, Ilkley, 59, 61–3
King's Rhapsody, 97
Kingsley, David, 172, 173
Kitty (author's housekeeper), 134
Knights of Madness, 97
Koon, Johnnie, 188–9
Koornhof, Dr Piet, 234
Kossof, David, 157

Lacey, Robert, 215
Lait, Betty, 69
Lait, Peter, 60, 70
Lambert, Jack, 222
Langdon-Down, Dr, 109–10
"Larkins, The", 157
La Rue, Danny, 165, 208
Lawrence, Tony, 222
Lawson, Vincent, 81, 82
Lawson, Wilfred, 181
Lawton, Sir Frank, 176
Laye, Evelyn, 176
Learoyd, T. M., 210
Lee, Norman, 123
Lee-Potter, Lynda (Lynda Berrison), 149–50, 217
Le Mans, 160–1

Le Mesurier, John, 181
Leno, Dan, 184
Leslie, Ann, 207
Let Sleeping Wives Lie, 209, 212
Letter, The, 32-3
Levene, Philip, 103
Lewin, David, 136
Lewsen, Charles, 239
Lieb, Alan, 206
Lieb, Cristi, 206
Lindwall, Ray, 190
Linstead, Sir Hugh, 176-7
Listener, 196
Lister, Clement, 66
Lister, Laurier, 232
Little Hut, The, 97
Littlewood, Joan, 197
Lock, Stock and Barrel, 159
Logan, Jimmy, 234, 235, 236
London Weekend TV, 238
Long March, The, 122
Lonsdale, Frederick, 38
Look After Lulu, 210, 211
Lord, Basil, 129, 135, 145, 147, 149, 177, 190
Lord's Taverners, 108, 163, 182, 183
Lorenzo, José Maria Perez, 199-200, 206
Love in a Mist, 141-6
Lovebirds, The, 151, 181
Lumley, Joanna, 222
Lyel, Viola, 177, 190
Lykiardopoulos, Nicholas 160-1
Lynn, Ralph, 187
Lynn, Vera, 108, 146, 165

Macbeth, 21
MacDonald, Mrs, 205
MacGivern, Cecil, 119,
McGoohan, Patrick, 123
MacGregor, Brenda, 28
Macrae, Arthur, 37
Madame Louise, 148-9, 220
Madden, Cecil, 116, 118, 118
Madeira, 111, 112, 113, 114-15
Magic Cupboard, The, 77, 80
Majorca, 127
Man and Superman, 34, 38
Manderson, Anne, 35-6, 204

Manderson, Miles (Tim), 35, 38, 47-8, 186, 204
Mangano, Silvano, 85
Mannock, P. L., 90
Manolin (Spanish handyman), 206
March, Reg, 137
Margaret, Princess, 200, 201
Margate, 65, 66-7
Marks, Alfred, 222, 226
Marriott, Anthony, 156, 209
Martin, George, 138
Mason-Rogers, Leslie, 67
Massey, Daniel, 159
Maugham, Somerset, 32
Maynard, Bill, 156
Melville, Alan, 192
Men of Affairs, 224, 227
Mentor Advertising, 137
Mercier, Nigel, 137
Mercier, Peter, 67, 68, 147, 169, 188, 191
Mercier, Sheila (author's sister), 3, 5, 17, 20, 28, 41, 55, 67, 96, 137, 169, 191, 210
Merrick, Simon, 212, 214, 217
Michaels, Louis, 237
Midsummer Night's Dream, A, 22
Miles and Miles Ltd, 35
Mills, James E., 38
Milltown, Lossiemouth, 50
Miss Learoyd's, 6
Mr Facey Romford's Hounds, 64
Mister Roberts, 97
Mitchell, Andrew, 225, 226
Mitchell, Julian, 67
Mitchell, Warren, 224, 226
Monck, Nugent, 21
Money for Jam, 210
Montgomery, James, 61
Moore, Gerry, 205
Moore, John, 220
Moore, Roger, 108
Moore, Stanley, 220
Morecambe, 208-9, 238
Morley, Robert, 65-6, 97
Morris, Colin, 70, 74, 80-1, 82, 89-90, 91, 93, 95, 102, 103, 105, 122, 123, 198

Morris, Julian, 105
Morris, Viera, 90, 102, 105
Moscow, 228
Mount, Peggy, 114, 147, 157
Mousetrap, The, 124
Muende, Dr, 179
Muller, Robert, 185
Musgrove, John, 8

Nap Hand, 214, 215
Nap's Adventure, 10
Nathan, David, 212
National Society for Mentally Handicapped Children, 108 109-10
National Theatre, 30, 38
Neilson, Claire, 222
Newcastle, 27, 212
Newley, Anthony, 126
News Chronicle, 91, 160
News of the World, 213
New Statesman, 197, 217
New Theatre: Cardiff, 228-30; Hull, 17; Oxford, 128
Newton, Robert, 77
Nichols, Dandy, 101
Nico Malan Theatre, Cape Town, 233
Night Must Fall, 14, 36, 48
Night We Dropped a Clanger, The, 172, 178, 180
Night We Got The Bird, The, 181, 182
Night We Sprang a Leak, The, see *Nothing Barred*
Noble, Larry, 74, 75, 90, 102, 103, 126, 129, 168, 191, 207
Noel-Baker, Philip, 14
Noggin (author's spaniel), 72
Nolan, Margaret, 214
No, No, Nanette!, 114
Noose, 55
No Plums in the Pudding, 193
Norden, Christine, 98-9
Nordic Films, 125
Normansfield, 108, 109, 110, 165, 177
Northern Dance Orchestra, 138, 139
No Sex Please – We're British, 156
Nothing Barred, 181

Nothing But The Truth, 36, 48, 60, 61, 173
Nottingham, 27, 81, 135
Not Wanted On Voyage, 151–2
Nureyev, Rudolf, 198

Observer, 93, 187, 197
Odd Couple, The, 183
"On a Slow Boat to China", 138
On Monday Next, 35, 170–1
One for the Pot, 149, 180, 187, 191, 192, 196, 209, 212
One Wild Oat, 220
Opera House: Harrogate, 36 (*see also* White Rose Players); Leicester, 86

Padbury, Wendy, 210
Paget-Bowman, Cecily, 129
Palace Theatre, Plymouth, 79
Palmer, Señor, 206
Parker, Cecil, 178
Parkhurst, Clive, 103
Parnes, Larry, 232, 237
Pastoria's Restaurant, 187
Patch, Wally, 74, 75, 77, 80, 81, 82, 86, 90, 93, 98, 101, 103, 106, 120, 121, 189
Patrick, John, 66
Pavilion, Bridlington, 68
Pavlow, Muriel, 177, 190, 234
Peacock, Addie, 29, 30, 32, 34–5, 36, 39
Peacock, William, 34
Percy, Edward, 37
Perfect Woman, The, 147, 148
Perkins, Toby, 168
Pertwee, Maya, 218–19, 228
Pertwee, Michael, 57, 87, 122, 185, 212, 213, 215, 218–19, 221, 224, 225–6, 228, 229, 231, 232, 233, 235
Pertwee, Roland, 87, 122
Pettigrew, James, 91
Phillip Raphael Ltd, 137
Phillips, Leslie, 178, 226
Piccadilly Theatre, 21, 198
Pickles, Wilfred, 108, 146
Piffard, Freddie, 180
Pinewood Studios, 225, 226
Pipe, Archie, 83
plant, Pamela, 102

Plantation Inn, 194–5
Platts, Antony, 7
Platts, Douglas, 7
Platts, Tony, 7
Plays and Players, 168
Playhouse, Newcastle, 212
Plaza Suite, 194
Pleasure Gardens, Folkestone, 135
Plomley, Roy, 123, 159
Plunder, 154, 155
Portrait in Black, 62
Posner, Geoffrey, 51, 117
Postman's Knock, 119–20, 139
Powell, Enoch, 110–11
Priestley, J. B., 37
Prince of Wales Theatre, Cardiff, 24, 166
Princess Royal, the, 187
Public Michief, A, 142, 212
Punt, Norman, 8

Quaglino's, 90, 122
Queen Elizabeth Slept Here, 150, 151

Radford, Basil, 70, 72, 77, 78–80
Radford, George, 69, 70, 72, 74, 76, 77, 81, 85–6, 103, 189
Radley, Malcolm, 162
RAF, 29, 32, 37, 41–5, 48–58
Raki, Laya, 126
Ramsden, Dennis, 210
Ramsden, Slim and Christine, 234
Rank Organisation, 75, 126, 136, 172, 225, 226
Rattle of a Simple Man, 173
Raven Hotel, Droitwich, 220–1
Raymond, Jack, 99
Raymond, Paul, 208
Raynor, William E., 74, 103, 150
Read, Dougie, 137
Reading, Donna, 222, 234, 236
Redgrave, Vanessa, 152
Redmond, Liam, 140
Reece, Brian, 149, 190

Reeves, Kynaston, 181
Relph, Warrant Officer, 53
Reluctant Heroes, 30, 53, 6 70–1, 73, 74–5, 79, 80, 8 89, 90–4, 97–100, 102– 116–19, 121, 122, 146, 15 152, 155
Reunion Theatre, 55, 60
Richards, Dick, 93
Richardson, Dorothy, 33
Richardson, Mrs, 33–4, 37
Richardson, Oliver, 33
Richmond Theatre, 127, 18 196
Ring Round The Moon, 96
Riscoe, Arthur, 149
Riverside Studios, 99
Rix, Ernest Bertie (author' uncle), 18, 19, 20, 58, 63 187
Rix, Fanny (author's mother) 4, 5, 21, 23, 28
Rix, Geoffrey (author's cousin), 20
Rix, Herbert Dobson (author' father), 5–6, 9–10, 18, 19, 37, 45, 57–8, 195–6
Rix, Jamie (author's son), 164 170, 178, 186, 207, 227 234, 237
Rix, John (author's cousin), 20
Rix, John Robert (author's uncle), 18–19, 20
Rix, Jonathan (author's son), 2, 35, 184, 186, 190, 202, 203, 207, 221, 227, 237,
Rix, Kenneth (author's cousin), 19, 20
Rix, Leslie (author's cousin), 20
Rix, Louisa (author's daughter), 35–6, 127, 137, 148, 158, 165, 178, 186, 207, 223–4, 227, 234, 237
Rix, Malcolm (author's brother), 3, 5, 20
Rix, Margaret (author's grandmother), 18
Rix, Nora (author's sister), 3, 5
Rix, Robert (author's grandfather), 18

Rix, Sheila (author's sister), see Mercier, Sheila
Rix, Shelley (author's daughter), 104–7, 108, 109, 110, 137, 186
Rix Theatrical Productions, 59, 74
Roberts, Merylin, 169
Robinson, F. A., 156–7
Roehampton, 163, 164
Rogers, Anne, 25
Romulus Films, 140, 146
Ronald, Tom, 138
Rose and the Ring, The, 10
Rothwell, Talbot, 123, 150, 151
Roy, Harry, 138
Royal Shakespeare Company, 238
Royle, Derek, 207, 214, 216
Russell, Christine, 191
Rutherford, Norman, 139, 183
Rye, Daphne, 56
Rymer, Dorothy, 26–7
Rymer, Dr Norman, 13

Sachs, Andrew, 149, 169, 210
Sailor Beware!, 35, 114
St Bede's 6, 7–8, 10–11
St James's Theatre, 21, 23, 28
St Martin's Theatre, 142
St Oswald, Roland, 206
St Paul's, 227
Salberg, Derek, 167, 228
Salmon, Lady, 110
Sanderson, Joan, 145, 167, 168
Saunders, Richard, 103
Scales, Prunella, 124
Scarborough, 40, 41, 44
Scott, Allan, 74
Scott, Terry, 177, 190, 191, 238
Seagulls over Sorrento, 96–7, 99, 125
Sears, Heather, 147
Secombe, Harry, 108
Second Mrs Tanqueray, The, 97
See How They Run, 35, 70, 192
Service, Robert, 18
Sharp, Anthony, 214

Shelley, Carole, 183
Shephard, Alan, 238
Shepherd, Honor, 33
Shepley, Michael, 147
Shepperton Studios, 147, 172, 181
Sherwin, Stuart, 191
Sherek, Henry, 122
Sherwood, Dr, 107
She's Done It Again, 168, 212, 213–17, 218, 219
Shiner, Ronald, 27, 97, 98, 99–100, 126, 147, 151, 152, 181, 206
Shotter, Winifred, 187
Sim, Sheila, 124
Simon, Neil, 194
Simple Spymen, 61, 125, 147, 148, 159, 165, 166, 167, 170, 179, 180, 184, 185
Sims, Joan, 147, 198, 224
Singer, Campbell, 55
"Six of Rix", 220
Slater, Betty, 107
Slater, Johnnie, 107, 120–1, 128, 129, 130, 131, 135, 145–6, 147, 149, 155, 170, 181
Slater, Simon, 107
Sleeping Partnership, 142
Smith, Maggie, 183
South Africa, 233–5
Spa Theatre, Bridlington, 68
Spain, 199–200, 202–7, 227
SPARKS, 108
Spastics Society, 108, 146
Spot of Bother, A, 220
Spring Cleaning, 38
Spring Model, 122–3
Stage, The, 21, 74, 128
Stage Cricket Club, 124, 148
Staircase, 173
Stand By Your Bedouin, 209, 210
Stars' Organisation for Spastics, 108, 146, 147
Steinbeck, John, 55
Stepham, Renee, 76, 80
Stern, Ernest, 21, 28
Strand Theatre, 177
Stratford, Jim, 223
Streatham Hill Theatre, 127
Stross, David, 14, 26

Stross, Raymond, 14
Sun, 207
Sunday Chronicle, 93
"Sunday Night at the London Palladium", 119
Sunday People, 101–2
Sunday Pictorial, 93
Sunday Times, 1, 93, 187, 197, 213, 215, 222
Surtees, Robert, 64
Suspect, 37
Swansea, 82
Swinson, Arthur, 123, 159
Sylvaine, Marie, 219
Sylvaine, Vernon, 148–9, 214
Sylvester, William, 122

Take it from Us, 97
"Talking Sport", 196
Tangier, 151–2
Taylor, Weston, 213
Tell the Marines, 87, 93, 122
Temple, Syd, 69
Terol, Pedro, 206
Terry-Thomas, 226
Thark, 154
Theatre Royal: Birmingham, 80; Hanley, 166; Nottingham, 27, 81; Windsor, 125, 148, 159
Theseus, 9
Thin on Top, 185
"This Is Your Life", 25, 118, 188, 189–90
Thomas, Basil, 181
Thomas, Nina, 222
Those Above, 142
Tilvern, Alan, 210
Times, The, 91, 168, 187, 213, 239
To Dorothy, a Son, 205
Toerien, Pieter, 233, 234, 238
Top of the Ladder, 97
Torquay, 24–5, 78
Touch and Go, 97
Touch of Fear, A, 152
Traveller's Tale, 126
Travers, Ben, 148, 154–5, 165, 173
Treacher, Bill, 210
Treasure Island, 24
Trespass, 64–5
Trewin, J. C., 149, 239

Trial and Error, 142
Trickett, Bert, 188
Triumph Productions, 237
Trueman, Freddie, 196
Turvey, Bill and Ann, 14–15
Twelfth Night, 22, 23, 28, 38
Tynan, Kenneth, 123

Upgreen – And At 'Em or
A Maiden Nearly Over, 182–3
Uproar in the House, 156, 209, 210, 211
Up To His Neck, 126

Vale of Laughter, 154
Victoria Palace, 156, 157, 170
Viking Theatre Company, 64
Voss, Stephanie, 198

Waller, Celia, 114
Waller, Jack, 114
Walls, Tom, 154
Walsh, Dermot, 74, 75–6, 88, 90, 95, 98, 103, 121, 122
Walsh, Michael, 86, 87, 170, 211
Walsh, Peggy, 86–7
Walter, Mr, 162, 163
Wanted, One Body, 173
Ward, Bill, 123
Wardle, Irving, 168, 213
Watch It Sailor, 35
Watergate Theatre, 57
Watson, Jimmy, 99
Watson, Moray, 222, 226

Watt, Tommy, 42, 44, 138–9, 156, 183
Wayne, Naunton, 78–9, 181
Webster, Jenny, 60
"Wednesday Magazine", 195
Weight, Lucy, 28
Weldon, Duncan, 237
West, Peter, 196
Western Morning News, 79
Westmorland, David Earl of, 172, 173
What a Drag, 193
What Every Woman Wants, 123, 150
"What's My Line?", 119, 182
What's On, 102
What The Doctor Ordered, 220
Wheldon, Huw, 116
Whitehall Theatre, 2, 5, 14, 27, 74, 80, 81, 85, 88, 89, 98, 101, 103, 115, 117, 119, 120, 123, 125, 127, 128, 135, 143, 147, 159, 168, 176, 179, 185, 195, 196–7, 207–8, 209, 210, 211, 212, 238
White Rock Pavilion, Hastings, 74, 122
White Rose Players, Harrogate, 29, 32, 34–5, 40, 59
Whiting, John, 38
Whitsun-Jones, Paul, 198
Who Is Sylvia?, 97
Who's Your Father?, 196
Will Any Gentleman?, 97, 220
Williams, Bransby, 124
Williams, Emlyn, 36–7, 64
Williams, Jack, 155–6

Williams, Martin, 228
Willis, Lord Ted, 126, 18:
Wilson, Cecil, 90
Wilson, David, 210
Wilson, Isobel, 186
Wilson, Jennifer, 210
Wilson, "Tug", 68–9
Winchester, Nancy and Tai ton, 206
Windsor, 124, 125, 127, 1 148, 159
Windsor, Barbara, 208
Winter Gardens, Morecam 208–9, 238
Without The Prince, 17, 35
Wolfit, Donald, 16, 17–21, 22–3, 24, 25, 28–30, 189
Wolf's Clothing, 142, 177, 1
Woolf, John, 140, 146
Worm's Eye View, 27, 80, 97
Wormwood Scrubs, 117
Wyndham's Theatre, 198

Yale, Appaline, 69–70
Yesterday and Today, 97
York House, 161–4
Yorke, Katherine, 64, 72
Yorkshire Evening News, 36
Young, B. A., 149
"You Too Can Be Dreamer", 138
You, Too, Can Have a Bo 156–7, 170
Yvonne Arnaud Theatr Guildford, 227, 232, 233